# THE HISTORY OF
# WINCHESTER FIREARMS
# 1866 - 1975

*fourth edition*

*by* GEORGE R. WATROUS,
JAMES C. RIKHOFF *and* THOMAS H. HALL

This fourth edition
of
*The History of*
*Winchester Firearms*
is dedicated to
Pete Kuhlhoff

**Library of Congress Cataloging in Publication Data**

Watrous, George R.
 The history of Winchester firearms, 1866-1975.

 First-2d editions published under title: Winchester rifles and shotguns; 3d ed. published in
1966 under title: The history of Winchester firearms, 1866-1966.
 Includes index.
 1. Winchester firearms. I. Title.
TS533.2.W37  1975    683'.4    75-9269
ISBN 0-87691-208-0

*Published by Winchester Press*
*205 E. 42nd St., New York 10017*
*Printed in the United States of America*

# CONTENTS

# MODEL INDEX

*Model numbers marked with an asterisk (*) are contractions of the year the model was developed and introduced. Model number not so marked were assigned arbitrary numbers.

Each illustration is conveniently numbered for easy reference.

# MODEL INDEX

*Model numbers marked with an asterisk (*) are contractions of the year the model was developed and introduced. Model number not so marked were assigned arbitrary numbers.

Each illustration is conveniently numbered for easy reference.

# PREFACE

*The History of Winchester Firearms 1866-1975* is the fourth edition of *Winchester Rifles and Shotguns,* the chronicle of George R. Watrous, first issued on February 3, 1943, and retitled in 1966 with the publication of the third edition in commemoration of Winchester's Centennial. That third edition, the first one offered to the general public and also the first hardcover edition, was edited by Thomas E. Hall, Curator of the Winchester Museum, and the late Pete Kuhlhoff, then the longtime gun editor of *Argosy Magazine.* This edition is dedicated to the memory of Pete Kuhlhoff.

The first and second editions were compiled by Watrous, who worked with Winchester from 1900 to 1946. Historical research brought forth much additional information concerning the birth of the Hunt breech loading, repeating rifle action, its successive developments that finally became the famous Henry Repeating Rifle, and still later improvements that made possible the first Winchester rifle, the Model 1866.

A summary of this information was included in the second edition, published in 1950. This edition gave a clear picture of the events leading up to the adoption of many Winchester models and the reason for their later discontinuance. Since Winchester firearms have been on the market for 110 years, detailed information on the older models is necessarily limited to available data permanently recorded in some form.

The third edition brought Winchester from the important post-World War II period up to the year of its hundredth anniversary in 1966. Since the period immediately after 1964 has been regarded as both important and controversial in Winchester's development, the coverage of the first so-called "post-'64" models is particularly crucial. Equally important was the listing of the first Winchester Commemorative — the Centennial '66 — offered to the general public on a national basis.

This fourth edition includes the Winchester Commemoratives, including the very limited specialized commemoratives issued for the Wyoming Jubilee in 1964 and the Nebraska Centennial in 1966, both of which were omitted in the third edition. It also includes the Winchester Air Guns, which were imported and sold from 1969 through 1974.

Perhaps one of the most interesting — and least known — sidelights of modern Winchester history is the story of the special Commemoratives marketed in Canada and Europe in the last few years. These special lever action Commemoratives are covered for perhaps the first time in print anywhere. In the same framework, the two Spanish-made Winchester double barrel shotguns (one side-by-side and one over-and-under) designed for marketing throughout the international market, including Canada, are brought to popular attention in the United States for the first time.

Throughout the years, this book has served as a storehouse of practical reference for Winchester salesmen, design engineers, researchers, gun experts — in short, for everyone who requires specifications, descriptions and historical facts about Winchester firearms. This edition provides a continuing and comprehensive record of each model and the part it played in the establishment of Winchester's reputation for arms of the highest quality.

THOMAS E. HALL  
*Curator, Winchester Museum*  
June 1975

JAMES C. RIKHOFF  
*Former Director, Winchester*  
*Public Relations*  
June 1975

# THE BIRTH AND DEVELOPMENT
## OF A BREECH LOADING REPEATER
### AND THE COMPANIES
## THAT SUCCESSIVELY DEVELOPED IT

# THE ROCKETBALL AND THE VOLITION REPEATER

*1. HUNT REPEATING RIFLE. CALIBER .54. PATENT MODEL 1849.*

In August 1848, U. S. Patent No. 5701 was granted to Walter Hunt of New York City for a conical lead bullet. It had a cavity in the base filled with powder and closed by a disc having a hole in the center to admit the flame from an independent priming unit. The bullet was described as a Rocket Ball.

Hunt, born in Martinsburg, New York, on July 29, 1796, was a machinist by trade and the inventor of a bewildering variety of items. On August 21, 1849, he was granted U. S. Patent No. 6663 for a lever action, breech loading, repeating rifle, described as the Volition Repeater. Hunt developed this firearm to use the Rocket Ball, described above. His ideas expressed in the patent were not only in themselves original in the extreme, but were also the beginning of a train of ideas that eventually led to the development of a series of breech loading repeating firearms—the Henry Repeating Rifle and the Winchester Repeating Rifle, Model 1866 being the most famous.

# JENNINGS LEVER ACTION
# REPEATING RIFLE

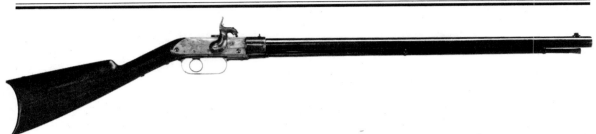

*2. JENNINGS BREECHLOADING RIFLE, FIRST STYLE. CALIBER .54. MADE AS A SINGLE SHOT. MANUFACTURED BY ROBBINS AND LAWRENCE OF WINDSOR, VERMONT. 1850 AND 1851.*

*3. JENNINGS BREECHLOADING RIFLE, SECOND TYPE. MADE AS A REPEATER WITH SMITH'S IMPROVEMENT. CALIBER .54. MANUFACTURED BY ROBBINS AND LAWRENCE. 1851 AND 1852.*

*4. MUZZLE LOADING RIFLE. CALIBER .54. MADE AT THE SHOP OF ROBBINS AND LAWRENCE FROM JENNINGS PARTS. SUCH GUNS WERE MADE IN 1852 TO CLEAN UP REMAINING STOCK.*

Hunt was teamed with a promoter, George A. Arrowsmith, who was also a model maker with a small machine shop in New York City. Hunt assigned his patents for the Rocket Ball and the Volition Repeater to Arrowsmith for development and promotion; he probably had been working with Arrowsmith under some form of agreement prior to the granting of the patents.

Arrowsmith's working machinist, a gunsmith by the name of Lewis Jennings, simplified and considerably improved Hunt's original design, for which he was granted a U. S. Patent on December 25, 1849. Thus he gave his name, in collector's parlance at least, to such firearms as were manufactured from this combination of ideas. Several crude working models were made up in a twenty-shot repeating design and Arrowsmith went to work promoting the firearm.

Arrowsmith soon found an interested capitalist in Courtlandt C. Palmer of Stonington, Connecticut, who at one time was President of the Stonington & Providence Railroad and a leading hardware merchant in New York City. Palmer purchased the patents of Hunt and Jennings from Arrowsmith and, in 1850, made arrangements with Robbins & Lawrence of Windsor, Vermont, for the manufacture of 5,000 Jennings rifles. The shop foreman at Robbins & Lawrence was Benjamin Tyler Henry, a master machinist, born in Claremont, New Hampshire, on March 22, 1821.

The names of Daniel B. Wesson, born in Worcester, Massachusetts, in 1825, and Horace Smith, born in Cheshire, Massachusetts, in 1808, were now added to the list of persons who became interested in the Hunt-Jennings repeating firearm. Both had acquired an extensive gunsmithing background. On August 26, 1851, U. S. Patent No. 8317 was granted to Horace Smith for a simplification and improvement of Lewis Jennings' design of December 25, 1849. Smith assigned his patent to Courtlandt C. Palmer, and firearms of this design were manufactured by Robbins & Lawrence during their contract with Palmer for Jennings' firearms.

Mr. Lawrence has left an interesting story of the production and testing of the Jennings rifle. He disclosed that the rapidity of fire had been increased so that a well-trained rifleman could fire at the rate of twelve shots a minute. Another important development, not usually credited to the Jennings-Volcanic series of firearms, was the use of loaded balls having grooves cut into the outside surface and filled with tallow. This reduced leading of the barrel, with consequent improvement in the accuracy of the balls in flight.

However, it became apparent that the whole system of repeating action was too complicated and not powerful enough to become commercially successful. Production was abandoned in 1852.

Palmer had lost considerable money in his venture into the firearms field. The rest of the group suffered, at least, keen disappointment in their failure to turn their dreams of a successful breech loading repeating rifle into reality.

There now occurs a time lag in which no record of progress appears, but Palmer, Smith, Wesson, and probably Henry were still carrying on further developments of a repeating action.

# SMITH AND WESSON

**5. SMITH AND WESSON PISTOL. CALIBER .38. MADE AT NORWICH, CONNECTICUT. BARREL LENGTH 8 INCHES. 1854 AND 1855.**

**6. SMITH AND WESSON PISTOL. CALIBER .30. MADE AT NORWICH, CONNECTICUT. BARREL LENGTH 4 INCHES. 1854 AND 1855.**

The next documentary record to appear is Patent No. 10535 granted to H. Smith and D. B. Wesson on February 14, 1854, for a repeating firearm. This new design departed in many respects from the previous Hunt-Jennings and Horace Smith designs, both in the action and in the loaded ball. The gun was of pistol size with a short curved pistol stock, and the tubular magazine under the barrel was slotted on the under side for nearly its full length.

Palmer had been furnishing funds for the experimental work. It is probable that both Smith and Wesson had been on his payroll, at least part-time, since the cessation of manufacture of the Jennings rifles. On June 20, 1854, Courtlandt C. Palmer, Horace Smith, and Daniel B. Wesson formed a limited partnership for the exclusive use and control of certain patent rights relating to cartridges and breech loading firearms. The patents involved in this partnership included the original Hunt, Jennings, and Horace Smith patents and the new Smith and Wesson patent granted the previous February.

The company factory was located at Norwich, Connecticut, and pistols manufactured were marked with the firm's name—Smith & Wesson. B. Tyler Henry, although his name does not appear in the partnership, was an employee of the firm. The original company under the name Smith & Wesson was short-lived. A new company was incorporated in July 1855 under the general laws of the State of Connecticut; it was known as the Volcanic Repeating Arms Company.

# VOLCANIC REPEATING ARMS COMPANY

7. *VOLCANIC PISTOL. CALIBER .38. MADE BY VOLCANIC REPEATING ARMS COMPANY, NEW HAVEN, CONNECTICUT. BARREL LENGTH 8 INCHES. 1856 AND 1857.*

9. *VOLCANIC PISTOL. CALIBER .38. MADE BY VOLCANIC REPEATING ARMS COMPANY, NEW HAVEN, CONNECTICUT. BARREL LENGTH 6 INCHES. 1856 AND 1857.*

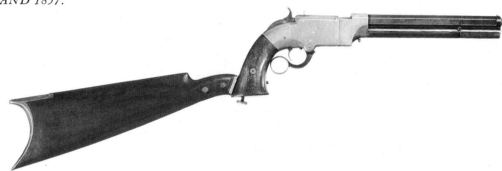

8. *VOLCANIC PISTOL. CALIBER .38. MADE BY VOLCANIC ARMS COMPANY, NEW HAVEN, CONNECTICUT. BARREL LENGTH 8 INCHES. MADE WITH DETACH-ABLE SHOULDER STOCK. 1856 AND 1857.*

Palmer, Smith, and Wesson were the incorporators of this new company. But among the subscribers to its stock appears the name of Oliver F. Winchester. This initial financial interest later led to his presidency of the company and to his further financial backing. Oliver Fisher Winchester was born in Boston, Massachusetts, on November 30, 1810. At the time of his purchase of stock in the Volcanic Repeating Arms Company, he was a manufacturer of men's clothing and other wearing apparel in New Haven, Connecticut.

The new company purchased the assets and patent rights from the former Smith & Wesson company. Courtlandt C. Palmer and Horace Smith stepped out as active participants.

Daniel B. Wesson had previously been working on the idea of a metallic rim fire cartridge as a better load for the repeating action. This idea had not been perfected; only an experimental action had been made for it. It was stipulated in an agreement, however, that the purchasers of the patents covering the repeating firearms would be allowed, royalty free, any further development of the metallic cartridge ideas that had been developed by Wesson.

Volcanic pistols and rifles were first manufactured at the old Smith & Wesson plant in Norwich with Wesson the shop superintendent. In February 1856, production started in a new plant located at New Haven. William C. Hicks was shop superintendent, Daniel Wesson having left the company. The ammunition department was organized in May 1856.

By August 1856, the Volcanic Repeating Arms Company was in financial difficulties, but was temporarily tided over by money borrowed from its principal stockholders. Early in 1857, a large part of the property was sold to Oliver F. Winchester to cover his loans to the company.

# NEW HAVEN ARMS COMPANY

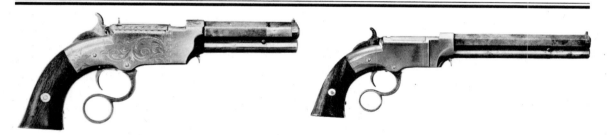

10. *VOLCANIC PISTOL. CALIBER .30. MADE BY NEW HAVEN ARMS COMPANY. BARREL LENGTH 3½ INCHES. 1858 TO 1860.*

11. *VOLCANIC PISTOL. CALIBER .30. MADE BY NEW HAVEN ARMS COMPANY, NEW HAVEN, CONNECTICUT. BARREL LENGTH 6 INCHES. 1858 TO 1860.*

12. *VOLCANIC RIFLE. CALIBER .38. MADE BY THE NEW HAVEN ARMS COMPANY, NEW HAVEN, CONNECTICUT. BARREL LENGTH 16 INCHES. 1858 TO 1860.*

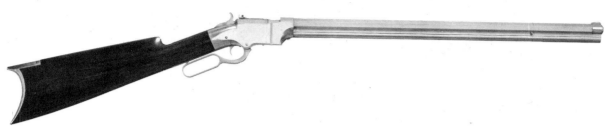

13. VOLCANIC RIFLE. CALIBER .38. MADE BY THE NEW HAVEN ARMS COM-
PANY, NEW HAVEN, CONNECTICUT. BARREL LENGTH 20 INCHES. 1858 TO
1860.

14. VOLCANIC RIFLE. CALIBER .38. MADE BY THE NEW HAVEN ARMS COM-
PANY, NEW HAVEN, CONNECTICUT. BARREL LENGTH 24 INCHES. 1858 TO
1860.

15. HENRY RIFLE. CALIBER .44 RIM FIRE. WITH IRON RECEIVER, HAS EARLY
TYPE BUTTSTOCK WITH ROUNDED HEEL. MADE BY NEW HAVEN ARMS
COMPANY, NEW HAVEN, CONNECTICUT. 1860 TO 1861.

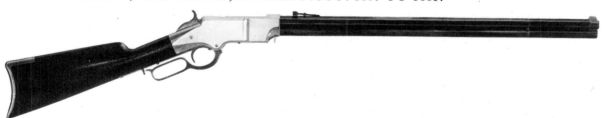

16. HENRY RIFLE. CALIBER .44 RIM FIRE. WITH BRASS RECEIVER. HAS EARLY
TYPE BUTTSTOCK WITH ROUNDED HEEL. MADE BY NEW HAVEN ARMS
COMPANY, NEW HAVEN, CONNECTICUT. 1861 AND 1862.

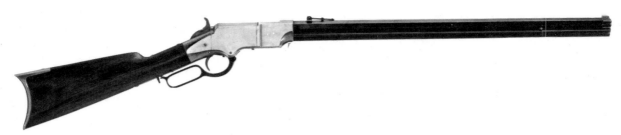

*17. HENRY RIFLE. CALIBER .44 RIM FIRE. HAS LATER TYPE BUTTSTOCK WITH SHARPER HEEL. MADE BY NEW HAVEN ARMS COMPANY, NEW HAVEN, CONNECTICUT. 1863 TO 1866.*

On April 25, 1857, The New Haven Arms Company was formally organized to take over and continue the business of the defunct Volcanic Repeating Arms Company. The New Haven Arms Company occupied the former Volcanic plant in New Haven and continued the manufacture of the Volcanic type of firearms, both in the pistol and rifle form. The firearms were still described as Volcanic but were now marked NEW HAVEN CONN. PATENT FEB. 14, 1854. In 1859, the plant was moved to a new location at No. 9 Artizan Street in New Haven.

Features common to all firearms of Smith & Wesson, Volcanic, and New Haven Arms Company manufacture included the tubular magazine under the barrel, slotted on the bottom side for nearly its entire length, with a spring-operated follower having a thumb piece moving outside the magazine tube.

Although many glowing tributes had been given to the excellence of the mechanism and rapidity of fire of the Volcanic firearms, the volume of sale was restricted by several features. The calibers were relatively small when compared with the large calibers commonly used in the single-shot arms of the period. Also, the cavity in the ball was too small, in relation to the total weight of the loaded ball, to hold a sufficient quantity of powder for adequate velocity and striking energy. The firearms lacked a satisfactory gas seal at the breech—a fault common to most of the early breech loading repeaters.

It became increasingly evident that if the New Haven Arms Company was to continue the manufacture and sale of repeating firearms, a radical change must be made to improve both the firearms and the ammunition, and to make the combination more attractive to prospective purchasers. B. Tyler Henry, now the shop superintendent, who had participated in the manufacture of all the successive developments of the Jennings-Volcanic action for nearly ten years, was given the task of redesigning the action for use with rim fire metallic cartridges. The first public record of Henry's direct participation in the design of the repeating action—demonstrating how well he accomplished his task—appears in U. S. Patent No. 30446, granted to B. Tyler Henry of New Haven, Connecticut, on October 16, 1860, for an "Improvement in Magazine Firearms."

New features of the Henry rifle consisted principally in the addition of a two-prong firing pin, striking on opposite sides of the flanged head of the rim fire cartridge, an extractor, and changes in the bolt and feeding mechanism. This system satisfactorily handled the loading and firing of the rim fire cartridge and the extraction and ejection of the empty fired shell. The slotted tubular magazine under the barrel was retained with a capacity of fifteen 44-pointed rim fire cartridges. The 44-flat, Henry caliber was added later. The chambering was identical for both cartridges.

The Henry rifle allowed a very rapid rate of fire, with satisfactory energy and striking power. As a repeater it had no equal and was approached only by the Spencer rifle, which had been

[ 8 ]

patented only a few months before Henry's patent was granted. Early catalogs establish the fact that the first regular production of the Henry rifle was in 1862.

In 1865, the President and Directors of the New Haven Arms Company began to consider changes in the Henry rifle and in the name of the company. Nathaniel Wheeler and James Wilson, directors of the company, advocated moving to Bridgeport, Connecticut. A portion of their Wheeler and Wilson Sewing Machine Company buildings was later rented for this purpose.

Oliver F. Winchester and others made application to the Legislature of the State of Connecticut for a Charter, which was granted by an Act of the Assembly on July 7, 1865. This Charter was originally issued to the Henry Repeating Arms Company, no doubt to capitalize on the popularity of the Henry rifle. However, the firm name was changed to "Winchester Repeating Arms Company" by a special Act of the Assembly in 1866. The incorporation was in complete effect on February 20, 1867. The Charter authorized the company to purchase and occupy lands and buildings and to carry on business in New Haven or in Bridgeport, or both. The final transfer of the assets of the New Haven Arms Company to the Winchester Repeating Arms Company was made on March 30, 1867.

# WINCHESTER REPEATING ARMS COMPANY

The physical assets of the old New Haven Arms Company were transferred to a portion of the Wheeler and Wilson Sewing Machine Company's buildings in Bridgeport, at East Washington Avenue and Hallett Street, and production was resumed by April 1867. Nelson King was the shop superintendent, B. Tyler Henry having left the company's employ before it moved to Bridgeport.

During the period of actual legal transfer, since the new Charter had been granted in 1866, the company had become known as the Winchester Repeating Arms Company. The first firearm to bear this name was listed as the Winchester Model of 1866 because it was developed in that year. Deliveries to the public did not begin until the summer of 1867.

# THE CIVIL WAR
## April 12, 1861 — April 26, 1865

At the beginning of the Civil War, the standard U. S. Infantry firearm was the U. S. Rifled Musket, Caliber 58, Model of 1855. This musket was loaded from the muzzle, using a paper cartridge with a charge of 60 grains of black powder and a hollow base, grooved, and lubricated lead bullet weighing 500 grains. The charge was ignited by a musket cap or with the Maynard tape primer.

However, the need for small arms was so great that any firearm capable of firing a shot was pressed into service. Arms made many years before the war, generally of the smooth bore, muzzle loading type and even of flintlock ignition, were put into use during the wartime emergency.

The years 1861-65 covered a transition period in the development of firearms. Some of the slightly more modern types of single shot breech loaders, as well as a few of the still more modern breech loading repeaters, such as the Spencer and Henry models, were used during the latter part of the war.

The Civil War was fought largely with muzzle-loading weapons. An interesting sidelight showing the nervous tension the troops underwent in using these single-shot weapons during the height of battle is taken from a Report of the Bureau of Ordnance, Navy Department, November 1864, Note B, page 39:

> The official report of the examination of the arms collected upon the battlefield of Gettysburg states that of the whole number received (27,574) we found at least 24,000 of these loaded; about one half of these contained two loads each, one fourth from three to ten loads each and the balance one load each.
>
> In many of these guns, from two to six balls have been found with only one charge of powder. In some, the balls have been found at the bottom of the bore with the charge of powder on top of the ball. In some as many as six paper regulation-caliber 58 cartridges have been found, the cartridges having been put in the guns without being torn or broken. Twenty-three loads were found in one Springfield rifle-musket, each loaded in regular order. Twenty-two balls and sixty-two buck shot with a corresponding quantity of powder all mixed up together were found in one percussion smooth-bore musket.
>
> In many of the smooth-bore guns Model of 1842, rebel make, we have found a wad of loose paper between the powder and ball and another wad of the same kind on top of the ball, the ball having been put in the gun naked. About six thousand of the arms were found loaded with Johnson & Dow's cartridges, many of these cartridges were about half way down in the barrels of the guns, and in many cases the ball end of the cartridges had been put into the gun first. The cartridges were found mostly in the Enfield rifle-musket.

The Civil War had emphasized the need to replace the old muzzle loaders with a more modern type. The firearm of the future must be a breech loading repeater and the ammunition of the fixed type of cartridge.

Worthy of repetition is Oliver F. Winchester's eloquent appeal for the adoption of a breech loading repeating firearm for the United States troops, made when he was President of the New Haven Arms Company.

> What would be the value of an army of one hundred thousand infantry and cavalry, thus mounted and armed with a due proportion of artillery, each artilleryman with a repeating carbine slung to his back? Certainly the introduction of repeating guns into the army will involve a change of the Manual of Arms. Probably it will modify the art of war; possibly it may revolutionize the whole science of war. Where is the military genius that is to grasp this whole subject, and so modify the science of war as to best develop the capacities of this terrible engine—the exclusive control of which would enable any government (with resources sufficient to keep half a million of men in the field) to rule the world?

# MODEL 1866 REPEATING RIFLE

18. PATENT MODEL WITH LOADING PORT IN SIDE OF RECEIVER. KING'S IMPROVEMENT 1866.

19. MODEL 1866 CARBINE. EARLY TYPE WITH FLAT SPRING COVER FOR LOADING PORT. MADE IN 1867.

20. MODEL 1866 CARBINE

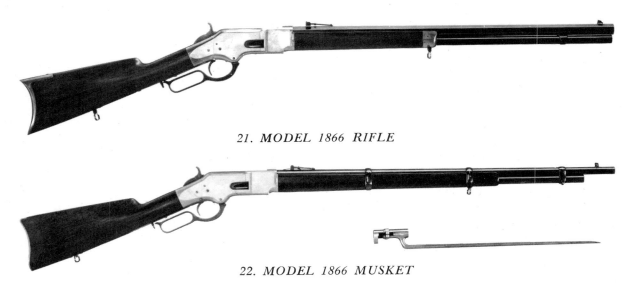

*21. MODEL 1866 RIFLE*

*22. MODEL 1866 MUSKET*

A weak point in the Henry rifle was its continuation of the Volcanic type of slotted magazine. The slot weakened the tube, making it subject to bending and it also allowed entry of mud and other foreign material when the firearm was dropped. To eliminate this objectionable feature, a different method of feeding the cartridges into the magazine and a change in the magazine tube itself was adopted for the Winchester Model 1866.

This arrangement was covered by U. S. Patent No. 55012 granted to Nelson King on May 22, 1866, assigned to Oliver F. Winchester on March 29, 1866, for a spring-closed loading port located on the right-hand side of the frame, directly at the rear of the magazine tube. By depressing the spring cover, the cartridges could be inserted one after another through the loading port directly into the magazine tube. As the magazine follower and the helical spring were placed within the magazine, the tube was completely closed on the outside. A new wooden forearm was installed.

This method of loading was much simpler and faster than loading the Henry rifle directly into the front end of the magazine tube. The opening and closing arrangement and the omission of the slot in the tube eliminated any possibility of foreign material entering and clogging up the magazine. The remainder of the mechanism of the Winchester Model of 1866 was essentially the same as the Henry rifle.

Winchester started manufacturing the Model 1866 in Bridgeport early in the spring of 1867. The Winchester Repeating Arms Company moved to New Haven in 1871, where the manufacture of the M/66 was continued.

## GENERAL SPECIFICATIONS OF THE M/66 RIFLE

| | |
|---|---|
| TYPE | Lever action repeating rifle, hammer, tubular magazine, solid frame. |
| STYLES | Sporting Rifle, Carbine, and Musket. The latter with either angular or saber type bayonet, introduced late in 1869. |
| BARRELS | Sporting Rifle, 24-inch, round or octagon. |
| | Carbine, 20-inch, round. |
| | Musket, 27-inch, round. |

| | |
|---|---|
| MAGAZINE | Tubular, full length, attached to and below the barrel. The magazine of the musket was slightly shorter than the barrel to allow for bayonet mounting. Capacity: |
| | Rifle and Musket — 17 Cartridges. |
| | Carbine — 13 Cartridges. |
| | Note: Although the Winchester catalogs listed the magazine capacity as 17 cartridges for the rifle and musket, and a check shows that these figures are correct, the M/66 rifle and musket were generally known as 15-shot repeaters. |
| TRIGGER | Plain type. |
| FIRING PIN | The M/66 was equipped with a Breech Pin Snapper which was a two prong firing pin, the prongs hitting on opposite sides of the cartridge rim. |
| CLEANING ROD | A jointed metal cleaning rod was carried in a hole in the butt stock, with access through a movable brass slide. Early production rifles had a hinged cover. |
| CHAMBER | 44 Flat Rim Fire and 44 Pointed Rim Fire (interchangeably). |
| FRAME | Brass (cast). |
| BUTT PLATE | Brass. |
| STOCK | Rifle type, straight grip. |
| | Carbine type, straight grip. |
| | Muskets were equipped with long wood stocks nearly the full length of the barrels. |
| LISTED WEIGHTS | Sporting Rifle, 24-inch, round—9 lbs. |
| | Sporting Rifle, 24-inch, octagon—9½ lbs. |
| | Carbine, 20-inch, round—7¾ lbs. |
| | Musket, 27-inch, round—8¼ lbs. |
| NUMBERS | Some of the M/66 rifles manufactured at Bridgeport have serial numbers, and some have not. |
| | On early production of '66s the serial number was located on left hand side of upper tang, inside the buttstock (buttstock has to be removed to see serial number). At about 20,000 serial range, the number was marked outside of the lower tang underneath the finger lever. At about number 125,000, the serial number was moved near the end of the lower tang. |

The Model 1866 was discontinued in 1898. Approximately 170,101 were made.

## Special Notes

The Winchester catalog of 1875 reads in part:

As in 1866 they abandoned the manufacture of the Henry rifle for the new model of that year, so they now abandon the manufacture of the model of 1866 and will (until something better can be produced) confine their works to the manufacture of the new model of 1873.

Factory records indicate, however, that during later years occasional small lots of M/66 firearms were manufactured; the record of the last firearm assembled bears the date August 1898. In 1891 1,020 M/66 component parts, on hand for many years, were used in the assembly of rifles chambered for the 44 "Henry" center fire cartridge and shipped to a firm in Brazil. In making up this lot of guns it was necessary to change the breech pin by discarding the Breech Pin Snapper, substituting a center fire firing pin and also inserting a threaded bushing in the face of the breech pin base with a hole in the center to allow the point of the firing pin to protrude and hit the primer. All other components were the same as previously used on the standard M/66, 44 caliber rim fire rifles, except for the chambering of the barrel.

Serial numbering of the Model 1866 Winchester was a continuation of that of the Henry. Actually, there was an overlapping in production of the two guns. Known examples of the Henry are numbered in the 14,000 range, with some known M/66s in the 12,000 bracket.

The first two or three thousand Model 1866s had flat brass receivers, similar to those of the Henry, without shoulders to butt against the wooden forearm. These guns also had flat spring covers for the loading port. Evidently, a very few of the first M/66s were made without the spring cover.

A second type or "New Model" 1866 saw production in the latter part of 1867. It has the more commonly known receiver and concave spring cover for the loading port. While the first type sometimes is called the "Improved Henry," in early company records it is referred to as the "Old Model" 1866 and the second version is called the "New Model."

The address "New Haven, Connecticut" was always stamped on the barrel of M/66s as the company offices and the warehouse were maintained in that city. However, the "Winchester" name did not appear on the very first examples of these guns. Early in 1869, after about nine or ten thousand had been produced, it became the practice to imprint the name on the barrel.

First M/66s were of rifle and carbine style. The musket was added to the line in 1869.

During 1870, as a result of the very large orders received from the Turkish and French governments for Winchester Model 1866 muskets and carbines, it was necessary to increase the plant capacity considerably. A stockholders' meeting held in August 1870 voted to purchase property in New Haven and to build shops there. Plans for the buildings were approved and work was started on the new plant in the fall of 1870. The last Bridgeport payroll was dated March 31, 1871; from then on the operation of the company has been carried on in New Haven.

The Model 1866 was followed by the Winchester Model 1873 Rifle.

## THOMAS GRAY BENNETT

The year 1870 is memorable in Winchester history. On the first day of August in that year, Thomas Gray Bennett entered the company's employ. Born in New Haven on March 22, 1845, he served as a volunteer during the Civil War and after being mustered out he entered the Sheffield Scientific School of Yale University and was graduated in the Class of 1870.

At a stockholders' meeting held on April 10, 1871, Bennett was elected Secretary of the company. He later served as Vice-President, remaining in that position until his election as President of the company in 1890. Through his interest in organization and processes of manufacturing, he had a very complete and practical knowledge of arms and ammunition. For many years he was as closely associated with the management of Winchester interests as was Oliver F. Winchester in the earlier years of the company.

On March 7, 1888, Winchester purchased one-half interest in the firm of E. Remington & Sons, which was dissolved and reorganized under the name Remington Arms Company with Marcellus Hartley as President and Thomas G. Bennett as Vice-President. Bennett served in this position until September 1896, when Winchester disposed of their Remington interests to Hartley & Graham. Thus, Thomas G. Bennett for a time served as Vice-President of both companies and for several years later as President of Winchester and Vice-President of Remington.

# MODEL 1873 REPEATING RIFLE

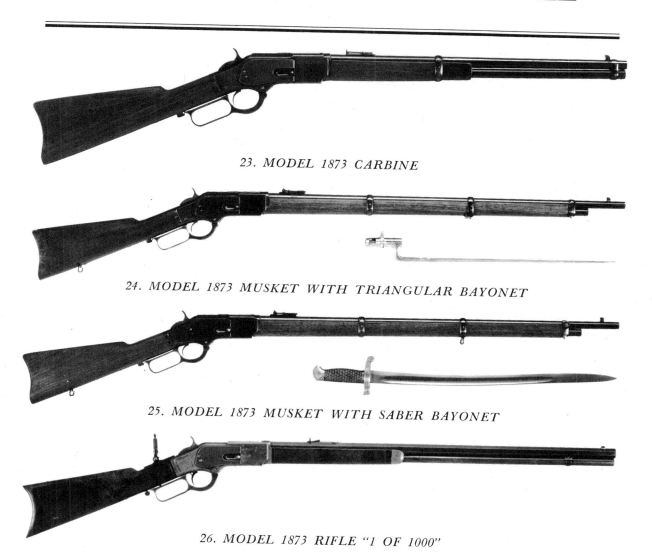

23. MODEL 1873 CARBINE

24. MODEL 1873 MUSKET WITH TRIANGULAR BAYONET

25. MODEL 1873 MUSKET WITH SABER BAYONET

26. MODEL 1873 RIFLE "1 OF 1000"

26A. CLOSE-UP OF MODEL 1873 "1 OF 1000" MARKING

27. MODEL 1873 RIFLE. HALF OCTAGON BARREL AND SHORT MAGAZINE

28. MODEL 1873 CARBINE MADE UNDER CONTRACT FOR THE SPANISH GOVERNMENT 1879.

29. MODEL 1873 MUSKET MADE UNDER CONTRACT FOR SPANISH GOVERNMENT 1879.

30. MODEL 1873 RIFLE. CALIBER .22 RIM FIRE

Standing out in Bennett's career with Winchester is his noteworthy work in connection with the Model 1873 rifle. It was only after long and diligent application to the problems involved in the perfection of a rifle that would be superior in every way to the Winchester Model 1866 that his efforts were crowned with success.

The Winchester Model 1873 was a great improvement over the Winchester Model 1866. Although built along the same general lines as the previous model, the principal changes were strengthening of the mechanism and the adaptation of the parts to handle the heavier center fire cartridges. A sliding lid or mortise cover, to keep water and dirt out of the action, was added to close the ejection port in the top of the frame. The brass frame and brass butt plates were discontinued in favor of forged iron, changed to steel in 1884. The wood forestock was lengthened considerably on the musket and the barrel length was increased from 27 inches to 30 inches. A half-octagon barrel for the sporting rifle was added, and a new set trigger for fine target shooting was listed as a special for those who desired this type of trigger.

The most accurate barrels were reserved for special orders—as shown by the following quotation from one of the early Winchester catalogs:

The barrel of every sporting rifle we make will be proved and shot at a target, and the target will be numbered to correspond with the barrel and be attached to it. All of these barrels that are found to make targets of extra merit will be made up into guns with set-triggers and extra finish and marked as a designating name, "one of a thousand," and sold at $100.00. The next grade of barrels, not quite so fine, will be marked "one of a hundred" and set up to order in any style at $20.00 advance over the list price of the corresponding style of gun.

The first M/73 rifle was listed in 44 W.C.F. caliber only. The 38 W.C.F. was first listed in 1880, and the 32 W.C.F. was first listed in 1882.

The Winchester 1885 Catalog lists a sporting rifle chambered for the 22 W.C.F. cartridge and also lists this cartridge separately with the notation "adapted to the Winchester Model 1873 and Single Shot Rifle." As no factory record can be found, it is the factory's opinion that no M/73s were furnished with this chambering, this caliber having been furnished only in the Single Shot Rifle, brought out by Winchester in 1885. Factory records show the first delivery of Model 1873 rifles to warehouse stock on September 20, 1873.

## GENERAL SPECIFICATIONS OF THE M/73 RIFLE CENTER FIRE

TYPE    Lever action repeating rifle, hammer, tubular magazine, solid frame.

STYLE    Sporting Rifle; Special Sporting Rifle; Carbine; Musket, with either angular or saber bayonet.

BARRELS    Sporting Rifle 24-inch, round, octagon, ½ octagon, 20-inch, octagon.
Carbine, 20-inch, round.
Musket, 30-inch, round.
Shorter barrels, round and octagon, 20, 18, 16, and 14 inches in length were also furnished on rifles and carbines. These shorter barrels were largely used by the rubber industry in South America. Extra length barrels and magazines, also extra heavy barrels round or octagon were furnished.

MAGAZINE    Tubular magazine.
Sporting Rifle, capacity 15 cartridges.
Sporting Rifle (short magazine), 6 cartridges.
Carbine, 12 cartridges.
Musket, 17 cartridges.

| | |
|---|---|
| TRIGGER | Plain type. |
| | A set trigger on sporting rifles was furnished as a special for those who desired this type of trigger. |
| CHAMBERS | Center Fire, 44 W.C.F. (44-40), 38 W.C.F. (38-40), 32 W.C.F. (32-20). |
| RECEIVER | Iron, forged. Later changed to steel. Listed in September 1, 1884, catalog. |
| STOCK | Rifle type, curved iron butt plate, straight grip. (Shotgun butt was first listed as a special in 1879.) |
| | Carbine type, carbine stock, straight grip. |
| | Pistol grip first listed in 1887. |
| | Muskets—long wood stock, nearly the full length of the barrel. |
| LISTED WEIGHTS | Sporting Rifle, 24-inch, octagon, 9 lbs.; 24-inch, ½ octagon, 8¾ lbs.; 24-inch, round, 8½ lbs. |
| | Carbine, 20-inch round—7¼-7½ lbs. |
| | Musket, 30-inch, round—9½ lbs. |
| CLEANING ROD | A jointed metal cleaning rod was carried in a hole in the butt stock with access through a slide in the butt plate. |
| SERIAL NUMBERS | M/73 rifles were serially numbered from 1 up, number being located near the end of lower tang. Letter following serial number refers to a minor change in the mechanism. |

The Model 1873 listed the following Winchester firsts:
1. Their first center fire firearm.
2. Their first firearm chambered for 22 caliber rim fire cartridges.
3. Their first set trigger as a special.
4. Their first shotgun butt type stock as a special (in 1879).
5. Their first selected barrels as a special.
6. Their first center fire cartridge, the 44 W.C.F. (44-40 Winchester).

M/73s chambered for center fire cartridges were discontinued in 1919, the final clean-up of the odds and ends being made in 1924 and 1925. Approximately 720,610 were made.

# MODEL 1873 RIFLE: RIM FIRE

Model 1873s, chambered for 22 Short rim fire and 22 Long rim fire cartridges (not interchangeable), were first announced in the catalog issue of 1884 which read in part:

> For convenience in carrying, the barrel, forearm, and magazine, fastened together, are attached to the frame by a taper pin. By drawing out this pin those parts may be separated from the frame, thus making the gun more easily packed in trunk or case.

This arrangement, used only on rifles chambered for 22 Short and 22 Long, was found unsatisfactory and was changed later to the same construction used on the M/73 center fire rifles (threaded shank).

Model 1873 rifles chambered for the 22 Short and 22 Long rim fire cartridges were of the same general type as the Model 1873 center fire sporting rifles.

Barrels 24- or 26-inch round, half octagon or octagon were furnished.

Magazine capacity: 22 Short, 25 cartridges; 22 Long, 20 cartridges.

A few Model 1873 rifles, chambered for the 22 extra long rim fire cartridges, were furnished on special order only.

The Model 1873 rim fire rifle was produced from 1884 to 1904. Approximately 19,552 were made.

It is generally conceded that the Winchester Model 1873 was the first repeating rifle made in this country chambered for 22 caliber rim fire cartridges. It was a very satisfactory firearm although its sale was considerably restricted by the general preference for the larger and more powerful calibers then in common use.

A note dated August 1, 1904, was inserted in the catalog, reading:

Having discontinued making Model 1873 rifles chambered for 22 caliber cartridges and our stock being exhausted, we cannot fill any further orders for them. Component parts for this model and caliber will be furnished as long as our stock lasts.

*Special Notes*

The introduction of the Model 1873 Winchester brought about the designation of the first Winchester as the Model 1866; until that time the guns had been referred to simply as "Winchesters."

About the first 30,000 had finger levers similar to the Model 1866 and a mortise cover with no groove on the underside. Early in 1879, a lug shaped piece fashioned on the top forward end of the finger loop of the operating lever was provided in order to make contact with a small pin, projecting from the under side of the receiver when the lever is closed. This device was a safety feature, for as long as the pin was extended the trigger could not be pulled.

In 1879, a new mortise cover with groove on underside, which slid on a mortise cover rib, was introduced. This rib was held to the top of the receiver by two short screws. About 1884 the mortise cover rib held on by two screws was changed. The receiver then was made with a rib machined as part of the receiver.

Finger lever catch was made as thumb screw for about the first 20,000, then made as a sliding catch.

Shortly after the Model 1873 center fire rifle was introduced by Winchester, the Colt Patent Firearms Company announced, in 1878, their single action army revolver with the 44 W.C.F. (44-40 Winchester) chambering. Winchester Model 1873 rifles and carbines, with their rugged construction and reliability in all kinds of weather, shared with this Colt revolver, using the same Winchester cartridges, the top position in the romance and history of the winning of the West— the frontier battles between Indians, cowboys, ranchers, sheriffs, and outlaws—during this turbulent period of American history. Carried in a saddle holster, the Winchester Model 1873 went with the westerner and frontiersman as a constant companion, provided his food, defended his possessions, and frequently saved his life and the lives of his family.

Model 1873 carbines were so popular that it was a common saying that "many a western baby cut his first teeth on the sling (saddle) ring of a Winchester Model 73 carbine." The Winchester Model 1873 was used by Buffalo Bill (Colonel W. F. Cody) on the Western plains and in exhibition work for nearly half a century. It was also the rifle referred to often in the famous dime novels of the 1880s and 1890s: "Crack-crack-crack went the Winchester, and fifteen Indians bit the dust."

The Model 1873 was successful from its introduction and played an important part in establishing the Winchester prestige and reputation for high quality firearms and ammunition. The Model 1873 was followed by the Winchester Model 1876 rifle and was succeeded later by the Winchester Model 1892 rifle.

# MODEL 1876 REPEATING RIFLE

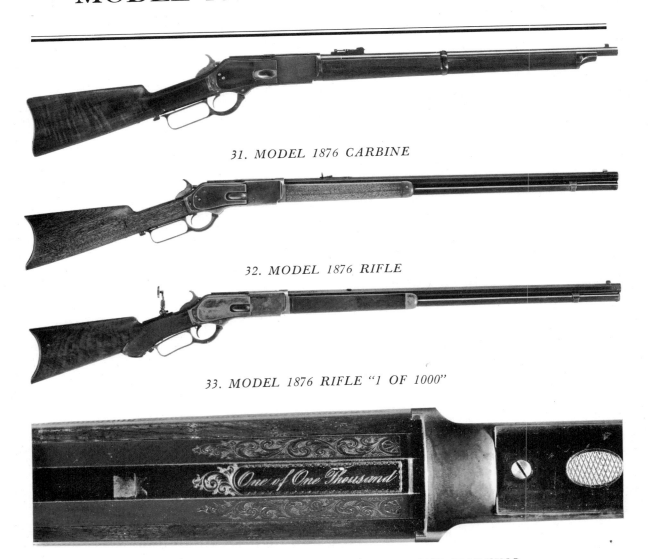

*31. MODEL 1876 CARBINE*

*32. MODEL 1876 RIFLE*

*33. MODEL 1876 RIFLE "1 OF 1000"*

*33A. CLOSE-UP OF MODEL 1876 "1 OF 1000" MARKING*

Although the popularity of the Winchester Model 1873 was such that a very large quantity of the various styles were manufactured, the cartridges used in them were relatively light in comparison with the heavier and more powerful calibers used in competitors' models of the single shot type. In response to continued demand for a repeating rifle to handle larger caliber cartridges with longer range and more effective striking power, Winchester went to work on a model for this purpose.

The new rifle was developed in 1876. Several sample firearms were made up and exhibited at the Centennial Exposition held in Philadelphia in the summer of that year and, because of this fact, the model was commonly referred to as the Winchester Centennial Model. The first public announcement of the Model 1876 was in a Winchester leaflet dated August 10, 1877, and covered the sporting rifle, target rifle, carbine, and musket, all chambered for the special 45-75 W.C.F. cartridge that Winchester had developed for this new model. The first shipment from the plant was made June 8, 1877.

The 45-75 Winchester cartridge, loaded with 75 grains of black powder and a 350-grain lead bullet, gave a striking energy of approximately 1,400 foot pounds, or more than double that of the 44-40 Winchester caliber.

The Model 1876 carbine with the 45-75 Winchester chambering was adopted as the official firearm of the Royal Northwest Mounted Police in Canada in 1883, and was used by them for many years. It was this carbine that helped put down the Riel rebellion in 1885.

The Model 1876 was basically the Winchester Model 1873 with several important changes and improvements. The receiver and other important parts were made larger and stronger to handle the larger calibers, the carbine barrel was increased from 20 inches to 22 inches in length, and the musket barrel length was increased from 30 inches to 32 inches. On both the carbine and musket the forearm was extended to nearly the full length of the barrel.

A special sporting rifle was furnished with a pistol grip stock and vernier rear and wind-gauge front sights. An express rifle was listed in 50 caliber using a 300-grain hollow point lead bullet with a copper tube inserted.

The 45-75 Winchester was the first caliber listed. The 50-95 Express and the 45-60 W.C.F. were added in 1879, the 40-60 W.C.F. in 1884.

## GENERAL SPECIFICATIONS OF THE M/76 RIFLE

| | |
|---|---|
| TYPE | Lever action repeating rifle, hammer, tubular magazine, solid frame. |
| STYLES | Sporting Rifle; Express Rifle; Carbine; Musket, with either angular or saber bayonet. |
| BARRELS | Sporting Rifle, 28-inch, round, octagon, ½ octagon. |
| | Express Rifle, 26-inch, round, octagon, ½ octagon. |
| | Carbine, 22-inch, round. |
| | Musket, 32-inch, round. |

The most accurate barrels were reserved for special orders as shown by the following quotation from one of the early Winchester catalogs:

The barrel of every sporting rifle we make will be proved and shot at a target and the target will be numbered to correspond with the barrel attached to it. All of these barrels that are found to make targets of extra merit will be made up into guns with set triggers and extra finish and marked as a designating name, one of a thousand, and sold at $100.00. The next grade of barrels not quite so fine will be marked one of a hundred and set up to order in any style at $20.00 advance over the list price of the corresponding style of gun.

| | |
|---|---|
| MAGAZINE | Tubular magazine.<br>Sporting Rifle, full magazine — 12 cartridges.<br>Carbine, full magazine — 9 cartridges.<br>Musket, full magazine — 13 cartridges.<br>(Short and full length magazines were furnished.) |
| TRIGGER | Standard Sporting Rifles, Express Rifles, Carbines, and Muskets were furnished with plain triggers.<br>(Set triggers were furnished as a special.) |
| STOCK | Rifle type, curved iron butt plate, straight grip.<br>Carbines and Muskets had extra long stocks.<br>A special Sporting Rifle was also furnished with a pistol grip stock as a standard.<br>Pistol grip stocks were furnished on other M/76s as a special. |
| LISTED WEIGHTS | Sporting Rifles, 28-inch, round—9¼ lbs.<br>Sporting Rifles, 28-inch, ½ octagon—9½ lbs.<br>Sporting Rifles, 28-inch, octagon—9¾ lbs.<br>Carbine, 22-inch, round—8¼ lbs.<br>Musket, 32-inch, round—8¾-9 lbs. |
| CLEANING ROD | A jointed metal cleaning rod was carried in a hole in the butt stock with access through a slide in the butt plate. |
| SERIAL NUMBERS | M/76 rifles were serially numbered from 1 up, located near the end of the lower tang. |

*Special Notes*

The Model 1876 became popular with those who desired a heavy caliber firearm in the repeating type. Fairly large quantities were sold, especially in England, India, Africa, and Canada. It was an early favorite of Theodore Roosevelt, who later became President of the United States.

Manufacture of the Winchester Model 1876 was discontinued in 1897; about 63,871 were made. The later and more modern Winchester rifles had become well established and, as smokeless powders were coming into general use, the older, black powder models were rapidly becoming obsolete.

The Model 1876 was followed by the development of the Winchester revolver and the announcement of the Double Barrel Breech Loading Shotgun.

# WINCHESTER PISTOL: REVOLVING TYPE

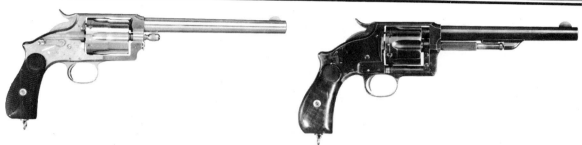

*34. & 35. EXPERIMENTAL REVOLVERS MADE BY HUGO BORCHARDT 1876*

*36. WINCHESTER EXPERIMENTAL REVOLVER MADE BY WILLIAM MASON 1883.*

The few hand-sized weapons ever considered by Winchester for addition to its line of firearms were developed in 1876. One was a single action revolver, with a surprisingly modern swing-out cylinder action, holding six 44 W.C.F. (44-40 Winchester) cartridges, developed by Hugo Borchardt who had come to Winchester from his former employment with the Colt Patent Fire Arms Company. The other had a lever on the right-hand side of the frame which when pressed down served as an extractor. Hugo Borchardt remained with Winchester for several years, went with the Sharps Rifle Company about 1880, and later returned to Germany with his design for an automatic pistol which was brought out in 1893.

On December 5, 1876, Amory Edwards, representing the Winchester Repeating Arms Company, submitted to the Ordnance Bureau of the United States Navy a sample of the revolver with a quantity of cartridges and copies of the instructions covering the method of operating the firearm, which read:

> To open: Take the pistol in the left hand, draw the rod on the under side toward the muzzle with the right hand and press it toward you. The revolving chamber opens toward you. The extractor is pressing down on the end of the rod, and it closes with a twist of the left wrist.

[ 23 ]

The revolver was also submitted to General Ordnitz of the Ordnance Department of the Russian Army.

Another similar revolver, but showing a number of improvements, was made in 1883. It was designed by William Mason, a former Colt employee, who at that time was Winchester's master mechanic and gun designer. This design had the same revolving cylinder and length of barrel used in the earlier model. The older form of extractor was omitted and replaced with a side rod ejector. This experimental revolver, of 44-40 Winchester caliber, closely approximated the design and appearance of the Colt Single Action Army Revolver, which at that time was commonly known as the Colt Frontier Revolver. None of these Winchester revolvers were listed in Winchester catalogs or price lists or were offered for public sale.

# BREECH LOADING SHOTGUNS: DOUBLE BARREL

*37. ENGLISH MADE DOUBLE BARREL SHOTGUN. SOLD THROUGH WINCHESTER'S NEW YORK STORE 1879 TO 1884.*

In 1878 an agent of Winchester, P. G. Sanford, was sent on a business trip to Birmingham, England. While there, he received instructions from the company to purchase a quantity of the cheaper grades of English double barrel, breech loading shotguns, for shipment to Winchester's New York City office because there was a shortage of shotguns in the New York area. At that time Winchester had no facilities for manufacture of such guns. It was believed that considerable additional business could be obtained by the importation and sale of English shotguns.

The arms were purchased from Messrs. W. C. McEntree & Company, Richard Rodman, C. G. Bonehill, and some of better grade from Messrs. W. C. Scott & Sons. After the arrival of the English guns in New York, they sold so rapidly that Winchester decided to purchase additional quantities of the better grades of English manufacture, to be marked with the Winchester name.

This new line, first announced on a loose-leaf insert in the Winchester catalog of 1879, consisted of Winchester Double Barrel Breech Loading Shotguns in 5 grades:

> Winchester Match Gun
> Winchester Class A
> Winchester Class B
> Winchester Class C
> Winchester Class D

Winchester in 1880 announced further details and prices of this new line as follows: The Winchester Match Gun and Classes A, B, and C were all furnished in 10 and 12 bore with either 30-inch or 32-inch laminated steel barrels. The Class D guns were furnished in the same gauges and barrel lengths, but were listed as having English twist barrels.

Retail prices were:

| | |
|---|---|
| Winchester Match Gun | $85.00 |
| Class A | 70.00 |
| Class B | 60.00 |
| Class C | 50.00 |
| Class D | 40.00 |

Club Gun, available, but little is known about it.

All of these guns were fitted with English walnut stocks, checkered grip and forearm, and were marked on the top rib:

*Winchester Repeating Arms Co.*
*(Match Gun) New Haven, Connecticut, U.S.A.*

This business continued on a very profitable basis for several years and Mr. Sanford made trips to England to purchase additional quantities of the Winchester-branded shotguns which were offered for sale only through the Winchester New York office. About 10,000 were imported.

During the early 1880s the New York office also sold Smith & Wesson, Colt, and several makes of European revolvers and pistols. In 1884, Winchester decided that as an American manufacturer interested in producing and selling its own products, it should discontinue the importation and purchase of other manufacturers' items. The balance of the stock of shotguns of English manufacture was sold to John P. Moore & Sons on May 12, 1884.

Winchester then began to consider the development of a shotgun that could be manufactured at its own plant, incorporating the lever action, repeating type of construction that the company had popularized for many years. These double barrel shotguns were followed by the Hotchkiss Repeater (Model 83 Rifle).

### OLIVER FISHER WINCHESTER

Oliver F. Winchester died on December 10, 1880, after having served as President of the company for many years. He had brought it up from the early days of the Volcanic Repeating Arms Company—a failing organization engaged in the manufacture of an impractical weapon—to the Winchester Repeating Arms Company, a successful organization with a capital stock issue of $1,000,000 and annual sales approximating that figure. He was succeeded by William W. Converse on March 2, 1881.

# WINCHESTER MODEL 1883 RIFLE
## (HOTCHKISS REPEATER
## or HOTCHKISS MAGAZINE GUN)

*38. HOTCHKISS MUSKET. FIRST STYLE 1879 AND 1880*

*39. HOTCHKISS CARBINE. SECOND STYLE 1880 TO 1883*

*40. HOTCHKISS SPORTING RIFLE WITH ENGRAVED RECEIVER. THIRD STYLE 1883 TO 1899. (CALLED MODEL 1883)*

Another new repeating rifle was shown at the Centennial Exposition at Philadelphia in 1876. It was the invention of an American, Benjamin B. Hotchkiss, who was engaged in the manufacture of artillery-sized weapons of various types, as well as other firearms. His factory was located at St. Denis, France, near Paris. The new model was covered by United States patents as well as various European patents.

In 1877, Winchester purchased from Hotchkiss the right to manufacture and sell the firearm. Their catalog issue of May 1, 1878, announced the rifle as the Hotchkiss Repeater with the statement: "These arms will not be in the market for some months, but models may be seen at our depot, 245 Broadway, New York."

It was found necessary to make many changes in the firearm originally introduced by Hotchkiss and for these improvements U. S. patents were granted to Winchester. To show that the gun was in process of being manufactured, the following is quoted from the May 1, 1879, Winchester catalog: "Samples can be seen at our works or at the New York Sales Office, 245 Broadway. Orders will be filled promptly after June 1, 1879."

The August 1, 1880, catalog listed the model as the Hotchkiss Magazine Gun. This name was in continued use until final changes were made and it was publicly announced as the Winchester Model 1883 in the catalog issue of January 1, 1884. This was the first bolt action rifle made by Winchester. The tubular magazine is located in the butt stock and the mechanism is operated by what was commonly known as the up-turn and pull-back bolt action.

## GENERAL SPECIFICATIONS OF THE M/83 RIFLE

| | |
|---|---|
| TYPE | Bolt action repeating rifle, tubular magazine, solid frame. |
| STYLES | Sporting Rifle; Carbine; Musket, with either angular or saber bayonet. |
| BARRELS | Sporting Rifle, 26-inch, round, octagon, ½ octagon. |
| | Carbine 24-inch, round; changed to 22½ inch, round in 1884. |
| | Musket 32-inch, round; changed to 28-inch, round in 1884. |
| MAGAZINE | M/83s were made with a tubular magazine in the butt stock holding six cartridges. |
| TRIGGER | Plain trigger. |
| | (Set triggers were furnished as a special.) |
| CHAMBER | 45-70-405 U.S. Government. |
| | The Winchester January 1884 catalog lists a sporting rifle chambered for a 40-65 Hotchkiss cartridge and also lists this cartridge separately with the notation "adapted to the Hotchkiss Repeating Rifle Model 1883." As both the sporting rifle and the cartridge were omitted from the September 1884 catalog, there is a question whether this rifle was ever furnished. No factory record can be found and it is thought that, although listed in the catalog, it was withdrawn later and never furnished. |
| STOCKS | Military type for muskets and carbines. Rifle type for the sporting rifles. Straight grip on muskets, carbines, and plain sporting rifle. Shotgun butt stocks also available. |
| LISTED WEIGHTS | Sporting Rifle 26-inch, round—8¼ lbs. |
| | 26-inch, octagon—8½ lbs. |
| | 26-inch, ½ octagon—8½ lbs. |
| | Carbine 24-inch, round—8½ lbs. |
| | 22½-inch, round—8¼ lbs. |
| | Musket 32-inch, round—9 lbs. |
| | 28-inch, round—9 lbs. |
| SERIAL NUMBERS | Hotchkiss Repeaters were serially numbered 1 up, the numbers continuing on the M/83. 1st and 2nd style numbered on left side top of receiver, 3rd style on underside of receiver in front of trigger guard. |

Manufacture of the Model 1883 was discontinued in 1899 and all surplus component parts were scrapped in 1913.

### Special Notes

The Model 1883 was a bolt action firearm designed for military use and was chambered for the 45-70 cartridge, the official cartridge of the United States Army at that time. It was an excellent weapon for military use and a reasonable quantity was sold for this purpose. However, it had a very limited sale as a sporting arm. Shooters generally preferred the older, lever action type of mechanism with which they were familiar.

On November 20, 1920, Winchester presented a Model 1883 rifle to the Hotchkiss Library of Sharon, Connecticut, founded in memory of Mr. B. B. Hotchkiss, the inventor of the Hotchkiss Repeater.

The Hotchkiss Repeater, later changed to Model 1883, was followed by the Winchester Single Shot Rifle.

### HOTCHKISS FIRST STYLE 1879 - 1880

Approximately 6,419 made. First style had a magazine cutoff and safety control contained in single unit, in form of a turn button on right side above trigger guard.

### HOTCHKISS SECOND STYLE 1880 - 1883

Approximately 16,102 made. Had magazine cutoff on right side, top of receiver, rear of bolt handle. Safety on left side of receiver opposite magazine cutoff.

### HOTCHKISS THIRD STYLE 1883 - 1899

Approximately 62,034 made. Had two piece stock.

# SINGLE SHOT RIFLE

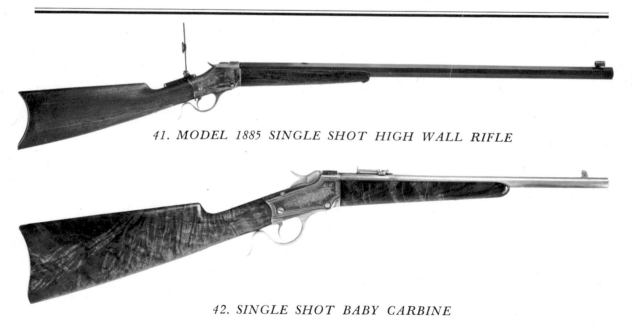

*41. MODEL 1885 SINGLE SHOT HIGH WALL RIFLE*

*42. SINGLE SHOT BABY CARBINE*

*43. SINGLE SHOT SCHUETZEN RIFLE. TAKEDOWN*

*44. SINGLE SHOT CALIBER .22 MUSKET*

*45. SINGLE SHOT SHOTGUN*

On October 7, 1879, U. S. Patent 220,271 was granted to John M. Browning of Ogden, Utah, covering a lever action, single shot rifle adaptable to heavy hunting caliber cartridges. John Browning and his brothers operated a small gunshop in Ogden. They manufactured a quantity of rifles under this patent, which they intended to sell to hunters and plainsmen needing powerful and accurate single shot rifles for hunting purposes.

According to the *History of Browning Guns,* a representative of the Winchester Repeating Arms Company saw the rifle before enough of them were completed to warrant their being put on sale by the Browning brothers. Winchester promptly started negotiations with the Brownings that ended in the purchase of all firearms and component parts that had been produced and also the right to manufacture under this patent, exclusively, from that time on.

It is Winchester's impression, however, that some of these Browning manufactured rifles had been sold privately, and it was their excellent performance in the field that brought them to the attention of Winchester and caused them to send a representative to Ogden to start negotiations with the Browning brothers. The purchase, made about 1883, was the beginning of Winchester's close association and business dealings with the Browning brothers, which continued for many years.

This was the first single shot rifle made by Winchester. The original announcement of this model appeared in the catalog of 1885 and read in part:

> The Winchester Single Shot Rifle. This gun has the old Sharpe's breech-block and lever and is as safe and solid as that arm. The firing pin is automatically withdrawn at the first opening movement of the gun and held back until the gun is closed. The hammer is centrally hung,

[ 29 ]

but drops down with the breech-block when the gun is opened and is cocked by the closing movement. It can also be cocked by hand. This arrangement allows the barrel to be wiped and examined from the breech.

In outline everything has been done to make the gun pleasing to the eye. It can be furnished either with or without set triggers, with barrels of all ordinary lengths and weights and for all standard cartridges, also with rifle and shotgun butt, plain or fancy wood, or with pistol grip.

The Winchester October 1886 catalog added the following: "All 22 Caliber Rim Fire rifles are fitted with a kicking extractor which throws the shell clear of the gun."

## GENERAL SPECIFICATIONS OF THE SINGLE SHOT RIFLE

TYPE
Lever action, single shot rifle, hammer, solid frame.
Takedown was first listed in June 1910.

STYLES
Plain Sporting Rifle, Special Sporting Rifle, Special Target Rifle, Schuetzen Rifle.
The Standard Schuetzen Rifle was described in Winchester catalogs as:

> Special Single Shot Rifle. Half octagon barrel, fancy walnut, checked pistol grip stock with Swiss cheek piece, nickel plated Swiss butt plate, case hardened frame, plain trigger with mid-range vernier peep and wind gauge sights, without slot cut in barrel for rear sight.

In the Winchester March 1897 catalog a new standard Schuetzen rifle was listed as:

### Winchester Schuetzen Rifle

> Octagon barrel 30 inch No. 3, fancy walnut checked pistol grip stock, with Swiss cheek piece, Schuetzen butt plate, (Helm Pattern) case hardened frame, double-set trigger, spur finger lever, palm rest, with mid-range vernier peep and wind gauge sights, without slot in barrel for rear sight, weighing 12 lbs., $61.00. With No. 4 barrel, weighing 13 lbs., $63.00.

The Schuetzen single shot rifle in takedown form was first listed in June 1910.

LIGHTWEIGHT CARBINE
This carbine was sometimes called the Baby Carbine and was first listed in March 1898 as: "Fifteen-inch round barrel, plain trigger, straight grip stock and forearm of plain wood, sling ring on frame, caliber 44 W.C.F., weight about $4\frac{1}{4}$ pounds."

MUSKET
The musket style was first listed but not pictured in the Winchester catalog for October 1886. This would probably have been 45-70, not 22 caliber rim fire. A musket was listed in the Winchester October 1905 catalog and was described as: "Standard and only style made. Round barrel, 28 inches long, chambered for 22 Long Rifle cartridge; weight about $8\frac{1}{2}$ pounds. Designed especially for military indoor target shooting and preliminary outdoor practice." This musket was later changed and was generally known as the "Winder" Musket in honor of Colonel C. B. Winder who assisted in its revamping. Muskets chambered for the 22 Short cartridge were first listed in the Winchester 1914 catalog.

20 GAUGE SHOTGUN
A 20 gauge single shot shotgun, in both solid frame and takedown, was first listed in 1914. The catalog listing of this 20 Gauge reads:
> The gun is made with 26-inch, full choked nickel steel barrel chambered for shells 3 inches in length and under. Its length overall is $41\frac{3}{4}$ inches,

length of stock 13-7/16 inches, drop at comb 1-7/16 inches, and drop at heel 2-11/16 inches. It weighs about 5½ pounds, it has straight grip stock and forearm of plain walnut and is fitted with a rubber butt plate. The receiver is matted on top along the line of sight, cylinder bore or modified choke barrels will be furnished instead of full choke, without extra charge and interchangeable barrels, full choke, modified choke or cylinder bore will be furnished for takedown guns. Matted barrels and matted rib barrels also will be furnished.

RIFLE BARRELS Round, octagon, and ½ octagon rifle barrels were furnished in several different styles, weights, and in various lengths. The October 1886 catalog covers the types and weights of barrels with the following statement:

To accommodate all tastes as to weights we shall make five sizes of barrels numbered from 1 to 5 and varying in weight:

No. 1 Barrel is the smallest and will be adapted to small caliber rim and center fire cartridges and will also take 22, 32, 38, and 44 W.C.F. cartridges. Guns with this size will weigh from 7 to 8 pounds varying according to caliber.

No. 2 Barrel is intended for small sizes of center fire cartridges and will weigh about 8½ lbs. If light guns are desired for the larger sizes of center fire cartridges, this barrel can be furnished for them.

No. 3 Barrel is intended for large sizes of military and sporting cartridges and will weigh from 9 to 10 pounds, varying according to caliber. With the same length and outside size, a 38 caliber will weigh about one half pound more than a 45 caliber.

All of the above barrels will be listed at the same price, viz: $5.00 for an octagon barrel of standard length.

No. 4 Barrel is made to accommodate those wanting a heavier gun, and will weigh from 10½ to 11 pounds. For this weight an additional charge of $2.00 will be made over the regular price.

No. 5 Barrel is the heaviest that can be made and will weigh about 12 pounds. For this weight an additional charge of $10.00 will be made over the regular price.

(Weights shown in the foregoing cover the complete weight of the gun with each style of barrel.)

No. 3½ Barrel was added in June 1910. The butt end of this barrel was the same size as the No. 4 and the muzzle end the same size as the No. 3 barrel. It was developed especially for chambering the 35 W.C.F. and 405 W.C.F. cartridges and weighed a bit more than the standard No. 3 Barrel.

TRIGGER Plain trigger was standard.
(Set triggers were furnished as special.)

CHAMBERS Chambered for all of the older standard calibers from 22 caliber to 50 caliber, both rim fire and center fire except cartridges of the rimless type. A few special order rifles were made for the rimless 6mm Lee and 30-06 cartridges.

FRAME Three different frames were used to cover the wide range of cartridges used in this model.

Frames were originally case hardened until August 1901, when change was made to the standard bluing method.

In 1908 the mainspring was changed from a flat spring attached to the barrel to a wire coil spring attached to the hammer and breechblock; also the hammer was made to remain at half cock instead of full cock when the action was closed.

STOCK    Plain Sporting Rifle, rifle type butt, straight grip.

Special Sporting Rifle, rifle type butt, pistol grip.

Schuetzen rifle, special Schuetzen type.

Musket, musket type.

CLEANING RODS    Standard equipment, brass rod with each 22 caliber arm, slotted hickory rod with all other calibers.

WEIGHTS    Weights varied in accordance with the caliber, style, and length of barrel.

SERIAL NUMBERS    Single Shot Rifles were serially numbered from 1 up, located near end of lower tang.

This model was discontinued about 1920; about 139,725 had been made. The Single Shot Musket was continued and listed as the Model 87. This was an arbitrary model number and should not have been used, as it conflicted with the Winchester M/87 shotgun, which was first listed in June 1887.

### Special Notes

The Single Shot model, with its three sizes of frames and six weights of barrels, with chambers ranging from the small 22 Short rim fire cartridge to the large 50 caliber center fire cartridges, covered practically the entire range of metallic ammunition calibers. The weights ranged from the light carbine chambered for the 44 W.C.F. (44-40) weighing 4¼ pounds with a 15-inch barrel to the Schuetzen rifle usually chambered for the 32-40 W.C.F. and 38-55 W.C.F. cartridges and weighing up to 13 pounds. The styles covered standard and special sporting rifles, an extra light carbine, special target rifles and the well-known Winder Musket; a large number of these were used for training United States troops during World War I.

The 20 gauge shotgun was announced in 1914, the year following the introduction of the Winchester Model 12, 20 gauge repeater. This Single Shot was added because of the immediate popularity of the 20 gauge in the repeating style, but was an unsuccessful venture and very few were sold.

The Single Shot Model was followed by the Winchester Model 1886 Rifle.

# MODEL 1886 REPEATING RIFLE

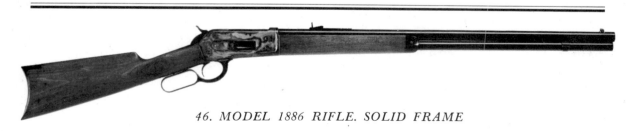

*46. MODEL 1886 RIFLE. SOLID FRAME*

*47. MODEL 1886 RIFLE. TAKEDOWN*

*48. MODEL 1886 SPORTING RIFLE. TAKEDOWN. ENGRAVED AND GOLD INLAID.*

*49. MODEL 1886 MUSKET*

*50. MODEL 1886 CARBINE*

Winchester had been giving considerable thought for some time to the adoption of a new repeating firearm capable of handling some of the powerful center fire cartridges of the period, especially the 45-70 caliber that was then the official cartridge adopted by the United States Government. The Winchester lever action Model 1876's locking device was not strong enough to handle the 45-70 Government caliber or some of the heavy bullet cartridges used in competitors' single shot firearms for long range, big game shooting. The Winchester Hotchkiss—which was the first bolt action repeating rifle made in this country—although chambered for the 45-70 Government caliber, had not proved generally acceptable to shooters for hunting purposes, due principally to its bolt action mechanism; they preferred the older type of lever action with which they were familiar.

Mr. Thomas G. Bennett had traveled to Ogden, Utah, in 1883 to negotiate with the Browning Brothers for their single shot rifle. While there, he obtained a crude model of a lever action repeater, designed to handle the long and powerful center fire cartridges. U. S. Patent 306,577 was granted to John M. Browning and Matthew S. Browning for this model on October 14, 1884, and assigned to the Winchester Repeating Arms Company. In making arrangements for the manufacturing rights for this model, Winchester agreed that part of the payment would be made in rifles. This would explain why barrels of some of the Model 1886s are marked, "Browning Bros. Ogden, Utah."

Winchester, in its final development of this model, made several changes from the original design, the most important being an improvement in the feeding mechanism. This change was covered by U. S. Patent 311,079 granted to William Mason on January 20, 1885, and assigned to the Winchester Repeating Arms Company by Mason, who at that time was Winchester's master mechanic and gun designer.

Factory records show the first delivery of Model 1886 rifles to warehouse stock was made on August 30, 1886.

The first public announcement of Winchester Model 1886 was in the catalog of October 1886 and read in part:

> This gun is adapted to 45-70 Government cartridges with 405 or 500 grain bullet, and to 45-90-300 or 40-82-260 cartridges especially made for it. The magazine is filled while the gun is closed, through a spring cover at the side, and is provided with a stop which permits the use of cartridges having the same shell of varying lengths less than the standard, thus the same gun will use 45-70-405 or 45-70-500 Government cartridges.

The M/86 as first listed in the Winchester October 1886 catalog was chambered for the following calibers:

45-70 U. S. Government
45-90 W.C.F.
40-82 W.C.F.
40-65 W.C.F., first listed in June 1887
38-56 W.C.F., first listed in June 1887
50-110 Express, first listed in Nov. 1887
40-70 W.C.F., first listed in Apr. 1894
38-70 W.C.F., first listed in Apr. 1894
50-100-450, first listed in Aug. 1895
33 W.C.F., first listed in Mar. 1903

## GENERAL SPECIFICATIONS OF THE M/86 RIFLE

TYPE
Lever action repeating rifle, hammer, tubular magazine, solid frame. Takedown was first listed in April 1894.

STYLES
Sporting Rifle, Fancy Sporting Rifle, Extra Light Weight Rifle (45-70) first listed in March 1897, Half Magazine Rifle.
Carbine was first listed in June 1887 and was made in solid frame only. The first Model 1886 carbines had the same type of forearm as the Model 1876 carbine. The forearm was practically the full length of the barrel. The change-over to the standard type of carbine forearm was made in 1889.
Elaborately ornamented M/86s were also furnished at special prices. A few M/86 muskets were made on special order (about 350).

BARRELS
Sporting Rifle, 26-inch, round, octagon, ½ octagon.
Fancy Sporting Rifle, 26-inch, octagon.
Extra Light Weight Rifle, 22-inch, round (nickel steel).
Carbine, 22-inch, round.

Shorter barrels, heavier barrels, extra length barrels, and extra length magazines were furnished at extra cost.

The furnishing of extra length barrels was discontinued in 1908.

MAGAZINES — Both full and half magazines were furnished.

Magazine capacities varied in accordance with the caliber and length of magazine.

TRIGGER — Plain type was standard.

Set triggers were furnished as a special. The first were single-set, changed to double-set in May 1895.

CHAMBERS — 45-70 U. S. Government (45-70 caliber in all weights of bullets could be used in this chamber).

45-90 W.C.F. (45-85 and 45-82 could be used in this chamber).

40-82 W.C.F. (40-75 could be used in this chamber).

40-65 W.C.F.

38-56 W.C.F.

40-70 W.C.F.

38-70 W.C.F.

50-100-450

50-110 Express

33 W.C.F.

The 40-82 W.C.F., 40-70 W.C.F., 40-65 W.C.F., 38-70 W.C.F., 38-56 W.C.F., and 50-100-450 were dropped in 1911. From September 1920 to January 1928, the Model 1886 was listed in 33 caliber only. From 1928 to July 1931 it was also listed in 45-70 caliber.

FRAME — First listed as case hardened, changed to standard blued finish in August 1901.

STOCK — Standard.

Sporting Rifle, rifle type butt, straight grip.

Fancy Sporting Rifle, rifle type butt, pistol grip.

Half Magazine Rifle, shotgun butt, straight grip.

Carbine, carbine type, straight grip.

Extras such as shotgun butt stock with either metal or hard rubber butt plate, special dimension stocks, straight or pistol grip, etc. were also furnished.

CLEANING ROD — Standard equipment, slotted hickory rod with each rifle.

WEIGHTS — Weights varied in accordance with the length, type of barrel, and the cartridge for which the arm was chambered.

SERIAL NUMBERS — Model 86s were serially numbered from 1 up. Located near end of lower tang.

Manufacture of the Model 1886 rifle was discontinued in 1935. Approximately 159,994 were made.

## Special Notes

The Winchester Model 1886 was the first repeating rifle to successfully employ the sliding vertical locks. The joint between the breech block and the barrel was effectively sealed and the simplicity of its mechanism seriously restricted the further sale of the older Winchester Model 1876 and Model 1883. The model had a remarkably fast and smooth action and was generally considered the most satisfactory lever action repeater ever made in this country.

The Model 1886 was followed by the Winchester Model 1887 shotgun.

# MODEL 1887 REPEATING SHOTGUN

*51. MODEL 1887 SHOTGUN*

The sale of English-manufactured double barrel shotguns bearing the Winchester name was discontinued in 1884. As the sale of these shotguns had proven a very profitable business, Winchester gave considerable thought to the development of a repeating shotgun that could be made by Winchester, incorporating the lever action it had popularized for many years.

In 1885, Winchester purchased the Browning brothers' patents covering a lever action repeating shotgun, together with a crude model embodying the ideas expressed in these patents. The first announcement of this new model, in 12 gauge, appeared in the June 1887 catalog as the Winchester Repeating Shotgun Model 1887. The 10 gauge was added in November 1887, starting with Serial No. 22,148.

This model was a pioneer in the shotgun field as it was the first lever action repeating shotgun made in this country.

The first guns were made with one extractor on left side. Breechblock stud was fastened by large flat head screw on right side. Double extractors began to be used between serial numbers 25,000 and 30,000 in 1889.

## GENERAL SPECIFICATIONS OF THE M/87 SHOTGUN

| | |
|---|---|
| TYPE | Lever action repeating shotgun, hammer, tubular magazine, solid frame. |
| STYLE | Standard style only. |
| | 12 gauge and 10 gauge riot guns were added in March 1898. |
| BARRELS | Made of rolled steel. |
| | 12 gauge, 30-inch and 32-inch, full choke. |
| | 10 gauge, 30-inch and 32-inch, full choke. |
| | 10 gauge Riot, 20-inch, cylinder bore. |
| | 12 gauge Riot, 20-inch, cylinder bore. |
| | 30-inch, full choke was standard on the 12 gauge, and |
| | 32-inch, full choke was standard on the 10 gauge. |
| | Damascus 3 blade and 4 blade barrels were furnished as a special at additional charge. |
| MAGAZINE | Tubular type. |
| | Capacity, four shells in the magazine and one in the carrier. |

| CHAMBERS | 12 gauge, chambered for 2⅝-inch shells. |
| | 10 gauge, chambered for 2⅞-inch shells. |
| FRAME | Case hardened. |
| STOCK | Plain wood, not checkered, pistol grip (English type), hard rubber butt plate. Also furnished in fancy wood, checkered or not checkered, special dimension stocks, etc. at extra cost. |
| FOREARM | Plain wood, not checkered. |
| LISTED WEIGHTS | 12 gauge, 30-inch barrel—about 8 lbs. |
| | 10 gauge, 32-inch barrel—about 9 lbs. |
| SERIAL NUMBERS | M/87 Shotguns were serially numbered, from 1 up, on underside of receiver, forward end. |

The manufacture of this model was discontinued in 1901; approximately 64,855 were made.

*Special Note*

The Model 1887 shotgun was of generous proportions, popular in its day, and continued in the line until 1901 when it was changed in some respects and reissued as the Model 1901, in 10 gauge only. The 12 gauge was not continued in the revamped model as the newer slide action repeater, the Model 1897 shotgun, had become well established.

The Model 1887 was followed by the Winchester Model 1890 rifle and was succeeded later by the Model 1901 shotgun in 10 gauge only.

# MODEL 1890 REPEATING RIFLE

*52. MODEL 1890 RIFLE. SOLID FRAME*

*53. MODEL 1890 RIFLE. TAKEDOWN*

Attention was next given to the idea of adopting a new repeating rifle, chambered for 22 caliber rim fire cartridges, to replace the older Model 1873 rifle, which had never achieved any great popularity in the rim fire chambering. John Browning was requested to develop a new model for this purpose.

Subsequently, U. S. Patent 385,238 was granted on June 26, 1888, to John M. Browning and Matthew S. Browning covering a magazine firearm. Under this patent the first Winchester repeating firearm of the sliding or trombone action was produced. It was announced in the November 1890 catalog as the Winchester 22 Caliber Repeating Rifle Model 1890. The announcement read in part: "Guns will be furnished with only 24-inch octagon barrels, plain triggers and straight grip stocks. We are not prepared to furnish longer barrels, set triggers or pistol grip stocks." Factory records show the first delivery of the M/90 to warehouse stock was made on December 1, 1890.

All Model 1890 rifles were made with the feeding mechanism and chambering for individual cartridges. The first production covered the 22 Short, the 22 Long, and the 22 W.R.F., the latter caliber having been developed by Winchester especially for this model. Individual chambering for the 22 Long Rifle cartridge was added in 1919.

## GENERAL SPECIFICATIONS OF THE M/90 RIFLE

TYPE
Repeating rifle with sliding forearm, hammer, tubular magazine, solid frame. Takedown was first listed in the December 1892 catalog. The solid frame was discontinued shortly after the introduction of the takedown. The first 15,500 were solid frame.

First receivers were case hardened, changed to blued as standard in August 1901.

In June 1906, a locking cut was made on front end, top of receiver, to allow breechbolt to drop in and lock bolt at forward end.

STYLES
Sporting Rifle, Fancy Sporting Rifle.

BARRELS
24-inch octagon.

MAGAZINE
Tubular magazine.

Capacity 22 Short, 15 cartridges; 22 Long, 12 cartridges; 22 W.R.F., 12 cartridges; 22 Long Rifle, 11 cartridges.

TRIGGER
Plain trigger.

Set triggers were not furnished on this model.

CHAMBERS
22 Short only.

22 Long only.

22 W.R.F. only.

22 Long Rifle only.

Chambers were listed as suitable only for the cartridge for which they were designed (not interchangeable).

STOCK
Rifle type, curved steel butt plate, straight grip.

Pistol grip stocks were later furnished as a special.

SLIDE HANDLE
Plain walnut, round with circular grooves, not checkered.

LISTED WEIGHTS
Standard Sporting Rifle—about 5¾ lbs.

Standard Fancy Sporting Rifle—about 6 lbs.

SERIAL NUMBERS
M/90 rifles were serially numbered on lower tang to No. 232,328; then on both front end of receiver and lower tang.

The manufacture of M/90 rifles was discontinued in 1932. The final clean-up of stock on hand was made in 1941. About 849,000 were made.

*Special Notes*

The Model 1890 was the most popular repeating rifle, using rim fire cartridges for general all around informal shooting purposes, ever produced by Winchester. For many years it was also generally considered the universal firearm for use in shooting galleries.

The Model 1890 was followed by the Winchester Model 1892 rifle, and was succeeded in 1932 by the Winchester Model 62 rifle.

# MODEL 1892 REPEATING RIFLE

*54. MODEL 1892 RIFLE. TAKEDOWN*

*55. MODEL 1892 CARBINE*

*56. MODEL 1892 MUSKET*

Due to the continued popularity of the 44-40, 38-40, and 32-20 Winchester Center Fire calibers used in the Model 1873 rifle, it was decided to develop a new and more modern rifle to handle them. This new model was of the same basic design as the Model 1886 and incorporated most of the special features of its action, including the double locking system. Some of the mechanism was simplified and the component parts were scaled down in size to handle the smaller calibers. The Model 1892 was first listed in the July 1892 catalog. Factory records show the first delivery of the M/92 rifle to warehouse stock on May 3, 1892.

The first chamberings were the 44-40, 38-40, and 32-20 Winchester calibers, which had previously been furnished in the Winchester 1873. The 25-20 chambering was developed especially for this model and was added in August 1895.

## GENERAL SPECIFICATIONS OF THE M/92 RIFLE

| | |
|---|---|
| TYPE | Lever action repeating rifle, hammer, tubular magazine, solid frame. |
| | Takedown was first listed in October 1893. |
| | (Carbines were made in solid frame only.) |
| STYLES | Sporting Rifle, Fancy Sporting Rifle, Carbine. |
| | Musket was first listed in March 1898. |
| | Elaborately ornamented M/92s were also furnished at special prices. |
| BARRELS | Rifles, 24-inch, round, octagon, 1/2 octagon. |
| | Carbine, 20-inch, round. |
| | Musket, 30-inch, round. |
| | Shorter barrels in 20, 18, 16, 15, and 14-inch lengths were also furnished on rifles and carbines. These barrels were used largely by the rubber industry in South America. |
| | Furnishing extra length barrels up to 36 inches at extra cost was discontinued in March 1908. |
| | The late Model 1892s were made with 20-inch barrels; if customer desired longer barrel, the Model 53 barrels were used. |
| MAGAZINES | 1/2, 2/3, and full magazines were furnished. |
| LISTED | Standard Rifle, 24-inch barrel, full magazine, 13 cartridges. |
| MAGAZINE | Standard Carbine, 20-inch barrel, full magazine, 11 cartridges. |
| CAPACITIES | Standard Carbine, 20-inch barrel, 1/2 magazine, 5 cartridges. |
| | Standard Musket, 30-inch barrel, full magazine, 17 cartridges. |
| TRIGGER | Plain type was standard. |
| | (Set triggers were furnished as a special.) |
| CHAMBER | 44 Win. (44-40), 38 Win. (38-40), 32 Win. (32-20), 25-20 Win. In 1936-38, a few were made in 218 Bee on special order only (not advertised). |
| STOCK | Plain wood, not checkered. |
| | Sporting Rifle, rifle type butt, straight grip. |
| | Fancy Sporting Rifle, rifle type butt, pistol grip. |
| | Carbine, carbine type, straight grip. |
| | Musket, musket type, straight grip. |
| | Extras, such as shotgun butt stock with either metal or rubber butt plates, special dimension stocks, straight or pistol grip, etc. were also furnished at extra cost. |
| SIGHTS | Ramp Sight Bases on M/92 carbines were authorized on November 12, 1931. A change in the sight equipment was necessitated by the use of the front ramp sight base. |
| CLEANING ROD | Standard equipment. A slotted hickory rod was furnished with each firearm. |

<table>
<tr><td>LISTED WEIGHTS</td><td>Rifle, 24-inch, round barrel, full magazine—about 6¾ lbs.<br>Rifle, 24-inch, octagon barrel, full magazine—about 7 lbs.<br>Carbine, 20-inch, round barrel, full magazine—about 5¾ lbs.<br>Carbine, 20-inch, round barrel, half magazine—about 5½ lbs.<br>Musket, 30-inch, round barrel, full magazine—about 8 lbs.</td></tr>
<tr><td>SERIAL NUMBERS</td><td>M/92s were serially numbered from 1 up.<br>Although the manufacture of M/92 rifles was discontinued in 1932, the carbines were continued in the line until 1941. Total production was about 1,004,067.</td></tr>
</table>

*Special Notes*

The Model 1892, like its predecessor, Model 1873, was immensely popular for many years throughout South America, Australia, and the Far East. The shorter barreled rifles and carbines in the 44-40 Winchester caliber far exceeded all other models in use in South America.

The Model 1892 was the second Winchester model to pass the 1,000,000 mark. The millionth M/92 rifle, chambered for the 32-20 Winchester cartridge, was appropriately engraved and presented to the then United States Secretary of War, Patrick Hurley, on December 17, 1932.

A carbine of the Winchester 1892 model was carried by Admiral Robert E. Peary on his trips to the North Pole.

The Model 1892 was followed by the Winchester Model 1893 shotgun.

# MODEL 1893 REPEATING SHOTGUN

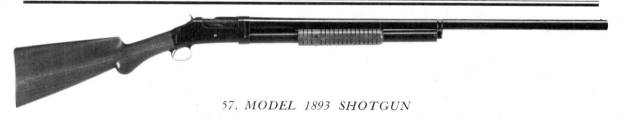

*57. MODEL 1893 SHOTGUN*

Until 1890 all firearms of Winchester manufacture were of the lever action type, except the Hotchkiss repeating rifle (Winchester M/1883). Christopher M. Spencer, who early in 1860 patented his lever action, rim fire, repeating rifle that competed with B. Tyler Henry's rifle of the same year and of similar type, came back into the firearms business with his new Spencer slide action, repeating shotgun in 1882. These guns were made by the Spencer Arms Company of Windsor, Connecticut.

In 1892 the Burgess shotgun was developed, using a sliding pistol grip to operate the mechanism, instead of a sliding forearm. This gun was manufactured by the Burgess Gun Company of Buffalo, New York.

As noted earlier, Winchester discontinued the importation of English made double barrel shotguns in 1884. Having no facilities for manufacturing this type of action, they purchased, in

1885, the Browning brothers' patents covering a lever action repeating shotgun. This new model was announced in June 1887 as the Winchester Repeating Shotgun Model 1887.

Departure from the former type of lever action to the more modern slide action mechanism dates from the announcement of the Model 1890 rim fire repeating rifle. Winchester needed a new model shotgun to more successfully compete with other manufacturers' models. So in 1890 a Browning brothers' patent was purchased. It covered a slide action shotgun having a visible hammer and with side ejection. Both before and after the start of manufacture of this new model, it was found necessary to make several changes in its construction. It was first publicly announced in the catalog of June 1893, as the Winchester Repeating Shotgun Model 1893, with the following note:

> This gun is operated by a sliding forearm below the barrel. It is locked by the closing motion and can be unlocked only by pushing forward the firing pin, which may be done by the hammer or by the finger. When the hammer is down, the backward and forward motion of the sliding forearm unlocks and opens the breech block, ejects the cartridge or fired shell and replaces it with a fresh cartridge.
>
> The construction of the arm is such that the hammer cannot fall or the firing pin strike the cartridge until the breech block is in place and locked fast. The trigger touches the sear only when the gun is closed—that is, the hammer cannot be let down except when the gun is locked. Having closed the gun and set the hammer at half-cock, it is locked both against opening and pulling the trigger. While the hammer stands at the full-cock notch, the gun is locked against opening.
>
> To open the gun, lift the hammer to full cock and push forward the firing pin, pulling back the action slide.

The M/93 was the first shotgun with a sliding forearm listed by Winchester.

## GENERAL SPECIFICATIONS OF THE M/93 SHOTGUN

| | |
|---|---|
| TYPE | Slide action repeating shotgun, hammer, tubular magazine, solid frame. |
| STYLES | Standard style only. |
| BARRELS | Made of rolled steel. |
| | 30-inch and 32-inch, full choke. 30-inch full choke was standard. |
| | Modified choke or cylinder bore barrels were furnished on special order. |
| | Damascus 3 blade and 4 blade barrels were furnished at additional cost. |
| MAGAZINE | Tubular magazine, holding 5 shells. |
| CHAMBER | 12 gauge, $2\frac{5}{8}$-inch shell only. |
| STOCK | Plain wood, not checkered, pistol grip (English type), hard rubber butt plate. |
| | Also furnished in fancy wood, checkered or not checkered, special dimension stocks, etc., at extra cost. |
| SLIDE HANDLE | Plain wood, rounded with semi-circular notches. |
| WEIGHT | Standard 12 gauge, 30-inch—about $7\frac{3}{4}$ lbs. |
| SERIAL NUMBERS | M/93 shotguns were serially numbered from 1 up. Located on underside of receiver near forward end. |

The manufacture of this model was discontinued in 1897. About 34,050 were made.

The Model 1893 shotgun was not an entirely satisfactory model. Mechanical weakness developed with the use of shells loaded with smokeless powders. Consequently the model was withdrawn from the market, revamped, and reissued later as the Winchester Model 1897 shotgun.

The Model 1893 was followed by the Winchester Model 1894 rifle and was succeeded by the Winchester Model 1897 shotgun.

# MODEL 1894 REPEATING RIFLE

*58. MODEL 1894 RIFLE. TAKEDOWN*

*59. MODEL 1894 RIFLE. HALF MAGAZINE*

*60. MODEL 1894 CARBINE. EARLY STYLE*

*60A. MODEL 1894 MUSKET WITH TRIANGULAR BAYONET (EXPERIMENTAL ONLY)*

60B. *MODEL 1894 MUSKET WITH SABER BAYONET*
*(EXPERIMENTAL ONLY)*

61. *MODEL 1894 CARBINE (CURRENT STYLE)*

62. *MODEL 1894 ANTIQUE CARBINE (CURRENT STYLE)*

62A. *MODEL 1894 CLASSIC*

With the development of successful smokeless powders for use in metallic cartridges, Winchester purchased U. S. Patent 524,702, granted to John M. Browning on August 21, 1894, for a lever action repeating rifle. This new model was announced in the November 1894 catalog as the Winchester Repeating Rifle Model 1894. The introductory words in this announcement were:

We believe that no repeating rifle system ever made will appeal to the eye and understanding of the rifleman as this will and that use will continue to warrant first impressions. These were prophetic words. This lever action model soon became famous throughout the world. With but few minor changes in its construction, it has been manufactured continuously, in various styles, for over seventy years.

The Model 1894 was the first lever action repeating rifle model placed on the market that was designed especially for cartridges loaded with smokeless powder. The new smokeless powder calibers were being developed for the new rifle, but there was a delay. So Winchester first announced the Model 1894, in solid frame style, chambered for the popular 32-40 and 38-55 black powder cartridges. Plain and fancy sporting rifles were manufactured with 26-inch octagon or round barrel, as well as in carbine style with 20-inch round barrel.

Factory records show that the first delivery of Model 1894 rifles to warehouse stock was made on October 20, 1894.

The two brand new, strictly smokeless cartridges, the 25-35 Winchester and the 30-30 Winchester, were included in the August 1895 catalog, with chamberings in a sporting model having a 26-inch round nickel steel barrel. This was Winchester's first listing of nickel steel barrels as standard equipment.

## GENERAL SPECIFICATIONS OF THE M/94 RIFLE

| | |
|---|---|
| TYPE | Lever action repeating rifle, hammer, tubular magazine, solid frame and takedown. Carbines were made in solid frame only. Takedown style was announced in February 1895. |
| STYLES | Sporting Rifle. Fancy Sporting Rifle. Extra Light Weight Rifle. Carbine. Elaborately ornamented M/94s were also furnished at special prices. |
| BARRELS | Sporting Rifle, 26-inch, round, octagon, or ½ octagon. Fancy Sporting Rifle, 26-inch, round, octagon, or ½ octagon. Extra Light Weight Rifle (1897 to 1918), 22-inch or 26-inch, round. Carbine, 20-inch, round. Extra length rifle barrels up to 36-inch were furnished at extra cost until March 1908, when this practice was discontinued. Barrels of less than 20 inches were also furnished. |
| MAGAZINES | 1/2, 2/3, and full length tubular magazines were furnished. Magazine capacities: Sporting Rifle, full magazine—8 cartridges. Sporting Rifle, takedown, ½ magazine—4 cartridges. Extra Light Weight Rifle, ½ magazine—3 cartridges. Carbine, full magazine—6 cartridges. Carbine, ½ magazine—4 cartridges. |
| TRIGGER | Plain type was standard. Set triggers were furnished as special. |
| CHAMBERS | 32-40 and 38-55, November 1894. 25-35 Winchester and 30-30 Winchester, August 1895. 32 Winchester Special, June 1902. 44 Magnum, January 1967. |
| STOCKS | Sporting Rifle, rifle type butt, pistol grip or straight grip, stock and forearm of plain walnut. Fancy Sporting Rifle, rifle type butt, pistol grip, fancy wood, checkered. Extra Light Weight Rifle, shotgun butt, straight grip. Fancy wood was special. Carbine, carbine type butt (changed to shotgun type butt stock in April 1937), straight grip. Extras such as shotgun butt stock with either metal or rubber butt plate, special dimension stock, straight or pistol grip were also furnished at extra cost. |
| SIGHTS | Dovetail front, open rear. Various type sights were supplied as extras. A front ramp sight base for M/94 carbines was authorized on Sept. 25, 1931. |

WEIGHTS       Sporting Rifle, 26-inch round barrel, full magazine—7¼ to 7¾ lbs.

Fancy Sporting Rifle, 26-inch octagon barrel, full magazine—7½ to 7¾ lbs.

Extra Light Weight Rifle, 22-inch round barrel, half magazine—7 to 7¼ lbs.

Carbine, 20-inch round barrel, full magazine—5¾ to 6¼ lbs.

SERIAL NUMBERS       M/94s are serially numbered, from 1 up, on the underside of the receiver near the forward end.

*Special Notes*

The addition of the new, specially developed smokeless powder cartridges—the 25-35 Winchester and the 30-30 Winchester—in a specially designed new rifle model having a nickel steel barrel, was a radical development because smokeless powders were then in their infancy and nickel steel barrels were new as standard equipment. Prior to this addition, the only rifle furnished by Winchester for use with smokeless powder was the Single Shot model chambered for the 30 U. S. Army (30-40 Krag), the cartridge used in the Krag-Jorgensen, bolt action, repeating rifle that had been adopted by the United States Army.

The Winchester Model 1894 has been called the "Klondike Model," probably because of its popularity in the Klondike Gold Rush of 1898.

The Model 1894 never had casehardened receivers as standard. However, according to early records a small number were casehardened. From 1916 until 1963, levers were listed as casehardened, and hammers by this process from 1916 to 1934. The sling (saddle) ring was omitted in 1925.

Manufacture of all M/94 rifles and the 25-35 Winchester caliber carbine was discontinued in 1936. Carbines chambered for the 30 Winchester (30-30) and for the 32 Winchester Special cartridge were continued in the line. The 25-35 Winchester was reinstated in 1940 and discontinued in 1950.

The Model 1894 was the first sporting gun to pass the 1,000,000 mark. The millionth 94, chambered for the 30-30 Winchester cartridge and appropriately engraved, was presented in 1927 to President Calvin Coolidge. The 1½ millionth Model 94 was presented to President Harry S. Truman on May 8, 1948. The 2 millionth was presented to President Dwight Eisenhower in 1953. The 2½ millionth 94 was assembled in 1961.

In 1964, to commemorate the 70th year of production of the Model 94, a variation of the carbine was introduced in 30-30 caliber only. It has a casehardened receiver with scroll decoration, brass saddle ring, and brass-plated spring cover.

In January 1967, Winchester announced that the Model 94 would be made in a "Classic" version, reflecting some of the popular specifications incorporated or brought back in the Centennial '66 Commemorative of the previous year. The Model 94 Classic came in both rifle (26-inch barrel) and carbine (20-inch barrel) models. The Classic model features octagonal barrels, steel butt plates, semi-fancy American walnut stocks, old-fashioned front sights and scroll work on the receiver. It was chambered for 30-30 Winchester only and was last listed in 1970. A saddle ring was packed with the gun. It was introduced as a milestone in the company's history as production passed 3,000,000 for the Model 94 since 1894.

Also in 1967, the Model 94 Magnum carbine, chambered for eleven 44 Magnum cartridges (including one in the chamber), was first listed in the catalog, but distribution did not take place until September 1968 because of production difficulties. Although the magnum version was not listed in the 1968 catalog, it was again listed in 1969 through 1971 and finally dropped in 1972. The 32 Winchester Special was last listed in 1973.

The standard Model 94 was renovated and a number of improvements incorporated in its design in 1971. A new steel carrier of sturdier block design replaced the earlier lighter-weight carrier, providing smoother, more positive feeding of cartridges from magazine to chamber. Improved linkage, achieved through a redesigned lever camming slot, resulted in easier and more rapid lever action. A new improved loading port cover was added to facilitate more rapid loading of cartridges.

As of January 27, 1975, a total of 4,146,278 Model 94 rifles and carbines had been manufactured.

The Model 1894 is unquestionably the most successful center fire lever action model ever produced by Winchester.

The Model 1894 rifle was followed by the Winchester Model 1895 rifle, and was succeeded in 1924 by a revamped rifle, the Winchester Model 55. The Model 1894 Carbine is still in production.

# MODEL 1895 REPEATING RIFLE

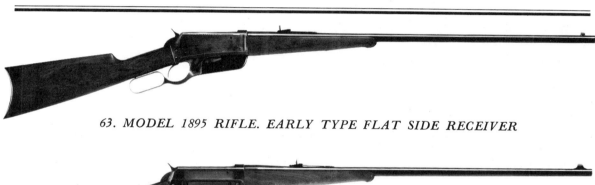

*63. MODEL 1895 RIFLE. EARLY TYPE FLAT SIDE RECEIVER*

*64. MODEL 1895 RIFLE. PISTOL GRIP*

*65. MODEL 1895 RIFLE*

[ 47 ]

66. *MODEL 1895 U.S. MUSKET*

67. *MODEL 1895 N.R.A. MUSKET*

68. *MODEL 1895 CARBINE*

69. *MODEL 1895 MUSKET. MADE FOR IMPERIAL RUSSIAN GOVERNMENT 1915 TO 1916.*

With the growing popularity of the new smokeless powders, the demand was rapidly increasing for hunting rifles of repeating type, capable of handling higher powered smokeless cartridges comparable to the military ammunition of the period. Winchester was ready to meet this demand with a new model. It was first listed in the June 1896 catalog as the Model 1895 rifle. This new model was produced under U. S. Patent 549,345 granted on November 5, 1895, to John M. Browning, covering a Box Magazine Firearm, assigned to the Winchester Repeating Arms Company.

The rifle was a strongly constructed lever action repeater and differed from preceding models in that the cartridges were held in a single column, non-detachable box magazine, rather than the traditional tubular magazine below the barrel. It was the first successful box magazine, lever action repeater ever placed on the market. During the first year of production, however, it was found desirable to make several minor changes from Browning's original design. The model was first chambered for the 30 caliber U. S. Army (30-40 Krag), the 38-72-275 Winchester, and the 40-72-330 Winchester cartridges.

The original announcement also listed the 236 U. S. Navy (6mm) chambering, but this caliber was never furnished in the Model 1895.

Factory records show the first delivery of Model 1895 rifles to warehouse stock was made on February 1, 1896.

## GENERAL SPECIFICATIONS OF THE M/95 RIFLE

TYPE
Lever action repeating rifle, hammer, non-detachable box magazine, solid frame.

Takedown, rifle only, was first listed on January 1, 1910.

Carbines and muskets were made in solid frame only.

STYLES
Sporting Rifle, Fancy Sporting Rifle, Carbine.

1. Musket with or without knife bayonet (8 inch blade)—chambered for 30 U. S. Army or 303 British.

2. Listed as:

Musket 30 Army Model 1895 U. S. Army Pattern.

This musket was adopted by the U. S. Army and was chambered for the 30 U. S. Army cartridge, 28-inch round nickel steel barrel, weight complete with knife bayonet, scabbard, and strap, about 9¾ pounds, 6 shot.

3. Model 1895 30 U. S. Army N.R.A. Musket.

This musket was first listed in the October 1905 catalog with the following description:

This is the regular Winchester Model 1895, 30 U. S. Army Musket but fitted with 30-inch instead of 28-inch barrel and Model 1901 Krag-Jorgensen Rear Sight. This style musket has been accepted by the National Rifle Association of America as conforming to the regulations governing arms for admission to the military contests of this association, and certificates will be issued for these guns upon application. They can be used in all matches—for "Any Military Arm"—shot under the rules of the National Rifle Association.

4. N.R.A. Musket, Model 1895, 30 Government cartridge, models 1903 and 1906.

This musket was first listed in the March 1908 catalog with the following description: "Twenty-four inch round nickel steel barrel, special butt plate, weight about 8½ pounds. Eligible for all matches—for 'Any Military Arm' —shot under rules of the National Rifle Association."

Elaborately ornamented M/95s were also furnished at extra cost.

BARRELS
Round, octagon, and ½ octagon barrels were furnished with various lengths depending on the style of arm, caliber, and length of barrel desired.

Barrels up to 36 inches in length were furnished for certain calibers at extra cost until March 1908 when the furnishing of extra length barrels for this model was discontinued.

MAGAZINE
Non-detachable box magazine.

Magazine capacities varied in accordance with the cartridge for which the arm was chambered.

TRIGGER
Plain trigger only.

Set triggers were not furnished on this model.

| | |
|---|---|
| CHAMBERS | 30 U. S. Army (30-40 Krag), 1896. |
| | 38-72 Winchester, 1896. |
| | 40-72 Winchester, 1896. |
| | 303 British, March 1898. |
| | 35 Winchester, March 1903. |
| | 405 Winchester, June 1904. |
| | 30 Government M/03, October 1905. |
| | 30 Government M/06, March 1908. |
| STOCKS | Sporting Rifle, rifle type butt, straight grip. |
| | Fancy Sporting Rifle, shotgun butt, straight grip. |
| | Carbine, carbine type butt, straight grip. |
| | Muskets, musket type butt, straight grip. |
| | A small number were made with pistol grip. |
| LISTED WEIGHTS | Weights varied in accordance with the length of barrel and the cartridge for which the arm was chambered. |
| SERIAL NUMBERS | M/95s were serially numbered from 1 up. Located on lower tang. |

About the first 5,000 Model 1895s were made with flat-sided receivers.

Manufacture of the Model 1895 rifle was discontinued in 1931, with the final clean-up of odds and ends in 1938. Approximately 425,881 were made.

### Special Notes

During the Spanish-American War a quantity of Model 1895 muskets, chambered for the 30-40 Krag cartridge, was sold for use by the United States Army.

The Model 1895 was one of the several Winchester rifles carried by Theodore Roosevelt on his famous hunting trip through Africa.

During 1915-16, a very large quantity of Model 1895 muskets (293,816) chambered for the 7.62mm Russian cartridge and fitted with clip guides in the top of the receiver and with bayonets was manufactured for the Imperial Russian Government. First 15,000 with 8 inch blade bayonets, balance with 16 inch blade sword bayonet.

The Model 1895 was considered a very satisfactory model. It was followed by the Lee Straight Pull model.

# LEE STRAIGHT PULL RIFLE

*70. LEE STRAIGHT PULL NAVY MUSKET*

## 71. LEE STRAIGHT PULL SPORTING RIFLE

In 1895 Winchester undertook the manufacture of the Lee Straight Pull Bolt Action Rifle for the United States Navy. Rights were obtained to manufacture the rifle and cartridge clip under patents granted to James Paris Lee and assigned by him to the Lee Arms Company.

The Lee Straight Pull model was essentially a military firearm and was claimed to be the first rifle ever designed in this country for clip loading. If this is true, Browning's design—which later became the Winchester Model 1895—must have been a close second, for his original design incorporated the clip loading feature. However, Winchester removed the clip loading arrangement before starting manufacture of the Model 1895. Production of this model was without the clip loading feature, except the muskets made on the Russian contract and chambered for the 7.62mm Russian cartridge.

Lee arms made for the United States Navy were of the musket style with a long wood stock running nearly the full length of the 28-inch nickel steel barrel. Sling swivels were attached. The rifle was equipped with a short knife shape bayonet and U. S. Navy scabbard. These arms were officially known as the U. S. Navy Rifle, Model 1895, Caliber 6mm Lee or 236. The 1895 in the above name represents the year of government adoption of the model and has no connection with the Winchester Model 1895, with which it is often confused. Many of the Lee muskets made on the U. S. Navy contracts were used during the Spanish-American War.

The Lee Straight Pull was first listed for commercial sale in the Winchester catalog of March 1897 and read in part:

> The Winchester Repeating Arms Company was awarded the contract for supplying these guns to the United States Navy and is now manufacturing on that contract; until its completion, none of these can be furnished to other parties, but when the contract is finished, which fact will be duly advertised, orders will be received and prompt delivery made.

The catalog description of the Navy model was Musket, U. S. Navy Model.

The Lee Straight Pull was the only arm ever made by Winchester with this type of bolt action straight pull mechanism.

## GENERAL SPECIFICATIONS OF THE LEE STRAIGHT PULL

| | |
|---|---|
| TYPE | Bolt action straight pull repeater, non-detachable box magazine, solid frame. |
| STYLES | Musket U. S. Navy model, with or without a knife bayonet and scabbard, U. S. Navy pattern. |
| | The Sporting Rifle was first listed in the November 1897 catalog. |
| BARRELS | Made of nickel steel. |
| | Sporting Rifle, 24-inch, round. |
| | Musket, 28-inch, round. |

| | |
|---|---|
| MAGAZINE | Non-detachable box magazine, capacity 5 cartridges. |
| | The cartridges could be inserted into the magazine one at a time or in a pack held together with a steel clip. |
| STOCK | Sporting Rifle, rifle type butt, steel butt plate, finger grooves in the front portion of the forearm, pistol grip. |
| | Musket, musket type with steel butt plate and pistol grip. |
| TRIGGER | Plain type. |
| CHAMBER | 6mm Lee (236 Caliber), smokeless powder. |
| LISTED WEIGHTS | Sporting Rifle, 24-inch round barrel—7½ lbs. |
| | Musket, 28-inch round barrel—8½ lbs. |
| SERIAL NUMBERS | Lee Straight Pull arms were serially numbered from 1 up. |
| | Located on top of receiver near forward end. |

Very few of the Lee Straight Pull firearms were sold for sporting use due to the small caliber and lightweight bullet of the 6mm cartridge, as shooters were accustomed to the larger calibers and heavier bullets then in general use. The manufacture of these guns was discontinued in the early 1900s with the final clean-up of odds and ends in 1916. About 20,000 were made, 1,700 as sporters.

### Special Notes

The catalog instructions covering the manipulation of the arm were:

The trigger having been pulled, grasp the cam-lever handle and pull the bolt smartly to the rear.

Grasp a clip or pack containing five cartridges between the thumb and first two fingers of the right hand and pushing the extractor to the left with the lowest cartridge, insert the pack in the magazine, either side up, keeping the clip close to the face of the bolt.

With the thumb on the pack near the head of the top cartridge, push it down until the cartridges are released from the clip, which will drop out through the bottom of the magazine in the course of firing—the cartridges are then raised by the follower until the top one touches the under side of the extractor and the upper portion of its head is in front of the bolt.

Close the gun by pushing the bolt forward smartly, thus entering a cartridge into the chamber.

The gun is now ready to be discharged and the bolt cannot be drawn back unless the bolt-release is pushed down or until the trigger is pulled which of course discharges the gun.

If it is not desired to fire the gun at once, the firing pin may be rendered inoperative by pulling up the firing-pin-lock on the left of the receiver until it clicks.

The firing-pin-lock must be pulled up with some force in order to overcome the tension of the mainspring. Pushing the firing-pin-lock down releases the firing-pin-striker and if the trigger is pulled, the gun will be discharged.

After firing draw the bolt back smartly, the empty cartridge case being extracted and ejected to the right. On again closing the bolt, another cartridge is pushed into the chamber.

The Lee Straight Pull was followed by the Winchester Model 1897 Shotgun.

# MODEL 1897 REPEATING SHOTGUN

*72. MODEL 1897 SHOTGUN. SOLID FRAME*

*73. MODEL 1897 SHOTGUN. TAKEDOWN. FANCY GRADE*

*74. MODEL 1897 TRENCH GUN*

This new model was a revamped and greatly improved Winchester Model 1893 shotgun with several important changes:

1. The frame was strengthened and made longer to handle a 12 gauge 2¾-inch shell, as well as the 2⅝-inch shell.

2. The frame at the top was covered so that the ejection of the fired shell was entirely from the side.

3. The gun could not be opened until a slight forward movement of the slide handle released the action slide lock. In firing, the recoil of the gun gave a slight forward motion to the slide handle and released the action slide lock which enabled the immediate opening of the gun. In the absence of any recoil, the slide handle had to be pushed forward manually in order to release the action slide lock.

4. A movable cartridge guide was placed on the right side of the carrier block to prevent the escape of the shell when the gun was turned sideways in the act of loading.

5. The stock was made longer and with less drop.

The Model 1897 shotgun was first listed for sale in the November 1897 catalog, in 12 gauge solid frame only. The 12 gauge takedown was added in October 1898, the 16 gauge takedown in February 1900.

# GENERAL SPECIFICATIONS OF THE M/97 SHOTGUN

**TYPE**

Slide action repeating shotgun, hammer, tubular magazine.

12 gauge, both solid frame and takedown.

16 gauge, takedown only.

**STYLES**

*Standard or Field Gun*

First listed in November 1897.

*Trap Gun*

First listed in November 1897. Discontinued in 1931. This trap gun was succeeded by the Special Trap Gun in 1931.

*Pigeon*

First listed in November 1897. Discontinued in 1939.

*Brush Gun*

First listed in November 1897. Discontinued in 1931. This Brush Gun was regularly furnished with a 26-inch cylinder bore barrel. In 1931 the Brush name was dropped and the gun was thereafter furnished as a Standard or Field Gun.

*Riot Gun*

Solid frame in 12 gauge was first listed in March 1898.

Discontinued in 1935. Takedown was first listed in 1921.

*Tournament*

First listed in June 1910. Discontinued in 1931. Succeeded by the Standard Trap Gun in 1931.

*Trench Gun*

Solid frame in 12 gauge was first listed in 1920. This was the same gun as had been furnished previously to the United States Army for trench work during World War I. Discontinued in 1935.

Takedown in 12 gauge was first listed in 1935. Discontinued in 1945.

*Standard Trap Gun*

First listed in 1931. Discontinued in 1939.

*Special Trap Gun*

First listed in 1931. Discontinued in 1939.

**BARRELS**

Made of rolled steel.

12 gauge Standard, 30-inch, full choke.

12 gauge Riot, 20-inch, cylinder bore.

12 gauge Trench, 20-inch, cylinder bore.

16 gauge Standard, 28-inch, full choke.

3 blade and 4 blade Damascus barrels were furnished at extra cost until they were discontinued in 1914.

**BARREL LENGTHS**

12 gauge, 32, 30, 28, and 26-inch.

16 gauge, 28, 26-inch; (30-inch barrel was added in 1930).

Matted barrels were furnished on special order at extra cost. M/97 barrels were never furnished with solid raised matted rib or ventilated rib.

**MAGAZINE**

Tubular Magazine.

12 gauge, capacity 5 shells.

16 gauge, capacity 5 shells.

By Presidential Proclamation signed February 2, 1935, based on the recommendation of the United States Biological Survey, the capacity of any automatic loading or repeating shotgun used in shooting migratory birds was specifically limited to three shots. This means two shells in the magazine and one shell in the chamber. On February 22, 1935, a special shape wood magazine plug was authorized to reduce the magazine capacity to two shells. One of these plugs was included in each carton containing an M/97 shotgun after that date.

CHOKES      Full choke, modified choke, cylinder bore.

Intermediate chokes, improved modified (¾ choke), and improved cylinder (¼ choke) were authorized on October 29, 1931.

Winchester No. 1 Skeet and Winchester No. 2 Skeet chokes were first listed in the July 1, 1940, catalog.

CHAMBERS      12 gauge, 2¾-inch shell.

16 gauge, 2⅝-inch shell (changed to 2¾-inch shell in 1931). Last listed in 1950.

STOCK      Plain walnut, not checkered, pistol grip (English type).

Changed to ½ pistol grip in March 1908.

M/97 Shotguns have been furnished with both steel and hard rubber butt plates.

Stocks used on the higher grade M/97s were made of better wood and checkered. The quality of wood and the amount of checkering varied according to the grade and style of the arm.

SLIDE HANDLES      Standard shape made of plain walnut, round with semi-circular grooves, not checkered.

Slide handles used on the higher grade M/97s were made of better wood, checkered, and were furnished in two types, standard shape and semi-beaver-tail shape.

The standard shape was the round handle with the grooves omitted. The beavertail shape was furnished in 12 gauge only. The quality of the wood used on these handles and the amount of checkering varied according to the style and grade of the arm. On June 25, 1945, a new standard slide handle was authorized. It was of different shape, slightly larger, nearly flat on the bottom side, with grooves on the sides only. This new shape slide handle was put into use during the latter part of 1947.

WEIGHTS      12 gauge, 30-inch barrel—about 7 lbs. 14 oz.

12 gauge Riot, 20-inch barrel—about 7 lbs. 2 oz.

12 gauge Trench, 20-inch barrel—about 7 lbs. 14 oz.

12 gauge, 28-inch barrel—about 7 lbs. 8 oz.

16 gauge, 28-inch barrel—about 7 lbs. 8 oz.

SERIAL NUMBERS      M/97s are serially numbered from 34,151 which followed the numbers used on the M/93 shotgun. Numbered on underside of receiver and underside of extension, if gun is takedown. Discontinued in 1957, approximately 1,024,700 were made.

*Special Notes*

The Model 1897 was the first shotgun manufactured by Winchester with the following features:

1. 12 gauge, with standard chambering for a 2¾-inch shell.
2. 12 gauge, in both solid frame and takedown styles.
3. Chambered for a 16 gauge shell.

The Model 1897 shotgun became popular immediately after its announcement and quickly outdistanced the sales of its principal competitors' models, the Spencer and Burgess guns. The Model 1897 is the most famous visible hammer type repeating shotgun ever made in this country and is still being used by a surprisingly large number of shooters who prefer the visible hammer type of mechanism.

The Model 1897 was followed by the Winchester Model 1900 rifle.

# MODEL 1900 SINGLE SHOT RIFLE

### 75. MODEL 1900 RIFLE

Winchester bought U. S. Patent 632,904 from the Browning brothers; it had been granted to John M. Browning in August 1899 for a single shot, rim fire firearm. Included was a rifle model embodying Browning's ideas expressed in the patent. When Winchester started to manufacture this new model, it was found necessary to make several changes from Browning's original design. After these changes were made, the arm was announced to the trade, in a flyleaf attached to the August 1899 catalog, as the Winchester Single Shot Rifle Model 1900. The announcement read in part:

> The Winchester Model 1900 single shot rifle is a serviceable low-priced gun designed to handle 22 Short or 22 Long Rim-Fire cartridges. Bullet breech caps may also be used in it if desired.
>
> It is a "Takedown" and can be taken apart easily and quickly; the operation consisting simply of unscrewing the thumb screw located underneath the forearm which releases the barrel and action from the stock.
>
> The action used on this gun is of the bolt type and is exceedingly simple, consisting of very few parts. When the gun is cocked, the action is locked against opening until the firing pin falls. This permits carrying the gun cocked without liability of the action jarring open. The gun is cocked by pulling rearward on the firing pin which is made with a knurled head to afford a good grip.
>
> The barrel of this rifle is round, 18 inches long, bored, and rifled with the same care and exactness that have made Winchester rifles famous the world over for their accurate shooting. It has a straight grip stock, the length of pull being 12¾ inches, drop at comb 1½ inches, drop at heel 2¾ inches.

Model 1900 rifles are fitted with open front and rear sights, the sights of every gun being lined up by shooting. The length of the Model 1900 from muzzle to butt is 33¼ inches.

The Model 1900 can be furnished only as described above. We cannot fill orders for this gun calling for any variation whatsoever from the standard.

## GENERAL SPECIFICATIONS OF THE M/1900 RIFLE

| | |
|---|---|
| TYPE | Bolt action, takedown, single shot rifle, cocked by pulling rearward on the firing pin head. |
| STYLES | Sporting rifle only. |
| BARREL | 18 inches, round only. |
| CHAMBER | 22 Short and 22 Long, interchangeably. |
| STOCK | Gum wood, finished to show the grain and natural color of the wood. Straight grip. |
| BUTT PLATE | The Model 1900 was made without a fitted butt plate. However, the form of a butt plate was rolled into the butt end of the stock. |
| SIGHTS | Open sporting sights. |
| WEIGHT | About 2¾ pounds. |
| SERIAL NUMBERS | The Model 1900 was not serially numbered. The manufacture of this model was discontinued in 1902. About 105,000 were produced. |

### Special Notes

This model was Winchester's first venture into the low priced 22 caliber, rim fire rifle field. It was manufactured to compete with other low priced rifles, particularly in foreign markets. It was Winchester's first application of the simple type of bolt action, cocked by pulling rearward on the knurled firing pin head. Adaptations of this cocking action were later used by most other firearms manufacturers in this country.

The Model 1900 was not very successful as it was a bit too light in weight and too cheaply constructed to compete with other manufacturers' models. After being redesigned, the revamped arm was announced to the trade as the Winchester Model 1902 Single Shot Rifle.

The Model 1900 was followed by the Winchester Model 1901 Shotgun and was succeeded by the Winchester Model 1902 Rifle.

# MODEL 1901 REPEATING SHOTGUN

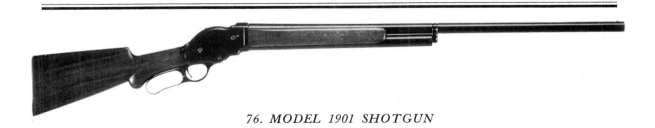

*76. MODEL 1901 SHOTGUN*

With the discontinuance of the Winchester Model 1887 lever action repeating shotgun in 1901, a redesign of this model was manufactured in 10 gauge only. Listed as the Winchester Repeating Shotgun Model 1901, it was placed on the market in January 1902.

The new model was very similar to the previous Model 1887 except that it was strengthened to withstand smokeless powders which were coming into more common use. A few minor changes and improvements were added. The frame was changed to a standard blued finish in place of the case hardening used on the Model 1887.

The Model 1901 was made in 10 gauge only. Since the popularity of the more modern, slide action Winchester Model 1897, in 12 gauge, was high and increasing, it was obvious that a 12 gauge in the older lever action type was unnecessary and would have little chance of selling in reasonably large quantities.

Factory records show that the first delivery of Model 1901 shotguns to warehouse stocks was made on August 27, 1901.

## GENERAL SPECIFICATIONS OF THE M/01 SHOTGUN

| | |
|---|---|
| TYPE | Lever action repeating shotgun, hammer type, tubular magazine, solid frame. |
| STYLES | Plain and Fancy. |
| BARRELS | Made of rolled steel. |
| | Standard barrel, 32-inch, full choke, modified and cylinder bore. |
| | Shorter barrels were supplied in these chokes and bore on special order at extra cost. |
| | 3 blade and 4 blade Damascus barrels were furnished at extra charge until they were discontinued in 1914. |
| MAGAZINE | Tubular type, capacity 5 shells. |
| CHAMBER | 10 gauge $2\frac{7}{8}$-inch shell. |
| RECEIVER | Blued finish. |
| STOCK | Plain wood, not checkered, pistol grip (English type), rubber butt plate. (Steel butt plates were also furnished.) |
| | Stocks of fancy wood, checkered and made to customer's special stock dimensions were furnished at additional charge. |
| LISTED WEIGHTS | Plain—$8\frac{3}{4}$ lbs. |
| | Fancy—9 lbs. |
| SERIAL NUMBERS | M/01 shotguns were serially numbered commencing with 64,856 which followed the numbers previously used on the M/87 shotgun. Located on underside of receiver. The manufacture of this model was discontinued in 1920; about 13,500 were made. |

The M/87 and the M/01 were the only 10 gauge shotguns ever produced by Winchester. The Model 1901 shotgun was followed by the Winchester Model 1902 rifle.

# MODEL 1902 SINGLE SHOT RIFLE

*77. MODEL 1902 RIFLE*

*77A. TARGET PISTOL MADE ON A 1902 ACTION. TYPE MADE BY EMPLOYEES FOR THEIR OWN USE.*

The Model 1902 rifle was of the same general design as the earlier 1900 model. The principal changes were:

1. The use of a special shape trigger guard with the rear end extended and curved to fulfill the purpose of a pistol grip.
2. A shorter trigger pull.
3. A blued steel butt plate.
4. The use of a rear peep sight in place of the open rear sight used on the M/1900.
5. The 18-inch round barrel, although the same length as the barrel used on the M/1900, was made heavier at the muzzle.

The Model 1902 rifle was first listed in the March 1903 catalog, chambered for 22 Short and 22 Long rim fire cartridges, interchangeably.

Factory records show the first delivery of Model 1902 rifles to warehouse stock was made on June 4, 1902.

## GENERAL SPECIFICATIONS OF THE M/02 RIFLE

| | |
|---|---|
| TYPE | Bolt action, single shot rifle, cocked by pulling rearward on the firing pin head, takedown. |
| STYLES | Standard rifle only. |
| BARREL | 18-inch round only. |
| CHAMBER | 22 Short and 22 Long, interchangeably. |

Chambering changed to 22 Short, 22 Long, and 22 Extra Long, interchangeably, in 1914.

Chambering changed again in 1927 to 22 Short, 22 Long, and 22 Long Rifle, interchangeably. This was the 1902-A. Also a new length sear added.

STOCK    Gum wood, straight grip, steel butt plate, changed in 1907 to composition butt plate.

SIGHTS    Open front sight and peep rear sight.

The peep rear sight was later discontinued as standard by the following notice: "On and after this date Model 1902 Single Shot Rifles will be furnished on all orders with open rear sights. Peep rear sight will be furnished on this model without extra charge if so specified—August 13, 1904."

LISTED WEIGHT    About 3 lbs.

SERIAL NUMBERS    M/02s were not serially numbered.

The manufacture of this model was discontinued in 1931. About 640,299 were made.

*Special Notes*

The Model 1902 was a great improvement over the Winchester Model 1900 rifle and, because of the change and its low price, sold in large quantities, especially through export channels.

A Model 1902 rifle was included in each Winchester Junior Rifle Corps Range Kit No. 1, which was first offered for sale about 1920.

The Model 1902 rifle was followed by the Breech Loading Cannon and was succeeded by the Winchester Thumb Trigger and Model 1904 rifles.

# MODEL 1898 BREECH LOADING CANNON

*78. MODEL 1898 BREECH LOADING CANNON*

This breech loading cannon was developed and patented by Charles H. Griffith, a Winchester employee, to supply a demand for a low priced 10 gauge cannon combining safety, simplicity of construction, and ease of manipulation.

It was originally announced to the trade in the March 1903 catalog as the Winchester Breech Loading Cannon. The announcement covering its description read:

This cannon consists of a 12-inch tapered, rolled steel barrel, cylinder bored, mounted on a shapely cast iron carriage, substantially built, which is supplied with two heavy wheels at the forward end $3\frac{5}{8}$ inches in diameter. The barrel and breech closure are proved and tested to withstand a much greater pressure than can be developed by any charge of black powder that can be loaded in a 10 gauge shell. The carriage and wheels are nicely japanned, the barrel blued, and breech closure hardened black giving the gun a very neat appearance. The length of the cannon over all is 17 inches, its height $7\frac{1}{4}$ inches and its width 7 inches.

## GENERAL SPECIFICATIONS OF THE BREECH LOADING CANNON

| | |
|---|---|
| TYPE | Breech Loading Cannon mounted on two wheels. |
| STYLES | Standard, black, or chromium plate finish. Rubber tires were added in 1930. |
| BARREL | 12-inch round, tapered, cylinder bore. |
| CHAMBER | 10 gauge $2\frac{7}{8}$-inch blank shell. |
| LISTED WEIGHT | About 14 lbs. |
| SERIAL NUMBERS | Breech Loading Cannon are not serially numbered. Numbers on underside of barrel and ring are identification numbers. Numbers on side of barrel were ones numbered for export. |

### Special Notes

This cannon is generally known in the New Haven factory as the M/98 Breech Loading Cannon, the arbitrary model number having been assigned to it some years ago for factory use.

The Model 1898 B. L. Cannon can be used for any purpose where a large amount of smoke and noise is desired, such as saluting, starting boat races, celebrations, etc. The chromium plated style is especially adaptable as a small yacht cannon. The cannon was never a large selling item. It was discontinued in January 1958. About 18,400 were made.

The Breech Loading Cannon was followed by the Winchester Model 1903 rifle.

# MODEL 1903 AUTOMATIC
# SELF-LOADING RIFLE

*79. MODEL 1903 RIFLE*

The first semi-automatic rifle put out by Winchester was also the first successful simple, blowback action rifle ever made in this country to handle 22 caliber rim fire cartridges. It was announced to the trade in the July 1904 catalog as the Winchester Automatic Rifle Model 1903.

The M/03 was developed and patented in 1903 by Thomas Crossley Johnson, who entered the employ of Winchester on November 30, 1885. During his long service with the company, he became nationally known as a successful designer and inventor of firearms.

The Model 1903 was a takedown rifle with a tubular magazine in the butt stock holding ten rim fire cartridges of a caliber specially designed for this model and known as the 22 Winchester Automatic Smokeless Cartridge.

The M/03 was the first automatic (self-loading) rifle and also the first hammerless repeating rifle made by Winchester.

Factory records show the first delivery of Model 1903 rifles to warehouse stock was made on March 2, 1903.

## GENERAL SPECIFICATIONS OF THE M/03 RIFLE

| | |
|---|---|
| TYPE | Automatic (self-loading) repeating rifle, hammerless, takedown. |
| | First guns had bronze firing pins, changed to steel in 1906. |
| STYLES | Plain Rifle and Fancy Rifle. |
| BARRELS | 20-inch, round only. |
| MAGAZINE | Tubular magazine in butt stock holding ten cartridges. |
| CHAMBER | 22 Winchester Automatic Rim Fire Smokeless only. |
| STOCK | Plain Rifle, plain walnut, straight grip. |
| | Fancy Rifle, fancy walnut, pistol grip. |
| | No variation from standard stock was allowed except pistol grip, fancy wood, checkered or not checkered. |
| LISTED WEIGHTS | Plain Rifle—5¾ lbs. |
| | Fancy Rifle—6 lbs. |
| SERIAL NUMBERS | M/03 rifles were serially numbered from 1 up. Located on underside of receiver and forward end of trigger guard extension. About 126,000 were made. |

The manufacture of this model was discontinued in 1932, when it was redesigned and reissued the following year as the Model 63, chambered for the 22 Long Rifle smokeless cartridge.

*Special Notes*

The Model 1903 was an automatic (self-loading) rifle with balanced breech bolt, simple blowback operated mechanism. This means that the breech bolt contains a quantity of metal proportioned to the weight and velocity of the bullet so that the shock of the recoil is absorbed by the breech bolt which in a sense balances the recoil. When the cartridge is fired, the bullet leaves the muzzle of the barrel before the breech bolt commences to move rearward. The design and weight of the breech bolt are so proportioned that there is no loss of velocity and energy of the bullet. In order to obtain the nicety of balance required to operate this type of mechanism, it was necessary for Winchester to develop a new cartridge for this model. With this self-loading type of mechanism, the trigger must be pulled and released for each shot. Trigger lock added December 1903, about serial No. 5,000.

The M/03 was the first successful simple blowback rifle ever made to handle rim fire cartridges.

The Model 1903 was followed by the Winchester Thumb Trigger rifle and was succeeded in 1933 by the Winchester Model 63 rifle.

# THUMB TRIGGER MODEL 99

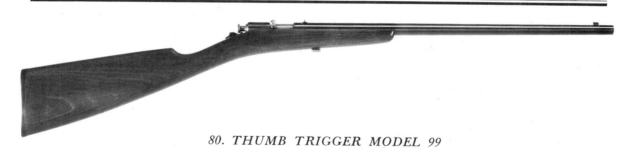

*80. THUMB TRIGGER MODEL 99*

This model was an adaptation of the Winchester Model 1902 rifle, with the patent for the Thumb Trigger mechanism granted to Thomas G. Bennett. The M/99 was first listed in the July 1904 catalog as a novelty in rim fire rifles.

Instead of the customary trigger and trigger guard on the underside of the stock, the trigger—which included the sear and extractor—was extended rearward beneath the head of the firing pin. Thus, the rifle could be fired by simply depressing the knurled top of the trigger with the thumb. It was claimed that with this style of trigger the shooter was not as apt to throw the gun off target as with the customary trigger. Except for this feature, the Winchester Thumb Trigger model was approximately the same as the original Winchester Model 1902 rifle chambered for the 22 Short and 22 Long rim fire cartridges.

An arbitrary model number was later assigned to this model, it being first listed as the Model 99 Thumb Trigger rifle in the 1920 Winchester catalog.

Factory records show the first delivery of Thumb Trigger rifles to warehouse stock was made on July 5, 1904.

## GENERAL SPECIFICATIONS OF THE THUMB TRIGGER RIFLE

| | |
|---|---|
| TYPE | Bolt action, thumb trigger, single shot rifle, cocked by pulling rearward on the firing pin head, takedown. |
| STYLES | Standard style only. |
| BARRELS | 18-inch, round only. |
| CHAMBER | 22 Short and 22 Long, interchangeably. |
| | Chambering changed in 1914 to 22 Short, 22 Long, and 22 Extra Long, interchangeably. |
| STOCK | Gum wood, shotgun butt, straight grip, no trigger or trigger guard on the stock. Composition butt plate, checkered. |
| WEIGHT | About 3 lbs. |
| SERIAL NUMBERS | Thumb Trigger rifles were not serially numbered. |

The manufacture of this model was discontinued in 1923. About 75,433 were made.

### Special Notes

The Thumb Trigger rifle was designed to compete with other low-priced rim fire rifles, particularly those of foreign manufacture. This rifle was very popular in Australia, and large quantities were shipped to that country.

The original announcement covering the description of this model reads:

The Winchester Thumb Trigger model is a novelty in 22 caliber rifles. It has the same simple and reliable bolt action which made the Winchester Model 1902 such a popular gun and caused it to be so widely imitated. It will handle either 22 Short or 22 Long rim fire cartridges. As its name indicates, the trigger which is located on the upper side of the grip at the rear of the bolt is operated by pressing down with the thumb.

Simplicity and quickness of action are features of the thumb trigger. It is also claimed that it is an aid to accurate shooting, as the shooter is not so apt to throw the gun off the object aimed at in pressing down the trigger as when pulling it in the old way.

The Thumb Trigger model is made with a rebounding lock. It is a takedown and is made with an 18-inch round barrel and a 13½-inch highly polished straight grip stock with checked rubber butt plate attached with fancy screws.

Notwithstanding the low price at which this rifle is offered, it is made with the same care as our other models. The sights are accurately set by shooting at a target.

This model was the only Winchester rifle ever made with a thumb trigger mechanism and was their first rifle listed with a rebounding lock.

The Thumb Trigger rifle was followed by the Winchester Model 1904 rifle.

[ 64 ]

# MODEL 1904 SINGLE SHOT RIFLE

*81. MODEL 1904 RIFLE*

Another variation of the Winchester Model 1902 bolt action was offered for sale in July 1904. It was listed as the Winchester Model 1904 Single Shot Rifle. The principal changes from the Model 1902 were a heavier barrel, 21 inches in length, and a larger special shape stock with a lip on the front end of the forestock. The rifle weighed four pounds, compared to three pounds for the Winchester Model 1902.

Factory records show the first delivery of Model 1904 rifles to warehouse stock was made on July 5, 1904.

## GENERAL SPECIFICATIONS OF THE M/04 RIFLE

| | |
|---|---|
| TYPE | Bolt action takedown, single shot rifle, cocked by pulling rearward on the firing pin head. |
| STYLES | Standard rifle only. |
| BARREL | 21-inch, round only. |
| CHAMBER | 22 Short and 22 Long, interchangeably. |
| | Chambering changed in 1914 to 22 Short, 22 Long, and 22 Extra Long, interchangeably. |
| | Chambering again changed in 1927 to 22 Short, 22 Long, and 22 Long Rifle, interchangeably. Also new length sear. This was the Model 1904-A. |
| STOCK | Gum wood, varnished, rifle shape with lip on forearm, straight grip. Blued steel butt plate, changed to hard rubber butt plate in 1925. |
| TRIGGER GUARD | Special shape trigger guard with the rear end extended and curved to fulfill the purpose of a pistol grip. |
| WEIGHT | About 4 lbs. |
| SERIAL NUMBERS | M/04 rifles were not serially numbered. |

The manufacture of this model was discontinued in 1931. About 302,859 were made.

The Model 1904 rifle sold at a price somewhat higher than the Winchester Model 1902. Both of these models were popular in Australia. They met the demand for rifles that could be imported at a low price, for use in shooting the practically inexhaustible supply of rabbits in that country.

Both the Winchester Model 1902 and 1904 sold in satisfactory quantities for many years, although both were widely imitated in cheaply constructed models of foreign manufacture. Due to its higher price, the Winchester Model 1904 was not quite as successful as the Model 1902. A M/04 rifle was included in each Winchester Junior Rifle Corps Range Kit No. 2, which was first offered for sale about 1920.

The Model 1904 rifle was followed by the Winchester Model 1905 rifle.

# MODEL 1905 SELF-LOADING RIFLE

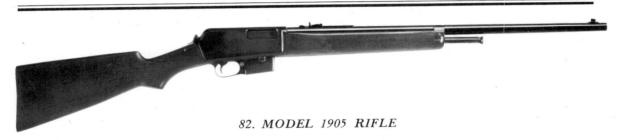

*82. MODEL 1905 RIFLE*

Following the announcement of the new Winchester Model 1903 Automatic (self-loading) rim fire rifle, Thomas C. Johnson turned his attention to the development of a new self-loading model along somewhat similar lines, but built to handle center fire cartridges. He was successful in this development. The new model was announced to the trade in the October 1905 catalog as the Winchester Self-Loading Rifle Model 1905. Two new center fire calibers had been developed especially for use in this new model, the 32 Winchester Self-Loading and the 35 Winchester Self-Loading smokeless cartridges.

In many respects the mechanism was similar to the Winchester Model 1903, but much larger and heavier to handle the more powerful center fire cartridges. The principal difference was in the magazine which was a five shot, single column, detachable box magazine.

The M/05 was the first Winchester self-loading model chambered for center fire cartridges, and also their first rifle equipped with a detachable box magazine.

Factory records show the first delivery of Model 1905 rifles to warehouse stock was made on August 12, 1905.

## GENERAL SPECIFICATIONS OF THE M/05 RIFLE

TYPE       Self-loading repeating rifle, hammerless, detachable box magazine, takedown.

STYLES     Sporting Rifle, Fancy Sporting Rifle.

| | |
|---|---|
| BARRELS | 22-inch, round only. |
| MAGAZINE | Detachable box magazine, holding 5 cartridges. |
| | Longer magazines, holding 10 cartridges, were first listed in October 1911. |
| CHAMBERS | 32 Winchester Self-Loading. |
| | 35 Winchester Self-Loading. |
| STOCK | Sporting Rifle, plain walnut, not checkered, hard rubber butt plate, straight grip (changed to pistol grip in March 1908). |
| | Fancy Sporting Rifle, fancy walnut, checkered, pistol grip. |
| | Fancy walnut, checkered or not checkered, special dimension stocks, etc. were also furnished at extra cost. |
| LISTED WEIGHTS | Sporting Rifle, 7½ lbs. |
| | Fancy Sporting Rifle, 8 lbs. |
| SERIAL NUMBERS | M/05 rifles were serially numbered from 1 up. Number located on underside of trigger guard plate and on left side of receiver. |

Due to its high price and the relatively low velocity cartridges used, the Winchester Model 1905 was never considered a popular model. Manufacture was discontinued in 1920. About 29,113 were made.

### Special Note

The definitive proof mark, "WP" in an oval, was put on all barrels in assembled guns, except 22 caliber, beginning July 17, 1905. The same stamp was applied to both receiver and barrel beginning in July 1908, and was put on all Winchester guns, including 22 caliber, as of October 1908.

A mail order proof stamp, "P" in an oval, was instituted to apply to barrels and receivers sent out from mail order department, beginning on May 31, 1913.

The Model 1905 was a self-loading rifle with a balanced breech bolt, simple blowback operated mechanism. This means that the breech bolt contains a quantity of metal proportioned to the weight and velocity of the bullet so that the shock of the recoil is absorbed by the breech bolt, which in a sense balances the recoil. When the cartridge is fired, the bullet leaves the muzzle of the barrel before the breech bolt commences to move rearward. The design and weight of the breech bolt are so proportioned that there is no loss of velocity and energy of the bullet. In order to obtain the nicety of balance required to operate this type of mechanism, it was necessary for Winchester to develop new cartridges for this model. With this self-loading type of mechanism, the trigger must be pulled and released for each shot.

The Model 1905 rifle was followed by the Winchester Model 1906 rifle.

# MODEL 1906 REPEATING RIFLE

*83. MODEL 1906 RIFLE*

To meet the demand for a slide action repeating rifle chambered for 22 caliber rim fire cartridges, that could be sold at a lower price than the Winchester Model 1890 rifle, Winchester announced a new model in the January 1907 catalog, listed as the Winchester Repeating Rifle Model 1906. This new model was essentially the Winchester Model 1890 action, but with a 20-inch round barrel in place of the longer 24-inch full octagon barrel on the earlier model. Also, the butt stock was changed to the shotgun type with a composition butt plate. The first rifles produced were chambered for the 22 Short cartridge only.

On April 12, 1908, changes were made in the feeding mechanism and in the chambering to handle the 22 Short, 22 Long, and 22 Long Rifle rim fire cartridges, interchangeably. This change, to accommodate three lengths of 22 caliber cartridges, was a popular one. Office records show a remarkable increase in sales after the change was made.

The M/06 was the first model listed by Winchester chambered for 22 Short, 22 Long, and 22 Long Rifle cartridges, interchangeably.

Factory records show the first delivery of Model 1906 rifles to warehouse stock was made on January 16, 1906.

## GENERAL SPECIFICATIONS OF THE M/06 RIFLE

| | |
|---|---|
| TYPE | Repeating rifle, with sliding forearm, hammer, tubular magazine, takedown. |
| STYLES | Standard Sporting Rifle. |
| | Expert rifles were first listed in the Winchester 1924 catalog in three styles: |
| |     1. Regular blued finish. |
| |     2. Nickel trimmed receiver, guard and bolt. |
| |     3. All metal parts full nickel trimmed. |
| | The Expert rifle was equipped with a pistol grip stock, special shape action slide handle, and a 20-inch round barrel. |
| BARRELS | 20-inch, round only. |
| MAGAZINE | Tubular magazine. |
| | Magazine capacities: 22 Short, 15 cartridges; 22 Long, 12 cartridges; 22 Long Rifle, 11 cartridges. |
| CHAMBER | 22 Short only. |
| | Chambering changed on April 12, 1908, to 22 Short, 22 Long, and 22 Long Rifle, interchangeably. |

| STOCK | Standard Sporting Rifle, plain wood, straight grip, composition butt plate. |
| | Expert Rifle, pistol grip. |
| SLIDE HANDLE | Standard rifle, plain wood, round with circular grooves. |
| | Expert rifle, plain wood, special turned shape, no grooves. |
| WEIGHT | About 5 lbs. |
| SERIAL NUMBERS | M/06 rifles were serially numbered on lower tang and underside of receiver. |

The popularity of the Winchester Model 1906 rifle continued for many years and large quantities were sold. In 1932 its manufacture was discontinued, with 848,000 made. The model was revamped and reissued the same year (1932) as the Winchester Model 62.

The Model 1906 Rifle was followed by the Winchester Model 1907 rifle and was succeeded in 1932 by the Winchester Model 62 rifle.

# MODEL 1907 SELF-LOADING RIFLE

*84. MODEL 1907 RIFLE*

Another center fire rifle of the self-loading type was placed on the market and first announced in the January 1907 catalog as the Winchester Model 1907 Self-Loading Rifle. This model was also designed by Thomas C. Johnson. It was an improved version of the Winchester Model 1905, made somewhat heavier to handle the new 351 Winchester Self-Loading smokeless cartridge developed especially for this new model. The new cartridge gave considerably higher velocity than the two special calibers used in the Model 1905.

Factory records show the first delivery of Model 1907 rifles to warehouse stock was made on November 24, 1906.

## GENERAL SPECIFICATIONS OF THE M/07 RIFLE

| TYPE | Self-loading repeating rifle, hammerless, detachable box magazine, takedown. |
| STYLES | Standard Rifle, Fancy Sporting Rifle, Police Rifle (authorized in December 1934). |
| | The Police Rifle had a special shaped stock, pistol grip, beavertail forearm, checkered steel butt plate, and was equipped with a 1¼-inch army type leather sling strap. The rifle was furnished with or without a knife bayonet and steel scabbard. Manufacture of the Police Rifle was discontinued in 1937. |

| | |
|---|---|
| BARREL | 20-inch, round. |
| MAGAZINE | Detachable box magazine holding 5 cartridges. Longer magazines holding 10 cartridges were first listed in October 1911. |
| CHAMBER | 351 Winchester Self-Loading. |
| STOCK | Standard Rifle, plain walnut, not checkered, hard rubber butt plate, pistol grip. The foregoing stock was discontinued and the Police stock with checkered steel butt plate and beavertail forearm was authorized on December 10, 1937. Fancy Sporting Rifle, fancy walnut, checkered. Fancy wood, checkered or not checkered, special dimension stocks, etc. were furnished at extra cost. |
| COMPONENT PARTS | A finger hook was added to the operating sleeve and the magazine release was made larger (authorized on June 3, 1948). |
| WEIGHTS | Standard Rifle—7¾ lbs. and 9 lbs. Police rifle with bayonet, scabbard, and sling strap—10 lbs. 14 oz. Police rifle without bayonet, scabbard, and sling strap—8 lbs. 14 oz. |
| SERIAL NUMBERS | M/07 rifles were serially numbered from 1 up on left side of receiver and below trigger guard plate. |

This model was discontinued in 1957. About 58,490 were made.

### Special Notes

The M/07 is a self-loading rifle with balanced breech bolt, simple blowback operated mechanism. This means that the breech bolt contains a quantity of metal proportioned to the weight and velocity of the bullet so that the shock of the recoil is absorbed by the breech bolt, which in a sense balances the recoil. When the cartridge is fired, the bullet leaves the muzzle of the barrel before the breech bolt commences to move rearward. The design and weight of the breech bolt are so proportioned that there is no loss of velocity and energy of the bullet.

In order to obtain the nicety of balance required to operate this type of mechanism, it was necessary for Winchester to develop a new cartridge for this model. With this self-loading mechanism, the trigger must be pulled and released for each shot. Due to the higher velocity cartridge used in this rifle, it was considerably more popular than the Winchester Model 1905 and was especially adaptable for law enforcement purposes. Model 1907 was sold to some extent to the Allies during World War I, particularly for arming airplanes.

The Model 1907 rifle was followed by the Winchester Model 1910 rifle.

# MODEL 1910 SELF-LOADING RIFLE

*85. MODEL 1910 RIFLE*

The Model 1907 self-loading rifle was followed by a new rifle of essentially the same action but made larger and heavier to handle a larger caliber cartridge developed especially for it. This new model was also developed by Thomas C. Johnson. It was first listed in the June 1910 catalog, chambered for the new 401 Winchester Self-Loading smokeless cartridge, using either a 200-grain or a 250-grain bullet.

Factory records show the first Model 1910 rifle was delivered to warehouse stock on February 1, 1910.

## GENERAL SPECIFICATIONS OF THE M/10 RIFLE

| | |
|---|---|
| TYPE | Self-loading repeating rifle, hammerless, detachable box magazine, takedown. |
| STYLES | Sporting Rifle, Fancy Sporting Rifle. |
| BARREL | 20-inch, round. |
| MAGAZINE | Detachable box magazine holding 4 cartridges. |
| CHAMBER | 401 Winchester Self-Loading, 200 or 250-grain bullet. |
| STOCK | Plain walnut, pistol grip, not checkered; hard rubber butt plate. Special dimension stocks, etc. were furnished at extra cost. |
| WEIGHTS | Sporting Rifle—8¼ lbs. |
| | Fancy Sporting Rifle—8½ lbs. |
| SERIAL NUMBERS | M/10s were serially numbered from 1 up, on underside of trigger guard plate and left side of receiver. |

The manufacture of this model was discontinued, the last of the rifles being sold in 1936. About 20,786 were made.

### Special Notes

The M/10 was a self-loading rifle with balanced breech bolt, simple blowback operated mechanism. This means that the breech bolt contains a quantity of metal proportioned to the weight and velocity of the bullet so that the shock of the recoil is absorbed by the breech bolt, which in a sense balances the recoil. When the cartridge is fired, the bullet leaves the muzzle end of the barrel before the breech bolt commences to move rearward. The design and weight of the breech bolt are so proportioned that there is no loss of velocity and energy of the bullet.

In order to obtain the nicety of balance required to operate this type of mechanism, it was necessary to develop a new cartridge for this model. With this self-loading type of mechanism, the trigger must be pulled and released for each shot.

Although the Model 1910 gave very satisfactory accuracy at relatively short ranges and was considered an excellent deer gun, it had a very limited sale.

The Model 1910 Rifle was followed by the Winchester Model 1911 shotgun.

# MODEL 1911 SELF-LOADING SHOTGUN

*86. MODEL 1911 SHOTGUN*

John M. Browning, about April 1899, in line with his usual custom, brought to Winchester a crude model of a new self-loading shotgun he had developed. Thomas C. Johnson worked with him in the preparation of suitable specifications for use in his patent application for the newly designed shotgun. Later during negotiations for the purchase of the patent rights and much to Winchester's surprise, it was found that Browning did not wish to dispose of the manufacturing rights, except on a royalty basis. This proposed arrangement was deemed unsatisfactory by Winchester and negotiations were dropped. In 1905, the Remington Arms Company brought out this Browning design, listed as the Remington Auto-Loading Shotgun Model 11.

Winchester had become interested in the self-loading type of action for shotguns but, unfortunately for Winchester, T. C. Johnson had effectively covered the special features necessary in a self-loading action for inclusion in John Browning's patent application. In order to develop a competitive model it was necessary to design an entirely different action—a difficult task, taking considerable time. The problem was finally solved and the new model was announced to the trade in the October 1911 catalog as the Winchester Self-Loading Shotgun Model 1911.

Factory records show the first delivery of Model 1911 shotguns to warehouse stock was made on October 7, 1911.

The Model 1911 shotgun was Winchester's first self-loading shotgun and also its first hammerless shotgun.

## GENERAL SPECIFICATIONS OF THE M/11 SHOTGUN

TYPE          Self-loading repeating shotgun, recoil operated, hammerless, tubular magazine, takedown.

| | |
|---|---|
| STYLES | Plain, Fancy. |
| | Trap and Pigeon models were first listed in January 1913. |
| BARRELS | 26-inch and 28-inch, full choke, modified choke, and cylinder bore. |
| | Matted barrels were furnished at extra cost. M/11s were never furnished with solid raised matted rib or ventilated rib barrels. |
| MAGAZINE | Tubular magazine, holding 5 shells. |
| CHAMBER | 12 gauge 2¾-inch shell. |
| STOCK | Made of birch, laminated (3 pieces), pistol grip, hard rubber butt plate. |
| | Plain or fancy wood, checkered or not checkered, special dimension stocks, straight or pistol grip were furnished at extra cost. |
| FOREARM | Made of birch with rock elm insert. |
| RECEIVER | Blued steel, matted along the line of sight. |
| LISTED WEIGHTS | Plain, 26-inch—7½ lbs. |
| | Fancy, 26-inch—8 lbs. |
| SERIAL NUMBERS | M/11 shotguns were serially numbered from 1 up, on underside of receiver. |

The manufacture of this model was discontinued in 1925. About 82,774 were made.

### Special Notes

The M/11 was a self-loading recoil operated shotgun designed to handle any of the 12 gauge loads then on the market. The recoil of this arm was divided, its main force being absorbed by a buffer at the lower front end of the receiver and the remainder by a similar device forming a cushion between the bolt and the rear end of the receiver.

After its introduction it was found necessary to make several changes in its construction to correct certain weaknesses that had developed. Although the M/11 had a fairly large sale, it was not considered a particularly satisfactory model.

The Model 1911 shotgun was followed by the Winchester Model 1912 shotgun.

### 1911-1918

From 1911-18 no new models of commercial rifles were announced. During 1911, 1912, and 1913 the company was busily engaged in the development and manufacture of their new Model 1911 self-loading and Model 1912 slide action repeating shotguns.

While the United States did not enter World War I until April 1917, participation in it by Winchester began with orders from the British Government in 1914. Large quantities were manufactured for the rapidly expanding British Army during 1915, 1916, and 1917. With entry of the United States in World War I, and until the end of the war in 1918, a very large portion of Winchester production facilities was engaged in the manufacture of war material for use by the United States.

# MODEL 1912 REPEATING SHOTGUN

*87. MODEL 1912 SHOTGUN (EARLY TYPE)*

*88. MODEL 12 SHOTGUN*

*89. MODEL 1912 TRENCH GUN*

*90. MODEL 12 SUPER PIGEON GRADE SHOTGUN*

*91. MODEL 12 SHOTGUN WITH HYDRO-COIL*

The Model 1912, developed and patented by Thomas C. Johnson, was the first Winchester shotgun of the slide action, hammerless repeating type. It was first listed in the January 1913 catalog in 20 gauge, with a 25-inch round nickel steel barrel. This was the first Winchester model to be chambered for 20 gauge. The 12 gauge and the 16 gauge were first listed in 1914, the 12 gauge Riot Gun in 1918, and the 28 gauge was authorized in 1934.

Factory records show the first delivery of Model 1912 shotguns to warehouse stock was made on August 30, 1912.

## GENERAL SPECIFICATIONS OF THE M/12 SHOTGUN

TYPE
    Slide action repeating shotgun, hammerless, tubular magazine, takedown.

STYLES
    Standard or Field Gun.

Tournament Grade, first listed in 1914, discontinued on July 2, 1931, to be succeeded by the Standard Trap Grade.

Trap Grade. First listed in 1914, discontinued on July 2, 1931, to be succeeded by the Special Trap Grade.

Riot Gun, introduced in 1918, last listed in 1963.

Trench Gun, introduced in 1918, thereafter made on special order only.

Standard Trap Grade, authorized on December 24, 1930, discontinued on September 15, 1939, to be succeeded by a new style M/12 Trap Gun.

Special Trap Grade. Authorized on December 24, 1930, discontinued on September 15, 1939.

Trap Gun—New Style. A new style of M/12 Trap Gun was authorized on July 21, 1938, discontinued in 1964.

Trap Gun—Ladies and Junior Model (20 gauge). This style of Trap Gun was authorized on October 22, 1939, discontinuance authorized on December 31, 1941.

Skeet Gun. Skeet guns with solid raised matted rib barrels were authorized on November 17, 1933.

Skeet guns with plain barrels were authorized on January 20, 1937, and last listed in 1947.

Skeet Gun, with Cutts compensator attached.

This style of skeet gun was authorized on August 4, 1938, in 12 gauge; 16 gauge and 20 gauge authorized on February 8, 1939, discontinued in 1940.

Guns with Cutts compensator were discontinued in 1954.

Heavy Duck Gun. M/12 Heavy Duck Gun in 12 gauge only, authorized on February 15, 1935, discontinued in 1963.

Pigeon Grade. Pigeon Grade was first listed in 1914; discontinued in 1941. Reintroduced in 1948; discontinued in 1964. Super Pigeon Grade introduced in 1965.

BARRELS
    *12 gauge:*

Plain barrels, 26, 28, 30, and 32-inch, first listed in 1914.

Matted barrels, on special order only, first listed in 1914.

Solid raised matted rib barrels, 26, 28, 30, and 32-inch, first listed in 1914.

Ventilated rib barrels, 30-inch, first listed in 1919.

26¾-inch ventilated rib barrels were authorized on October 21, 1935.

A new Winchester ventilated rib on Skeet, Trap, and Pigeon Grade guns was introduced in 1960.

*16 gauge:*

Plain barrel, 26-inch first listed in 1914, 28-inch first listed about 1927, 30-inch was authorized on November 24, 1930.

Matted barrels, special order only, first listed in 1914.

Solid raised matted rib barrels, 26-inch first listed in 1914, 28-inch first listed about 1927, 30-inch authorized on November 24, 1930.

*20 gauge:*

Plain barrel, 25-inch, first listed in January 1913.

26-inch barrel, first listed in 1927.

28-inch barrel, first listed in 1927.

30-inch barrel was authorized on November 24, 1930.

Matted barrels, on special order only, first listed in January 1913.

Solid raised matted rib barrel, 25-inch, first listed in January 1913.

A revised edition of the Winchester 1935 catalog reads:

"The 25-inch barrel in the M/12, 20 gauge has been made obsolete."

*28 gauge. Discontinued in 1960:*

Plain barrels, 26-inch and 28-inch, authorized on November 9, 1934.

Solid raised matted rib barrels, 26-inch and 28-inch, authorized on November 9, 1934.

CHOKES

Full choke, modified choke, and cylinder bore.

Intermediate chokes—improved modified choke (¾ choke) and improved cylinder choke (¼ choke)—were authorized on October 29, 1931.

Winchester No. 1 Skeet choke and Winchester No. 2 Skeet choke were authorized in 1935.

CHAMBERS

12 gauge, 2¾-inch shell.

12 gauge heavy duck gun, 3-inch shell.

16 gauge, 2-9/16-inch shell.

Chambering changed to 2¾-inch shell in 1927.

20 gauge, 2½-inch shell.

Chambering changed to 2¾-inch shell in 1925.

28 gauge, 2⅞-inch shell.

STOCKS

*Standard or Field Gun*

A new style stock was authorized for general use on all Standard or Field Guns on November 6, 1934. This stock is of slightly different dimensions, with a shorter grip than the stock previously used. Made of plain walnut, not checkered, with pistol grip and hard rubber butt plate.

*Skeet Gun*

The skeet gun stock was used after the introduction of M/12 skeet guns on November 17, 1933. It was the same as the standard or field gun stock, except it was made of selected walnut with checkered stock, full pistol grip, pistol grip cap, and a hard rubber butt plate.

*Trap Gun*

Trap gun stocks were made of selected walnut with either pistol grip or straight grip and equipped with a rubber recoil pad. Trap gun with Monte Carlo stock was authorized on December 18, 1940.

*Heavy Duck Gun*

Heavy duck gun stocks were made of plain walnut, not checkered, and equipped with a Winchester rubber recoil pad.

A reduction in the length of pull, from 14 inches to 13⅝ inches, was authorized on January 10, 1936.

A change in the drop at heel dimension, from $2\frac{1}{2}$ inches to $2\frac{3}{8}$ inches, was authorized on December 20, 1938.

A Hydro-Coil butt stock (to reduce apparent recoil) with matching forearm, was available on Model 12 Trap and Skeet Guns during 1964 — ivory color or simulated walnut, regular stock with Skeet Gun, Monte Carlo comb or regular stock with Trap Gun.

SLIDE HANDLES

*Standard or Field Gun*

Standard shape, made of plain walnut, round with circular grooves, not checkered. On April 6, 1944, a new standard slide handle was authorized, of a different shape, slightly larger, nearly flat on the bottom side and with grooves on the sides only. This new slide handle was put into use during the latter part of 1946. In 1953, a new action slide handle, longer, shaped full in the center, and tapered at both ends, was introduced.

*Skeet Gun*

Extension slide handle, semi-beavertail shape, made of selected walnut, checkered. A new extension slide handle, which is shorter and of a slightly different shape than the older handle, was authorized as standard equipment on December 19, 1934.

*Trap Gun*

Extension slide handle, semi-beavertail shape, selected walnut, checkered.

Note: A special shaped semi-beavertail slide handle was furnished on trap and skeet guns in 12 gauge only, principally on special orders. This handle was larger than the standard slide handle and smaller than the extension handle. Never very popular, it was discontinued in 1934. However it was reinstated, and a few 12 gauge Standard Skeet Guns were sold equipped with this type handle until discontinued on November 1, 1940.

*Heavy Duck Gun*

Standard shape, made of plain walnut, round with circular grooves, not checkered.

MAGAZINE

Tubular magazine.

Capacity, 5 shells.

Note: By Presidential Proclamation, signed February 2, 1935, and based on the recommendation of the U. S. Biological Survey, the capacity of any automatic loading or repeating shotgun used in shooting migratory birds is specifically limited to three shots. This means two shells in the magazine and one shell in the chamber. On February 22, 1935, a special shape magazine wood plug was authorized to reduce the magazine capacity to two shells. One of these plugs has been included in each carton containing a M/12 shotgun since that date. The only exception to this was the Heavy Duck Gun, which had the plug inserted in the magazine.

RECEIVERS

Straight-line matting on top of receiver.

Receivers sandblasted on the top portion were authorized on February 10, 1939, for use on M/12 skeet and trap guns.

CARTRIDGE GUIDE

A cartridge guide, attached to the ejection side of the carrier, was authorized in 1938. Its purpose is to avoid any possibility of a loaded shell dropping out of the ejector port when short length shells are used.

[ 77 ]

*Standard or Field Gun*
12 gauge, 30-inch barrel—7 lbs. 5 oz.
16 gauge, 28-inch barrel—6 lbs. 9 oz.
20 gauge, 28-inch barrel—6 lbs. 5 oz.
28 gauge, 26-inch barrel—7 lbs. 3 oz.
*Skeet Gun*
12 gauge, 26-inch barrel—7 lbs. 5 oz.
16 gauge, 26-inch barrel—6 lbs. 12 oz.
20 gauge, 26-inch barrel—6 lbs. 11 oz.
*Trap Gun*
12 gauge, 30-inch barrel—8 lbs. 2 oz.
*Heavy Duck Gun*
12 gauge, 30-inch barrel—8 lbs. 9 oz.

SERIAL NUMBERS    M/12 shotguns are serially numbered from 1 up, on underside of receiver, forward end, and underside of receiver extension.

## Special Notes

The introduction of the M/12 shotgun with its hammerless slide action mechanism was an innovation. It soon became so popular that it was generally known as The Perfect Repeater.

Considered an ideal gun for small game shooting, it also has gained an enviable reputation at traps and on the skeet field.

Modified takedown M/12 Featherweight was introduced in 1959 and discontinued in 1962.

Winchester presented the 1,000,000th M/12 shotgun to Lieut. General Henry H. Arnold, Chief of the Army Air Forces, on August 30, 1943. This gun was a 12 gauge with a 30-inch full choke, matted rib barrel, with fancy skeet stock and extension slide handle engraved:

Number 1,000,000
Model 12 WINCHESTER Repeating Shotgun
Presented to
LIEUT. GEN. HENRY H. ARNOLD and the ARMY AIR FORCES
As a Tribute to America's Aerial Gunners
by
WINCHESTER REPEATING ARMS COMPANY
Division of
WESTERN CARTRIDGE COMPANY

The Model 12 was discontinued as a standard production model in December 1963. About 1,968,307 were made during this initial period.

The Model 12 continued to be made as a special order Super Pigeon Grade in 12 gauge only in the Winchester Custom shop from 1963 until the present. The Super Pigeon Grade Model 12 is available in standard barrel lengths and features full fancy American walnut stock and forearm and is custom built to exact individual measurements, along with choice of three distinctive receiver engravings.

In 1972, because of popular insistence, the Model 12 was reintroduced in the regular line with production trap, skeet and field guns in 12 gauge only and standard barrel lengths (26-, 28- and 30-inch), all with ventilated rib. The new production Model 12 shotguns are precisely like the old Model 12 down to interchangeable parts. As of January 12, 1975, a total of 2,022,172 Model 12 shotguns of all types had been manufactured.

The Model 1912 was followed by the British Enfield Pattern No. 14 Rifle and the United States Rifle Caliber 30, Model of 1917.

# BRITISH ENFIELD RIFLES
# PATTERN NO. 14 RIFLE

*92. BRITISH ENFIELD RIFLE. PATTERN NO. 14 RIFLE*

In 1915, 1916, and 1917, Winchester manufactured a large quantity of Enfield No. 14 rifles for the British Government. These rifles were chambered for use with the 303 British Mark VI round nose and the 303 British Mark VII pointed bullet cartridges.

They were serially numbered on right front of receiver.

Discontinued in 1917; about 245,866 were made.

# MODEL 1917 U.S. CALIBER 30

*93. U.S. MODEL 1917 ENFIELD*

When the United States entered World War I in 1917, it was imperative that large quantities of rifles for U. S. troops be obtained in the shortest possible time. Winchester had no special equipment for the production of the United States standard service rifle, so the company purchased from the British Government the equipment that had previously been used to produce the British Enfield Pattern No. 14 Rifle.

Changes were made in the equipment to adapt the rifle for handling the United States Service, 30-06 Springfield, ammunition. The name of the pattern was changed to the United States Rifle, Caliber 30, Model of 1917.

At the factory this rifle was known as the G17R and also as the Winchester M/17 Rifle. The first delivery of a few sample M/17 rifles was made in May 1917 and the first quantity production in August 1917.

## GENERAL SPECIFICATIONS OF THE M/17 RIFLE

| | |
|---|---|
| TYPE | Bolt action repeater, non-detachable magazine, solid frame. |
| STYLE | Military musket equipped with bayonet, scabbard, and sling strap. |
| BARREL | 26-inch, round. |
| MAGAZINE | Non-detachable box magazine holding 5 cartridges. |
| CHAMBER | 30-06 Springfield. |
| STOCK | Plain walnut, musket type, oiler and thong case carried in a recess in the butt stock, pistol grip. |
| SIGHTS | Military type, both front and rear sights protected by lateral wing guards. |
| BAYONET AND SCABBARD | Equipped with Model 1917 bayonet and bayonet scabbard. |
| LISTED WEIGHT | Total weight of arm with oiler and thong case, and bayonet, 10 lbs. 5 oz. |
| SERIAL NUMBERS | M/17s were serially numbered from 1 up on right front of receiver. Also stamped with a letter to indicate the place of manufacture and with numbers indicating the month and year of manufacture. |

M/17 rifles were produced only for the United States Government and were not listed in Winchester catalogs or price lists. About 545,511 were made.

### Special Note

The company presented a Model 1917 rifle of Winchester manufacture to President Woodrow Wilson on January 18, 1919.

The United States Rifle Caliber 30, Model of 1917, was followed by the Browning Machine Rifle, Model of 1918.

# MODEL 1918 BROWNING RIFLE
## (Browning Light Machine Gun)

*94. MODEL 1918 BROWNING AUTOMATIC RIFLE*

The Browning Machine Rifle, Model of 1918, was engineered by Winchester from a crude model constructed by John M. Browning. Although the official name of this rifle was the Browning Machine Rifle, Model of 1918, it was known in the factory as the G18M, the M/18, and also as the Browning Light Machine Gun.

It was designed as a shoulder arm with air cooled, gas operated mechanism; its operation was described in the U. S. Handbook as follows:

> Expanding powder gases furnish the energy for the operation of the gun. After the gun is fired and the bullet passes the gas port in the barrel, the live powder gases expand through the gas port into the gas cylinder and impinge against the head of the piston. This sudden blow forces the piston to the rear, compressing the recoil spring and storing up energy for the return movement. The various lugs and cams actuate the feeding, firing, extraction, and ejection, and also control the operation of the gun.

Although usually operated as a full automatic, by setting a change lever, it could also be used as a semi-automatic with the trigger pulled and released for each shot.

Factory records show the first delivery of M/18 rifles in April 1918.

## GENERAL SPECIFICATIONS OF THE M/18 RIFLE

| | |
|---|---|
| TYPE | Automatic machine rifle, gas operated, detachable box magazine. |
| STYLES | Standard rifle only. |
| BARREL | 24-inch, round. |
| MAGAZINE | Detachable box magazine holding 20 cartridges. |
| CHAMBER | 30-06 Springfield. |
| STOCK | Plain walnut, pistol grip. |
| SIGHTS | Sights graduated up to 1600 yards. |
| WEIGHTS | Rifle with magazine empty—15 lbs. 15 oz. |
| | Rifle with magazine filled—17 lbs. 6 oz. |

This machine rifle was manufactured for the United States Government only; 47,123 were made, and it was never listed in Winchester catalogs or price lists. Serial numbered on top front of receiver.

The Browning Machine Rifle Model of 1918 was followed by the Winchester Model 52 Rifle.

# MODEL 52 REPEATING RIFLE

*95. MODEL 52 TARGET RIFLE. FIRST STYLE. SLOW LOCK*

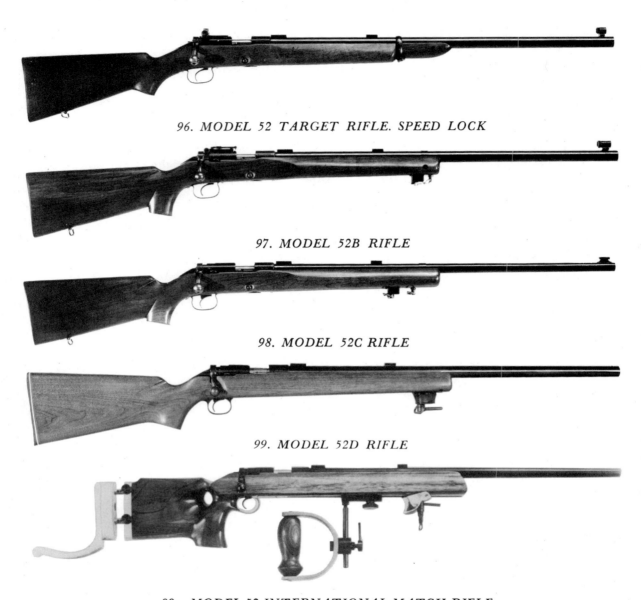

96. MODEL 52 TARGET RIFLE. SPEED LOCK

97. MODEL 52B RIFLE

98. MODEL 52C RIFLE

99. MODEL 52D RIFLE

99A. MODEL 52 INTERNATIONAL MATCH RIFLE

*99ʙ. MODEL 52 INTERNATIONAL PRONE TARGET RIFLE*

*100. MODEL 52 SPORTING RIFLE*

The general use of bolt action military rifles during World War I had made the troops bolt-action conscious. At the end of the war in 1918, there was an increasing interest in small bore match shooting and a growing demand for a high grade military type, bolt action, accuracy rifle built along the lines of the United States service arm, but designed and chambered especially for 22 Long Rifle rim fire ammunition. This interest was prompted, to a considerable extent, by the lack of suitable ranges where the service rifles and their high velocity, long range 30-06 Springfield ammunition could be used with safety.

Winchester's answer to the demand was a new model known as the Model 52, the pioneer rifle of its type, designed especially for small bore match shooting. A few of these rifles were produced for testing purposes and were first shown to shooters in Camp Caldwell, New Jersey, at the National Rifle Matches held in August 1919.

One of the important features of this new model was its detachable box magazine, curved to handle the flanged head of the rim fire cartridge. Patents were granted to Thomas C. Johnson for both the rifle and its box magazine.

Factory records show the first delivery of commercially made Model 52 rifles to warehouse stock on September 18, 1920.

## GENERAL SPECIFICATIONS OF THE M/52 RIFLE

| | |
|---|---|
| TYPE | Bolt action repeating rifle, detachable box magazine, solid frame. Made as single shot in Model 52D, 1961. |
| STYLES | Target Rifle, with standard weight barrel. |
| | Target Rifle, with heavy weight barrel. |
| | A few rifles with heavy barrels were manufactured on special orders commencing about 1927. This type was first listed as standard in 1933. |
| | Sporting Rifle, with light weight barrel. Authorized on February 5, 1934; discontinued in December 1958. |
| | Bull Gun, with extra heavy barrel. Authorized on February 8, 1939; production discontinued in 1960. |

International Match Rifle with precision rifled lead-lapped barrel and International style stock introduced in 1969. An International Prone Target Rifle variation was introduced in the 1975 catalog.

BARRELS
Target Rifle, standard weight, 28-inch, round. Lug forged on barrel for front sight base.

Target Rifle, heavy weight, 28-inch, round.

Sporting Rifle, light weight, 24-inch round. Ramp forged on barrel for front sight base, sight cover attached.

Bull Gun, extra heavy weight, 28-inch, round.

TELESCOPE BASES
Originally M/52 barrels were drilled and tapped for Winchester telescope bases designed for use with Winchester 3A and 5A, and Lyman telescopes. These bases had a 6.2-inch center-to-center spacing. With this spacing graduation adjustments gave a decimal point reading of 1.2-inch at 100 yards for each minute-of-angle on the rear mount.

A change in the bases and the spacing to be used was authorized on January 11, 1933. These new bases had a specially shaped Fecker type notch added on the right-hand side of both bases.

They are known as the Winchester Combination Telescope Sight Bases and are satisfactory for use with Winchester, Lyman, Fecker, and Unertl telescopes. Bases are spaced 7.2 inches center-to-center to give a graduation adjustment reading of 1 inch at 100 yards for each minute-of-angle graduation on the rear mount.

CHAMBER
22 Long Rifle.

RECEIVER
Flat Top Receiver.

This style has a sight slot on top of the receiver to fit the base of a Winchester No. 82 rear sight. It is also used on M/52 rifles equipped with receiver sights made by other manufacturers and using this style of sight base.

Flat top receivers were discontinued in 1947.

Round Top Receiver.

This type of receiver was authorized for general use on June 18, 1936. It is drilled and tapped on the left-hand side of the receiver to fit receiver sights made by other manufacturers and using this method of attachment.

MAGAZINE
Detachable box magazine holding five 22 Long Rifle cartridges. Longer magazines holding ten 22 Long Rifle cartridges were also furnished at extra cost. A Single Loading Adaptor was authorized on March 13, 1935. This adaptor is similar in appearance to the standard 5-shot magazine except that it has a flexible straight line cartridge guide affixed to the top of the magazine in place of the regular magazine follower.

STOCKS
Target Rifle, standard weight barrel. The original stock was made with a finger groove on each side of the forearm. This stock was discontinued in 1932 and a new target stock without finger grooves was adopted in its place. Stock made of plain walnut, not checkered, pistol grip, checkered steel butt plate. Target Rifle, heavy barrel. The original stock was of a semi-beavertail shape, known as the match type. This stock was discontinued in 1936 and a new type of stock known as the Marksman No. 1 was adopted in its place.

Stock made of plain walnut, not checkered, pistol grip, checkered steel butt plate.

The Marksman No. 1 stock was designed for use with telescope sights and special high iron sight combinations.

The Marksman No. 2 stock, authorized on December 22, 1937, was designed for use with standard height iron sight combinations and has been furnished on M/52 rifles with either standard weight or heavy weight barrels.

Bull Gun, extra heavy barrel. Marksman No. 1 stock, made of plain walnut, not checkered, pistol grip, checkered steel butt plate.

Sporting Rifle, light weight barrel. Sporting type stock with cheek piece made of selected walnut, pistol grip with hard rubber pistol grip cap, forearm tip made of black plastic material, checkered steel butt plate.

An International "free style" stock was introduced in 1969 with thumb hole, adjustable butt plate and forearm handle. A modified International stock (no thumb hole or adjustable butt plate of forearm handle) was introduced for prone target shooting in 1975.

**ADJUSTABLE SLING SWIVEL BASE** An adjustable sling swivel base was authorized as standard equipment on all M/52 rifles (except the Sporting Rifle) on August 27, 1935. The addition of this adjustable sling swivel base necessitated a change in M/52 stocks. The forearm was extended forward approximately 1¼ inches in order that the swivel base might be located in its proper position.

This adjustment swivel has 5 positions, which, with the sling strap in its free position, gives a total adjustment of 3¼ inches for the hand rest.

**SWIVEL BOWS AND SLING STRAPS** M/52 Target rifles and Bull guns are equipped with 1¼ inch swivel bows, without sling strap.

The M/52 sporting rifle is equipped with 1-inch quick detachable swivels and 1-inch army type leather sling strap.

**SPEED LOCK** The original speed lock was added in August 1929. It was discontinued and a new type of speed lock was adopted in May 1937.

**SAFETY** The original safety, located on the left-hand side of the receiver, was discontinued in 1937 in favor of a new type. The new safety is located on the right-hand side of the receiver ahead of the bolt handle and is operated by moving a thin, slightly curved thumb piece rearward to lock and forward to release.

**SIGHT COMBINATIONS** M/52 rifles are furnished with any suitable sight combinations desired.

**WEIGHTS** When offered:
Target Rifle, standard weight barrel—9¾ and 10 lbs.
Target Rifle, heavy barrel—11 and 12 lbs.
Bull Gun, extra heavy barrel—13 lbs.
Sporting Rifle, light weight barrel—7¼ lbs.

**TYPES** M/52, 1920 to 1929, original slow lock.
M/52, 1929 to 1932, first speed lock.
M/52A, introduced in 1932, receiver and locking lug strengthened.
M/52B, introduced in 1935, adjustable sling swivel assembly and single shot adaptor added.

M/52C, introduced in 1947, vibration-free trigger mechanism, easily adjusted. M/52D, introduced in 1961, single shot rifle. Free floating barrel with adjustable bedding device. New stock with hand-stop and adjustment channel.

SERIAL NUMBERS    M/52 rifles are serially numbered from 1 up, on forward end of receiver, left side.

### *Special Notes*

The Model 52 rifle, from the time of its introduction, has been the leading arm in the development of small bore accuracy shooting.

Many changes have been made in the rifle from time to time to keep in step with the rapidly changing conditions affecting small bore match shooting and, as a result of such changes, numerous patents have been granted to Winchester for new features incorporated in the Model 52 as now manufactured.

Since its introduction in 1919, the Model 52 has been a world leader in bringing out new features and in the development of better and more consistent accuracy, and has tremendously increased the popularity of small bore match shooting. It is still being manufactured in standard weight barrel and heavy weight barrel models.

Model 52D barreled actions were first offered in the 1965 catalog.

In response to increased interest in International competition, the M/52 International Match Rifle was introduced in 1969. It featured a "free style" stock with thumb hole and adjustable butt plate and forearm handle as well as a precision rifled lead-lapped 28-inch barrel. A variation for International prone target shooting was first listed in 1975. This ultra-modern styled prone stock features a high cheek piece on line with the line of the barrel.

As of September 24, 1974, a total of 124,489 Model 52 rifles of all types had been manufactured.

The Model 52 rifle was followed by the Winchester Model 20 shotgun.

# MODEL 20 SINGLE SHOT SHOTGUN

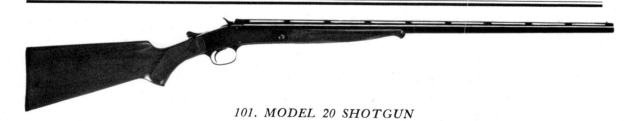

### *101. MODEL 20 SHOTGUN*

At the close of World War I, Winchester possessed manufacturing facilities greatly expanded over previous production requirements. In addition to the many new products then being considered for manufacture, some attention was given to the development of several types of single shot shotguns barreled for small gauges, which could be developed at little expense and put into production quickly to make use of a portion of the idle equipment in the Gun Department.

In 1920 three different models of single shot shotguns in the lower priced groups were placed on the market by the company. The first of these models was listed as the Model 20 Single Shot Shotgun. This model, designed with a visible hammer, was of the top lever break-down type, chambered for the 410 gauge 2½-inch shell. It was the first Winchester use of the break-down action, and the first Winchester chambering for the 410 gauge shell.

Factory records show the first delivery of Model 20 shotguns to warehouse stock was made in March 1919.

## GENERAL SPECIFICATIONS OF THE M/20 SHOTGUN

| | |
|---|---|
| TYPE | Single barrel shotgun, top lever break-down type, single shot, hammer. |
| STYLES | Standard style only. |
| BARREL | 26-inch, round, full choke. |
| CHAMBER | 410, 2½-inch shell. |
| STOCK | Standard plain walnut, not checkered, pistol grip, hard rubber butt plate. Checkered stock on special order. |
| FOREARM | Special shape with lip on front end. |
| LISTED WEIGHT | About 6 lbs. |
| SERIAL NUMBERS | M/20 shotguns were serially numbered from 1 up. Located on forward end of trigger guard and underside of receiver. |

The manufacture of M/20 shotguns was discontinued in 1924, and the remaining stock on hand was sold in 1931. About 23,616 were made.

### Special Notes

The M/20 was designed as a small compact shotgun for small game shooting and for practice shooting on midget clay targets. One of these guns was packed in each Winchester Junior Trap Shooting Outfit.

The Winchester 1920 Catalog description of this outfit reads:

### A New Shooting Game for the Entire Family

The shooting novelty of the year for young and old will be the Winchester Junior Trap Shooting Outfit. A whole new field of sport is packed into a neat, strong hand case that can be placed in the back of an automobile on trips to the country or seashore, or carried conveniently in the hand.

Besides the new and graceful 410 Winchester Shotgun, a little beauty and a fine arm, the outfit includes the Winchester Midget Hand Trap with which the shooter can throw the little clay targets at which he shoots, or have them thrown for him by any companion of his outing; 150 Winchester 410 gauge loaded shells, 100 clay targets, steel cleaning rod, gun grease, gun oil, and rust remover. All packed in a rugged handsome case 30 x 8½ x 6 inches. The total weight of outfit complete, including everything necessary for the sport of trap shooting, is about 40 pounds.

The M/20 was also sold singly and, although it was an excellent arm mechanically, it was a bit too high priced for large sales and therefore not considered a particularly successful model.

The Model 20 shotgun was followed by the Winchester Model 36 shotgun.

# MODEL 36 SINGLE SHOT SHOTGUN

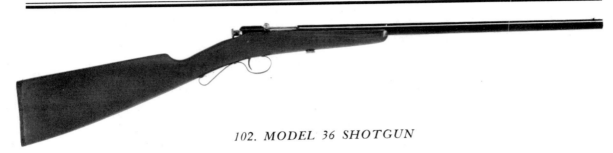

*102. MODEL 36 SHOTGUN*

The Model 36 was the second of the low priced single shot shotguns to be announced in the March 1920 Winchester catalog. This was a bolt action single shot shotgun in takedown form. It was cocked by pulling rearward on the knurled firing pin head—the same cocking mechanism that was used previously on several of the early Winchester rim fire single shot rifles.

Factory records show the first delivery of Model 36 shotguns to warehouse stock in March 1920.

## GENERAL SPECIFICATIONS OF THE M/36 SHOTGUN

| | |
|---|---|
| TYPE | Bolt action single shot shotgun, cocked by pulling rearward on the firing pin head, takedown. |
| STYLES | Standard style only. |
| BARREL | 18-inch, round only. |
| CHAMBER | 9mm Long Shot, 9mm Short Shot, and 9mm Ball, interchangeably. |
| STOCK | Plain wood, one piece stock and forearm, special shape trigger guard to fulfill the purpose of a pistol grip, composition butt plate. |
| LISTED WEIGHT | About 2¾ lbs. |
| SERIAL NUMBERS | M/36 shotguns were not serially numbered. |

The manufacture of this model was discontinued in 1927; about 20,306 were made.

### Special Notes

The construction of the M/36 shotgun was practically the same as the Winchester M/02 rifle and it was placed on the market as a low-priced arm for shooting small vermin. Although listed as a shotgun and chambered for the rim fire 9mm loaded paper shot shell, it could also be properly classed as a rifle, for it interchangeably takes the rim fire ball shell.

It was expected that the Model 36 would have a large sale, especially in the southern states, but its sale was disappointingly low. The gun was too small in size, weighing only 2¾ pounds, and lacked firing power due to the small gauge and short range of the ammunition. The Model 36 was the only shotgun ever made in this country chambered for the 9mm shot and ball cartridges, although other types of guns chambered for this ammunition had previously been made in Europe.

The Model 36 shotgun was followed by the Winchester Model 41 shotgun.

# MODEL 41 SINGLE SHOT SHOTGUN

*103. MODEL 41 SHOTGUN*

This model was the third of the low priced single shot shotguns to be announced in the March 1920 Winchester catalog.

The Model 41 was a single shot takedown with a bolt action, using the same cocking arrangement as the Winchester Model 36. It was, however, a very much better designed and constructed model.

Factory records show the first delivery of Model 41 shotguns to warehouse stock in 1920.

## GENERAL SPECIFICATIONS OF THE M/41 SHOTGUN

| | |
|---|---|
| TYPE | Bolt action single shot shotgun, cocked by pulling rearward on the firing pin head, takedown. |
| STYLES | Standard style only. |
| BARREL | 24-inch, round, full choke. |
| CHAMBER | 410 2½-inch shell. Chambering changed in 1933 to 3-inch shell. |
| STOCK | Plain walnut, one piece stock and forearm, pistol grip, hard rubber butt plate. Straight grip was furnished at no increase in price. Checkered stocks were available on special order. |
| WEIGHT | About 4½ lbs. |
| SERIAL NUMBERS | M/41 shotguns were not serially numbered. |

The manufacture of this model was discontinued in 1934; about 22,146 were made.

### Special Note

The Model 41 was the first shotgun of its type and price class made in this country. It was worthy of a much higher volume of sale but was handicapped by its relatively high price for a single shot.

The Model 41 was followed by the Winchester Model 53 rifle.

# MODEL 53 REPEATING RIFLE

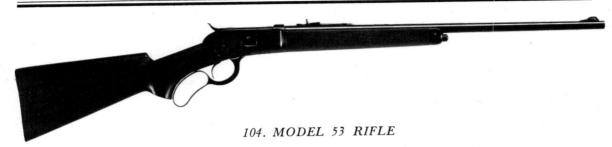

*104. MODEL 53 RIFLE*

The older Winchester Model 1892 lever action rifle was furnished in a great variety of styles, types and lengths of barrel, magazine capacities, etc., in both solid frame and takedown. However, the sale of many of the individual variations had dropped to a point where it was no longer profitable to continue their manufacture. In order to keep the Model 1892 rifle action on the market, it was decided in 1924 to discontinue all of the items in the Model 1892 rifle line and continue the manufacture of the rifle in only one standard style, barrel type and length, magazine capacity, etc., in solid frame and takedown style. After some modernization, the new rifle was placed on the market as the Winchester M/53. However, some of the older style M/92 rifles were sold as late as 1934.

This change did not affect the Model 1892 carbine which was continued in the line until 1941.

The principal changes incorporated in the new model, announced as the Winchester Model 53 in the 1924 catalog, included a 22-inch, round barrel, shotgun type butt stock with a checkered steel butt plate, and a change in sight equipment.

Factory records show the first delivery of Model 53 rifles to warehouse stock was made in August 1924.

## GENERAL SPECIFICATIONS OF THE M/53 RIFLE

| | |
|---|---|
| TYPE | Lever action repeating rifle, hammer, tubular magazine, solid frame and takedown. |
| STYLES | Sporting Rifle only. (Carbines were not furnished in this model.) |
| BARRELS | 22-inch, round only. |
| MAGAZINE | Tubular magazine holding six cartridges. |
| CHAMBERS | 25-20 Win., 32 Win. (32-20), 44 Win. (44-40). |
| STOCK | Plain walnut, not checkered, shotgun butt, straight grip, checkered steel butt plate. |
| | Rifle or shotgun butt stocks, either straight grip or pistol grip, fancy walnut, checkered or not checkered furnished at extra cost. |
| WEIGHT | Standard rifle—about 5½ to 6 lbs. |
| SERIAL NUMBERS | M/53 rifles were serially numbered concurrently with the Model 1892, on underside of receiver. |

The manufacture of this model was discontinued in 1932; about 24,916 were made.

Although the Winchester Model 53 rifle was in some respects a more modern rifle than its predecessor, it was not a large seller. After revamping, it was later reissued as the Winchester Model 65 rifle.

The Model 53 rifle was followed by the Winchester Model 55 rifle and was succeeded in 1933 by the Winchester Model 65 rifle.

# MODEL 55 REPEATING RIFLE

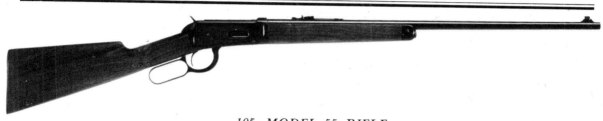

*105. MODEL 55 RIFLE*

The older Winchester Model 1894 lever action rifle was furnished in a great variety of styles, types and lengths of barrels, magazine capacities, etc. in both solid frame and takedown. The sale of many of the variations had gradually dropped to a point so low that it was no longer profitable to continue their manufacture.

To keep the Model 1894 rifle action on the market, it was decided in 1924 to discontinue all of the variations in the Model 1894 rifle line and continue the manufacture of the rifle in only one standard type. The design was modernized in both solid frame and takedown style, and placed on the market under a new Winchester model number. However some of the older style M/94 rifles were sold as late as 1936.

This change did not affect the Model 1894 Carbine, which was continued and is still being manufactured.

The principal changes incorporated in the new model, announced as the Winchester Model 55 in the 1924 catalog, included a 24-inch, round barrel, shotgun type butt stock with a checkered steel butt plate, and a change in sight equipment.

Factory records show the first deliveries of Model 55 rifles to warehouse stock were: takedown in August 1924, solid frame in 1931.

The first chambering listed was the 30-30 Winchester; the 25-35 Winchester and the 32 Winchester Special chamberings were added on January 3, 1927.

## GENERAL SPECIFICATIONS OF THE M/55 RIFLE

TYPE            Lever action repeating rifle, hammer, tubular magazine, solid frame and take-
                down.
STYLES          Carbines were not furnished in this model. Sporting rifle only.

| | |
|---|---|
| BARRELS | 24-inch, round only. |
| MAGAZINE | Tubular magazine holding 3 cartridges. |
| CHAMBERS | 25-35 Win., 30 Win. (30-30), 32 Win. Spec. |
| STOCK | Plain walnut, not checkered, shotgun butt, straight grip, checkered steel butt plate. |
| | Rifle or shotgun butt stocks either straight grip or pistol grip, fancy walnut, checkered or not checkered, furnished at extra cost. |
| WEIGHT | Standard rifle, about 6¾ to 7 lbs. |
| SERIAL NUMBERS | M/55 rifles were serially numbered independently to about No. 2868, then numbered with Model 1894s, on underside of receiver. |

The manufacture of this model was discontinued in 1932; about 20,580 were made.

### Special Note

Although the Winchester Model 55 was in some respects a more modern rifle than its predecessor, it did not enjoy large sales. It was revamped and reissued later as the Winchester Model 64 rifle.

The Model 55 rifle was followed by the Winchester Model 54 rifle and was succeeded in 1933 by the Winchester Model 64 rifle.

# MODEL 54 BOLT ACTION RIFLE

*106. MODEL 54 RIFLE*

*107. MODEL 54 CARBINE*

For a number of years Winchester had been developing a high grade repeating rifle of the bolt action type built along military lines. Also in process was a new center fire cartridge, with velocity approximating 3,000 foot seconds, that could be used in the new rifle. During the development of the rifle, several models of various design were made up for testing purposes. Cartridges used were the 30-06 Springfield and the new one, which in its development stage was known as the 27 W.C.F.

The final development of the new rifle and the new cartridge was in 1925. They were announced to the trade in the December 1925 catalog as the Winchester Bolt Action Rifle Model 54, and the 270 Winchester cartridge. Initial chamberings were for the 270 Winchester as well as the 30-06 Springfield. Additional calibers were added later.

Factory records show the first delivery of Model 54 rifles to warehouse stock was made on April 21, 1925.

## GENERAL SPECIFICATIONS OF THE M/54 RIFLE

| | |
|---|---|
| TYPE | Bolt action repeating rifle, non-detachable box magazine, solid frame. |
| STYLES | Standard Rifle. |
| | Carbine, added in 1927. |
| | Sniper's Rifle, added in 1929. |
| | NRA Rifle, added in 1931. |
| | Super Grade, added in 1934. |
| | Target Rifle with heavy barrel, added in 1935. |
| | National Match Rifle, added in 1935. |
| CHAMBERS | 270 Winchester, in 1925. |
| | 30-06 Springfield, in 1925. |
| | 30 Winchester (30-30), in 1928. |
| | 7mm, in 1930. |
| | 7.65mm, in 1930. |
| | 9mm, in 1930. |
| | 250-3000 Savage, in 1931. |
| | 22 Hornet, in 1933. |
| | 220 Swift, in 1936. |
| | 257 Roberts, in 1936. |
| BARRELS | Standard Rifle, 24-inch, round. |
| | Standard Rifle, 20-inch, round (added in 1934). |
| | Carbine, 20-inch, round. |
| | Sniper's Rifle, 26-inch, round, heavyweight. Changed to 26-inch, round, extra heavy, in 1935. |
| | NRA Rifle, 24-inch, round. |
| | Super grade, 24-inch, round. |
| | Target Rifle, 24-inch, round, heavyweight. |
| | National Match Rifle, 24-inch, round. |
| | Exception: All 220 Swift barrels were 26-inch, round. |
| | Note: Forged ramp front sight bases on rifle and carbine barrels were authorized on March 20, 1931. |
| TELESCOPE BASES | M/54 Standard Rifles and Carbines were drilled and tapped on the receiver for a rear telescope sight base. The barrels were not drilled for a front telescope sight base. |
| | M/54 National Match Rifle, Target Model with heavy barrel, and the Sniper's Rifle were regularly equipped with both front and rear telescope sight bases. |

These bases were furnished with either 6.2 inch or 7.2 inch center-to-center-spacing.

STOCKS · Standard Rifle. Plain walnut, stock and forearm checkered, pistol grip, scored steel butt plate, changed to checkered steel butt plate in 1930.

Carbine. Plain walnut, not checkered, finger groove in each side of forearm, pistol grip, scored steel butt plate.

Sniper's Rifle. Plain walnut, not checkered, pistol grip, checkered steel butt plate. Changed in 1936 to special target design stock.

NRA Rifle. Made of selected walnut, checkered pistol grip, checkered steel butt plate.

Super Grade. Made of selected walnut with cheek piece, checkered forearm tip made of black plastic material, pistol grip with hard rubber pistol grip cap, checkered steel butt plate.

Target Rifle. Plain walnut, checkered, pistol grip. Changed in 1936 to special target design stock, not checkered. Scored steel butt plate, changed to checkered steel butt plate in 1930.

National Match Rifle. Special target design stock, plain walnut, not checkered, checkered steel butt plate.

SWIVEL BOWS AND SLING STRAPS · Standard Rifles and Carbines were equipped with 1¼-inch swivel bows (no sling strap).

National Match Rifle, Target Rifle, Heavy Barrel, and the Sniper's Rifle were equipped with 1¼-inch swivel bows and a 1¼-inch army type leather sling strap.

Super Grade Rifle was equipped with 1-inch quick detachable swivels and a 1-inch army type leather sling strap and with front sight cover.

MAGAZINE · Non-detachable box magazine, holding 5 cartridges.

SPEED LOCK · The M/54 speed-lock was added in September 1932.

SIGHTS · M/54 rifles were furnished with any suitable sight combination desired.

WEIGHTS · Standard Rifle, 24-inch barrel—7¾ lbs.
Standard Rifle, 20-inch barrel—7½ lbs.
National Match Rifle—7¾ lbs.
Sniper's Rifle—11¾ lbs.
Super Grade Rifle—8 lbs.
Carbine—7¼ lbs.

SERIAL NUMBERS · M/54 rifles were serially numbered, on top front of receiver, right side.

The manufacture of this model was discontinued in 1936; 50,145 were made.

### Special Note

The M/54 was Winchester's first bolt action rifle designed for heavy, high velocity ammunition. It was a popular arm for sporting use, and was also used to a considerable extent for match accuracy shooting with the 30-06 Springfield chambering. Later several changes were made in its construction, many new features were added, and it was reissued as the Winchester Model 70.

The Model 54 rifle was followed by the Winchester Model 56 rifle and was succeeded in 1936 by the Winchester Model 70 rifle.

# MODEL 56 BOLT ACTION RIFLE

*108. MODEL 56 RIFLE*

This model was the first Winchester rim fire rifle in the bolt action, box magazine, medium price class. It was announced in the price list issue of January 3, 1927, as the Winchester Bolt Action, Box Magazine Rifle, Model 56.

Factory records show the first delivery of Model 56 rifles to warehouse stock was made on August 6, 1926.

## GENERAL SPECIFICATIONS OF THE M/56 RIFLE

| | |
|---|---|
| TYPE | Bolt action repeating rifle, detachable box magazine, solid frame. |
| STYLES | Sporting Rifle, Fancy Sporting Rifle. |
| BARREL | 22-inch, round only. |
| CHAMBERS | 22 Short (dropped in 1929). 22 Long Rifle. |
| MAGAZINE | Detachable box magazine. 22 Short magazine, 5 cartridges. 22 Long Rifle magazine, 5 cartridges. Extra long magazines, holding either ten 22 Long rifle or ten 22 Short cartridges, were also furnished at extra cost. |
| STOCK | Sporting Rifle, plain walnut, not checkered, pistol grip, checkered steel butt plate. Fancy Sporting Rifle, fancy walnut, checkered, pistol grip, checkered steel butt plate. Stocks used on both rifles were made with a lip on the front of the forearm. |
| WEIGHTS | Sporting Rifle—4¾ lbs. Fancy Sporting Rifle—5 lbs. |
| SERIAL NUMBERS | M/56 rifles were serially numbered on front end of receiver, right side. |

The manufacture of this model was discontinued in 1929; about 8,297 were made.

The Winchester Model 56 was designed as a small, compact, and well constructed sporting arm. However, because of its light weight for a fairly high priced rifle, it was not generally accepted by shooters.

The Model 56 rifle was followed by the Winchester Model 57 rifle.

# MODEL 57 BOLT ACTION RIFLE

### 109. MODEL 57 RIFLE

The Model 57 was essentially the same mechanically as the Winchester Model 56, but was equipped with heavier stock, a sight combination suitable for target shooting, and swivel bows attached to the stock. It was first announced in the January 3, 1927, price list.

Factory records show the first delivery of Model 57 rifles to warehouse stock was made in August 1926.

## GENERAL SPECIFICATIONS OF THE M/57 RIFLE

| | |
|---|---|
| **TYPE** | Bolt action repeating rifle, detachable box magazine, solid frame. |
| **STYLE** | Target Rifle. |
| **BARREL** | 22-inch, round only. |
| **CHAMBERS** | 22 Short (dropped in 1930). |
| | 22 Long Rifle. |
| **MAGAZINES** | Detachable box magazine. |
| | 22 Short magazine, 5 cartridges. |
| | 22 Long Rifle magazine, 5 cartridges. |
| | Extra long magazines, holding either ten 22 Long Rifle or ten 22 Short cartridges, were furnished at extra cost. |
| **STOCK** | Target type, plain walnut, not checkered, pistol grip, checkered steel butt plate, stock equipped with swivel bows. |
| **WEIGHT** | About 5 lbs. |
| **SERIAL NUMBERS** | M/57 rifles were serially numbered, front end of receiver, right side. |

The manufacture of this model was discontinued in 1936; about 18,600 were made.

Although the Model 57 had a fair sales volume, it was too light in weight and the barrel was too short to meet the general requirements of a target rifle.

The Model 57 was followed by the Winchester Model 58 rifle.

# MODEL 58 RIM FIRE RIFLE

*110. MODEL 58 RIFLE*

The Winchester Models 1902 and 1904, 22 rim fire caliber, were reasonably low priced and for many years sold in large quantities, especially in certain foreign countries. About 1927, the sale of these models began to slip badly. Many cheap imitations, made in Europe and the United States, were marketed at much lower prices than the Winchester models. In an attempt to hold this business, Winchester developed and offered for sale in the January 3, 1928, price list a new model known as the Model 58 Rim Fire Rifle.

Factory records show the first delivery of Model 58 rifles to warehouse stock was made in January 1928.

## GENERAL SPECIFICATIONS OF THE M/58 RIFLE

| | |
|---|---|
| TYPE | Bolt action, single shot rifle, cocked by pulling rearward on the firing pin head, takedown. |
| STYLES | Standard rifle only. |
| BARREL | 18-inch, round only. |
| CHAMBERS | 22 Short, 22 Long, and 22 Long Rifle, interchangeably. |
| STOCK | Plain wood, no butt plate, straight grip. |
| WEIGHT | About 3 lbs. |
| SERIAL NUMBERS | M/58 rifles were not serially numbered. |

The manufacture of this model was discontinued in 1931; about 38,992 were made.

The Model 58 was of the same general type as the Winchester Model 1902. But it was cheaply constructed, having a small butt stock and forearm made from a flat board with the corners edged, instead of the customary turned type of stock used on the Models 1902 and 1904 rifles.

The January 3, 1928, retail price of the Model 58 was $5.50, the Model 1902 was priced at $7.05, and the Model 1904 listed at $8.45. Regardless of its lower price, the Model 58 was not a successful model and only a small quantity was sold.

The Model 58 rifle was followed by the Winchester Model 59 rifle.

# MODEL 59 RIM FIRE RIFLE

*111. MODEL 59 RIFLE*

Shortly after the low priced Winchester Model 58 rifle was placed on the market, it was realized that this model could not successfully compete with other makes of low priced single shot rifles, particularly in foreign countries. So Winchester started the development of a new model to supersede it. The new model used the same mechanism as the Model 58, but had a barrel 23 inches in length and a turned wood pistol grip type stock with a composition butt plate. The weight of the rifle was increased to 4½ pounds, compared to 3 pounds for the Model 58.

The new model was placed on the market in May 1930, listed as the Winchester Model 59 Rim Fire Single Shot Rifle.

Factory records show the first delivery of Model 59 rifles to warehouse stock was made in May 1930.

## GENERAL SPECIFICATIONS OF THE M/59 RIFLE

| | |
|---|---|
| **TYPE** | Bolt action single shot rifle, cocked by pulling rearward on the firing pin head, takedown. |
| **STYLE** | Standard rifle only. |
| **BARREL** | 23-inch, round only. |
| **STOCK** | Plain wood, pistol grip, composition butt plate. |
| **CHAMBERS** | 22 Short, 22 Long, and 22 Long Rifle, interchangeably. |
| **WEIGHT** | About 4½ lbs. |
| **SERIAL NUMBERS** | M/59 rifles were not serially numbered. |

The manufacture of this model was discontinued in 1930; about 9,293 were made.

The Model 59 was not well received by the trade and its sale was a great disappointment. However, Winchester went to work revamping the Model 59, made a successful job of it, and announced the new model in 1931 as the Winchester Model 60 Rim Fire Rifle.

The Model 59 rifle was followed by the Winchester Model 21 Shotgun and was succeeded by the Winchester Model 60 Rifle in 1931.

# MODEL 21 DOUBLE BARREL SHOTGUN

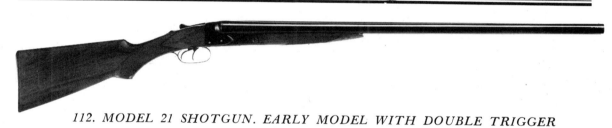

*112. MODEL 21 SHOTGUN. EARLY MODEL WITH DOUBLE TRIGGER*

*113. MODEL 21 SHOTGUN*

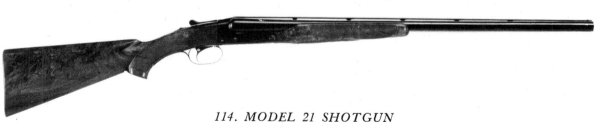

*114. MODEL 21 SHOTGUN*

For several years Winchester engineers had been developing a double barrel hammerless shotgun that for perfection of design, simplicity of parts, quality of material, and precision of manufacture would be outstanding in this type of arm. The first announcement of such a model was made in the Winchester price list of January 2, 1931, the Winchester Model 21 Shotgun.

The Model 21 was the first double barrel shotgun manufactured at the Winchester plant. The only previous double barrel shotguns to bear the Winchester name were of the breech loading type with visible hammers and hammerless. They were made in England, imported and sold in Winchester's New York store from 1879 to May 12, 1884.

The January 2, 1931, announcement of the new Winchester Model 21 included:

Standard Grade

Double Trigger, plain extractors or selective ejection

Single Trigger, plain extractors or selective ejection

with the following note: "Standard grade, double trigger, 12 gauge guns now available. Other styles of Model 21 not available until April 1, 1931."

Factory records show the first delivery of Model 21 double trigger shotguns to warehouse stock was made in March 1930 and the first with single triggers in March 1931.

## GENERAL SPECIFICATIONS OF THE M/21 SHOTGUN

| | |
|---|---|
| TYPE | Double Barrel, breech loading shotgun, hammerless, break-down. |
| STYLES | Standard. |
| | Tournament Grade. Added in 1932 and discontinued in 1936. |
| | Trap Grade. Added in 1932 and discontinued in 1940. |
| | Trap Gun, Standard Grade, added in 1940. |
| | Skeet Gun, Standard Grade, added in 1933. |
| | Skeet Gun, Tournament Grade, added in 1933 and discontinued in 1936. |
| | Skeet Gun, Trap Grade, added in 1933 and discontinued in 1940. |
| | Custom Built, added in 1933 and discontinued in 1941. |
| | Duck Gun, added in 1940. |
| | De Luxe, added in 1942. |
| | In 1959 regular production was discontinued. In January 1960 the "Custom" was reinstated; as of that date, the Custom Grade, Pigeon Grade, and Grand American were the only Model 21s available. |
| BARRELS | 12 gauge. Raised matted rib barrels, 32-inch, 30-inch, 28-inch, and 26-inch were first listed in 1931. Ventilated rib barrels, 32-inch, added in 1932; 30-inch, added in 1933; 26-inch, added in 1938; and 28-inch, added in 1947. |
| | 16 gauge. Raised matted rib barrels, 30-inch, 28-inch, and 26-inch were first listed in 1931. Ventilated rib barrels, 26-inch, added in 1938; 28-inch, added in 1947. |
| | 20 gauge. Raised matted rib barrels, 30-inch, 28-inch, and 26-inch were first listed in 1931. Ventilated rib barrels, 26-inch, added in 1938; 28-inch, added in 1947. |
| | 28 gauge. Made on 20 gauge frame, special order only, was added in 1936. |
| | 410 bore (gauge). A few were made on special order only. |
| CHOKES | Full choke, modified choke, cylinder bore. |
| | Intermediate chokes, improved modified choke (¾ choke), and improved cylinder choke (¼ choke), were authorized on October 29, 1931. |
| | Winchester No. 1 Skeet choke and Winchester No. 2 Skeet choke were authorized in 1933. |
| STANDARD | 12 gauge, 2¾-inch shell. |
| CHAMBERS | 12 gauge Duck Gun, 3-inch shell. |
| | 16 gauge, 2¾-inch shell. |

| | |
|---|---|
| | 20 gauge, 2¾-inch shell. |
| | 28 gauge, 2⅞-inch or 2½-inch shell. |
| STOCKS | Standard. Selected walnut, checkered, pistol grip, hard rubber butt plate. |
| | Trap Gun. Selected walnut, checkered, pistol grip, rubber recoil pad. |
| | Skeet Gun. Selected walnut, checkered, pistol grip, no butt plate. Butt end of stock checkered in lieu of a butt plate. |
| | Duck Gun. Selected walnut, checkered, pistol grip, rubber recoil pad. |
| | De Luxe. Full fancy American walnut, fancy checkering, pistol grip. |
| | All M/21s were furnished with either pistol grip or straight grip stocks at no extra charge. |
| STOCK DIMENSIONS | In addition to the standard stock dimensions of each style, all M/21s were furnished to customers' special dimensions (within certain limits) at no extra charge. |
| STANDARD FOREARMS | M/21 forearms were furnished in two styles, standard shape and beavertail shape. |
| | A change in these forearms was authorized in 1941. "Beavertail forearms used on selective ejection. M/21s in 12 gauge only are to be made in two sizes—a shorter forearm to be added for use on guns with either 26-inch or 28-inch barrels; the regular forearm to be continued for use only on M/21s with 30-inch or 32-inch barrels." |
| STANDARD SAFETY | Standard, equipped with automatic safety. |
| | Skeet Gun, equipped with non-automatic safety. |
| | Trap Gun, equipped with non-automatic safety. |
| | Duck Gun, equipped with automatic safety. |
| | Note: M/21 shotguns were furnished with either automatic safety, non-automatic safety, or no safety on special order only. |
| SERIAL NUMBERS | M/21 shotguns are serially numbered from 1 up, on upper tang. |

Authorization was issued on November 19, 1941, to discontinue the manufacture of M/21 shotguns with plain extractors.

Authorization was issued on June 8, 1944, to discontinue the manufacture of M/21 shotguns with double triggers.

As of January 1, 1950, Model 21 shotguns were manufactured in the single trigger, selective ejection style only.

*Special Note*

The Winchester Model 21 embodies in a modern, double barrel, hammerless shotgun, perfection of design and craftsmanship, precision of manufacture, quality of material, and is outstanding in its remarkable shooting qualities. This shotgun has contributed its full share to Winchester's reputation for arms of the highest quality. It is now produced only in Custom Grade, Pigeon Grade, and Grand American on special order only at premium prices.

As of January 1975, approximately 33,000 Model 21 shotguns of all types had been manufactured.

The Model 21 shotgun was followed by the Winchester Model 60 rifle.

# MODEL 60 RIM FIRE RIFLE

*115. MODEL 60 RIFLE*

This model continued the same single shot action that was used on the Winchester Model 59. Some changes were made to eliminate the weak points that had been found in the previous model.

Additional changes were made in 1932. The length of the barrel was increased from 23 inches to 27 inches and one inch was added to the overall length of the stock and forearm in 1933.

The Winchester Model 60 was first announced in the January 2, 1931, price list.

Factory records show the first delivery of Model 60 rifles to warehouse stock was made in December 1930.

## GENERAL SPECIFICATIONS OF THE M/60 RIFLE

| | |
|---|---|
| **TYPE** | Bolt action single shot rifle, cocked by pulling rearward on the firing pin head, takedown. |
| **STYLE** | Sporting rifle only. |
| **BARREL** | 23-inch, round tapered. |
| | Barrel length increased to 27 inches in 1933. |
| **STOCK** | Plain wood, shotgun butt, pistol grip, composition butt plate. Stock and forearm overall length increased in 1933 from 26¼ inches to 27¼ inches with no change in length of trigger pull. |
| **CHAMBERS** | 22 Short, 22 Long, and 22 Long Rifle, interchangeably. |
| | Note: The following changes were made in 1932. |

A.  The bolt, bolt handle, and trigger were chromium plated.

B.  A trigger spring was added to hold the trigger forward, allowing easier assembly of the rifle.

C.  An opening in the top of the bolt was added.

D.  In place of the S stamped on the firing pin, future production was to be stamped Safe and Fire, these words to be visible through the opening in the top of the bolt.

E.  The firing pin shank was changed to a longer shank and with straight knurling instead of the older diamond knurling.

**SEAR**  An extra notch was added on the bottom of the sear to relieve the pressure on the sear spring when the sear was in its extracted position. With this change, a 22 Long Shot cartridge was ejected satisfactorily.

| WEIGHT | About 4¼ lbs. |
| SERIAL NUMBERS | M/60 rifles were not serially numbered. |

The manufacture of this model was discontinued in 1934; about 165,754 were made.

## Special Note

The Model 60 was a well-constructed rifle and sold in reasonably satisfactory quantities in a large field of competitive models, until it was revamped and reissued as the Winchester Model 67.

The Model 60 was followed by the Winchester Model 62 rifle and was succeeded in 1934 by the Winchester Model 67 rifle.

On December 22, 1931, Winchester was purchased by Western Cartridge Company interests and continued to operate under the name Winchester Repeating Arms Company until December 31, 1938, when the name was changed to:

**WINCHESTER REPEATING ARMS COMPANY**
Division of Western Cartridge Company

This name was continued until December 30, 1944, when it was changed to:

**WINCHESTER REPEATING ARMS COMPANY**
Division of Olin Industries, Inc.

In 1954, Olin Industries, Inc. merged with Mathieson Chemical Corporation and became known as Olin Mathieson Chemical Corporation, with Winchester-Western as a Division.

Under Western Cartridge Company, Olin Industries, Inc., and Olin Mathieson Chemical Corporation management, the Winchester line of firearms has been given a great deal of attention. Many of the older models were revamped and a program for development of new and improved models has been in effect.

# MODEL 62 REPEATING RIFLE

### 116. MODEL 62 RIFLE

In 1890, Winchester announced the Model 1890 slide action repeating rifle, individually chambered for certain 22 caliber rim fire cartridges. This model had a visible hammer, a tubular magazine, and a 24-inch octagon shape barrel. It later became the most famous rim fire repeater ever made by Winchester. For many years it was generally accepted as the standard arm for shooting-gallery use.

In 1932 Winchester revamped the Model 1890, using essentially the same action but with several modern features added. This included a shotgun type of butt stock in place of the rifle butt stock used on the Model 1890; an increase in the magazine capacity; a round, tapered 23-inch barrel; and a change in the rifling, chambering, and feeding mechanism to allow the use of 22 Short, 22 Long, and 22 Long Rifle cartridges interchangeably.

The Model 62 rifle was first listed in the June 21, 1932, price list.

Factory records show the first delivery of Model 62 rifles to warehouse stock was made in April 1932.

## GENERAL SPECIFICATIONS OF THE M/62 RIFLE

| | |
|---|---|
| TYPE | Repeating rifle with sliding forearm, hammer, tubular magazine, takedown. |
| STYLES | Sporting Rifle, Gallery Rifle. |
| BARREL | 23-inch, round tapered. |
| MAGAZINE | Tubular magazine. |
| | Capacity: 22 Short, 20 cartridges; 22 Long, 16 cartridges; 22 Long Rifle, 14 cartridges. |
| | Note: To facilitate charging the magazine from loading tubes, the loading port on the 22 Short, Gallery rifle was changed from its older keyhole form to approximately triangular form with the wide end rearward (authorized on May 12, 1936). |
| CHAMBERS | 22 Short, 22 Long, and 22 Long Rifle, interchangeably. |
| | 22 Short only in Gallery Rifle. |
| STOCK | Plain walnut, straight grip, steel butt plate. Checked composition butt plate in place of steel was authorized on December 11, 1934. |
| LOCKING SYSTEM | In the original M/62 locking system the slide handle must be moved approximately ¼-inch to the rear before the bolt starts the opening movement. |
| | On May 12, 1938, authorization was given to change this locking system and adopt the system that was formerly used on the M/90 rifle—the initial rearward movement of the slide handle starts the opening movement of the bolt. |
| SLIDE HANDLE | A new style, longer slide handle was authorized on February 2, 1939. In 1949, the slide handle was again changed to semi-beavertail type. |
| WEIGHT | About 5½ lbs. |
| SERIAL NUMBERS | M/62 rifles are serially numbered on underside of receiver. |
| | The Model 62-A was introduced in January 1940, Serial No. 99,200, with changes made inside the receiver. |

The Model 62 was discontinued in 1958; about 409,475 were made.

The Model 62 rifle was followed by the Winchester Model 61 rifle.

# MODEL 61 REPEATING RIFLE

## 117. MODEL 61 RIFLE

For a considerable number of years, competitive manufacturers had been producing rim fire repeating rifles of the slide action, hammerless type, and equipped with a tubular magazine.

During this entire period, Winchester's only competitive repeating rifles were the Model 1890 and Model 1906. Both models have slide actions and tubular magazines, but are equipped with a visible hammer. In response to a continued demand for a Winchester hammerless rim fire, slide action, repeating rifle, the Winchester Model 61 was developed and placed on the market. It was first listed in the June 21, 1932, price list.

Factory records show the first Model 61 rifle was delivered to warehouse stock in June 1932.

## GENERAL SPECIFICATIONS OF THE M/61 RIFLE

| | |
|---|---|
| TYPE | Repeating rifle with sliding forearm, hammerless, tubular magazine, takedown. |
| STYLES | Sporting Rifle, round barrel; Sporting Rifle, octagon barrel. A special rifle to handle 22 Long Rifle Shot Cartridges was authorized June 13, 1939, last listed January 1945. This rifle has a special boring, line matting on top of the receiver, and was equipped with a standard shotgun front sight (no rear sight). |
| BARRELS | 24-inch round, 22 Short, 22 Long, and 22 Long Rifle, interchangeably. |
| | 24-inch octagon, 22 Short only. |
| | 24-inch octagon, 22 Long Rifle only. |
| | 24-inch octagon, 22 W.R.F. only. |
| | 24-inch round, 22 Long Rifle Shot. |
| MAGAZINE | Tubular magazine. |
| | Magazine Capacities: 22 Short, 20 cartridges; 22 Long, 16 cartridges; 22 Long Rifle, 14 cartridges; 22 W.R.F., 15 cartridges; 22 Long Rifle Shot, 14 cartridges. |
| CHAMBERS | 22 Short, 22 Long, 22 Long Rifle, interchangeably. |
| | 22 Short only. |
| | 22 Long Rifle only. |
| | 22 W.R.F. only. |
| | 22 Long Rifle Shot. |
| | 22 Winchester Magnum Rim Fire, introduced in March 1960. |
| STOCK | Plain walnut, pistol grip, checkered steel butt plate. |

| | |
|---|---|
| SLIDE HANDLE | A new shape, longer slide handle was authorized on December 8, 1938. |
| WEIGHTS | Round barrel rifle—about 5½ lbs. |
| | Octagon barrel rifle—about 5¾ lbs. |
| SERIAL NUMBERS | M/61 rifles are serially numbered on underside of receiver and on forward end of trigger guard plate. |

### Special Note

The Winchester Model 61 was developed as a modern, hammerless 22 caliber rim fire repeating rifle, incorporating all of the modern features of this type of arm. This model sold in reasonably satisfactory quantities although handicapped to some extent by the much earlier introduction of the hammerless action by competitive manufacturers.

The Model 61 was discontinued in 1963; about 342,001 were made.

The Model 61 rifle was followed by the Winchester Model 60A Target rifle.

# MODEL 60A TARGET RIFLE

*118. MODEL 60A RIFLE*

This model used the same mechanism as the older Model 60 standard rifle, but it was changed by the use of an accuracy barrel, target sights, and a target type stock with a 1¼-inch Kerr web sling strap attached.

The Model 60A Target rifle was first announced in the Winchester March 1, 1933, price list.

Factory records show the first delivery of this model to warehouse stock was made in August 1932.

## GENERAL SPECIFICATIONS OF THE M/60A TARGET RIFLE

| | |
|---|---|
| TYPE | Bolt action single shot rifle, cocked by pulling rearward on the firing pin head, solid frame. |
| STYLE | Target rifle only. Specially designed for accuracy shooting. |
| BARREL | 27-inch, round tapered. |
| CHAMBER | 22 Long Rifle. (Although listed as chambered for the 22 Long Rifle cartridge, it could be used with 22 Short, 22 Long, and 22 Long Rifle cartridges interchangeably.) |
| STOCK | Plain walnut, semi-beavertail forearm, pistol grip, checkered steel butt plate, a 1¼-inch Kerr web sling strap was included. |

| | |
|---|---|
| BOLT | Opening in top of bolt to show "Safe" in black and "Fire" in red. |
| CHROMIUM PLATING | The bolt, bolt handle, and trigger were chromium plated. |
| SIGHTS | Square top military blade front sight, and a Lyman 55W receiver sight. |
| WEIGHT | About 5½ lbs. |
| SERIAL NUMBERS | M/60A Target rifles were not serially numbered. |

The manufacture of this model was discontinued in 1939; about 6,118 were made.

*Special Note*

The M/60A Target rifle was a well constructed and accurate arm. But because it was too light-weight to meet the demand for a low-priced accuracy rifle, it never had a large sale.

The M/60A Target rifle was followed by the Winchester Model 63 rifle.

# MODEL 63 AUTOMATIC (SELF-LOADING) RIFLE

*119. MODEL 63 RIFLE*

This model was a revamping of the first Winchester self-loading rifle, the Model 1903, which was chambered only for a rim fire caliber especially developed for it and known as the 22 Winchester Automatic cartridge. Later, due to the popularity of the 22 Long Rifle cartridge, there was a rather insistent customer demand that an additional chambering be furnished for the 22 Long Rifle cartridge.

The Model 1903 was of a balanced simple blowback type action. So the 22 Long Rifle chambering could not be added except by making many important and expensive changes in the design of the rifle. No definite action to furnish the 22 Long Rifle chambering was taken until 1932, when Winchester decided to discontinue the manufacture of the Model 1903, make the necessary changes, and furnish the new rifle, chambered only for the 22 Long Rifle cartridge, as the Winchester Model 63.

The first announcement of the new model was in the Winchester March 1, 1933, price list.

Factory records show the first delivery of Model 63 rifles to warehouse stock was made in February 1933.

## GENERAL SPECIFICATIONS OF THE M/63 RIFLE

TYPE
: Automatic (self-loading) repeating rifle, hammerless, takedown, tubular magazine in butt stock.

STYLE
: Sporting rifle only.

BARRELS
: 20-inch, round; discontinued in 1936.
: 23-inch, round; authorized on December 13, 1934.

MAGAZINE
: Tubular magazine in butt stock. Capacity, 10 cartridges.

CHAMBER
: 22 Long Rifle Super Speed and 22 Long Rifle Super-X, interchangeably.

STOCK
: Plain walnut, not checkered, pistol grip, steel butt plate.

LOCKING DEVICE
: The first M/63 rifles were equipped with the same style of locking device that was used on the M/03 rifle. To take down the rifle equipped with this style of locking device, it was necessary to press the takedown screw-lock down through a slot in the tang to release the lock from the ratchet knurling on the collar of the takedown screw.
: A new style of locking device for the M/63 was authorized on December 11, 1933. To take down a M/63 Rifle equipped with this new style locking device, simply turn the takedown screw to the left until fully released.

WEIGHT
: About 5¾ lbs.

SERIAL NUMBERS
: M/63 rifles are serially numbered on underside of receiver and forward end of trigger guard.

The Model 63 was discontinued in 1958. About 174,692 were made.

### Special Note

The M/63 was a worthy successor to the M/03 rifle, being chambered for the popular 22 Long Rifle Super Speed and 22 Long Rifle Super-X cartridges. This model was automatic (self-loading), with balanced breech bolt recoil operated mechanism. This means that the breech bolt contains a quantity of metal proportioned to the weight and velocity of the bullet so that the shock of the recoil is absorbed by the breech bolt, in a sense balancing the recoil. When the cartridge is fired, the bullet leaves the muzzle of the barrel before the breech bolt commences to move rearward. The design and weight of the breech bolt are proportioned so that there is no loss of velocity and energy of the bullet. With this self-loading type of mechanism, the trigger must be pulled and released for each shot.

The Model 63 rifle was followed by the Winchester Model 64 rifle.

# MODEL 64 REPEATING RIFLE

*120. MODEL 64 RIFLE*

**120A. MODEL 64 RIFLE, LAST VERSION (1972-1973 ONLY)**

This model was a revamped Winchester Model 55 rifle, using the older action but with several changes in design. It was first announced in the March 1, 1933, price list as the Winchester Model 64 Lever Action Repeating Rifle.

Important changes from the Model 55 were: magazine capacity increased; stock changed to pistol grip; forged ramp on barrel for front sight base and front sight cover; lighter trigger pull; deer rifle style was added; made in solid frame only.

Factory records show the first delivery of Model 64 standard rifles to warehouse stock was made in February 1933, and Model 64 Deer rifles in May 1933.

## GENERAL SPECIFICATIONS OF THE M/64 RIFLE

| | |
|---|---|
| TYPE | Lever action repeating rifle, hammer, tubular magazine, solid frame. |
| STYLES | Sporting Rifle, Deer Rifle. |
| BARRELS | Sporting Rifle, 24-inch, round. |
| | Sporting Rifle, 20-inch, round (added in 1934). |
| | Sporting Rifle, 219 Zipper, 26-inch, round (added in 1938). |
| | Deer Rifle, 24-inch, round. |
| | Deer Rifle, 20-inch, round (added in 1934). |
| | Note: All M/64 rifles have a forged ramp on the barrel for the front sight base and are equipped with a front sight cover. |
| MAGAZINE | Tubular magazine, holding 5 cartridges. |

| | |
|---|---|
| CHAMBERS | 25-35, 30 Winchester (30/30), 32 Winchester Special. |
| | 219 Zipper added in 1938, discontinued in 1941. |
| STOCK | Sporting Rifle: Plain walnut, not checkered, shotgun butt, pistol grip, checkered steel butt plate. |
| | Deer Rifle: Plain walnut, checkered, shotgun butt, pistol grip with hard rubber pistol grip cap, checkered steel butt plate. Equipped with 1-inch quick detachable swivels and 1-inch army type leather sling strap. |
| LISTED WEIGHTS | Sporting Rifle, 24-inch round barrel—about 7 lbs. |
| | Sporting Rifle, 20-inch round barrel—about 6¾ lbs. |
| | Deer Rifle, 24-inch round barrel—about 7¾ lbs. |
| | Deer Rifle, 20-inch round barrel—about 7½ lbs. |
| SERIAL NUMBERS | M/64 rifles are serially numbered on underside of receiver. Numbered along with Model 1894s, first discontinued in 1957; about 66,783 were made in original version. Reintroduced in 1972; last listed in 1973. |

*Special Notes*

The Model 64 was an up-to-date rifle of the lever action type, chambered for popular caliber cartridges, and is considered a very satisfactory arm by hunters who prefer this type of action.

Sales were in rather limited quantities, due to the considerably lower prices of the Winchester Model 94 carbine having the same action and chamberings.

When Winchester introduced their National Rifle Association Commemorative Rifle (see Commemorative section for more information) in 1971, its styling evoked memories of the old Model 64 that had been discontinued some 14 years before. Consequently, the company decided to bring back the Model 64 in its regular line in 1972. The new version was identical to the old Model 64 except that it incorporated the minor design changes in the Model 94-type action that had been integrated through the years and its appearance was somewhat altered in that the pistol grip and lever curve were less pronounced in the latest version. The latest Model 64 did not receive the reception the company had hoped for and it was dropped from the line again at the close of 1973 and was no longer listed. It was chambered in 30-30 Winchester caliber only. A total of 8,251 rifles were made in the reintroduced run between 1972 until the close of 1973.

The Model 64 rifle was followed by the Winchester Model 65 rifle.

# MODEL 65 REPEATING RIFLE

*121. MODEL 65 RIFLE*

This model is a revamped Winchester Model 53 rifle, using the older action but with several changes in equipment. It was first announced in the March 1, 1933, price list as the Winchester Model 65 Lever Action Repeating Rifle.

Important changes from the Model 53 were: magazine capacity increased; stock changed to pistol grip; forged ramp on barrel for front sight base, and front sight cover; lighter trigger pull; made in solid frame only.

Factory records show the first delivery of Model 65 rifles to warehouse stock was made in March 1933.

## GENERAL SPECIFICATIONS OF THE M/65 RIFLE

| | |
|---|---|
| TYPE | Lever action repeating rifle, hammer, tubular magazine, solid frame. |
| STYLE | Sporting Rifle only. |
| BARRELS | Standard, 22-inch, round. |
| | 218 Bee, 24-inch, round (added in 1939). |
| | Note: All M/65 rifles have a forged ramp on the barrel for the front sight base and are equipped with a front sight cover. |
| MAGAZINE | Tubular magazine holding 7 cartridges. |
| CHAMBERS | 25-20 Winchester. |
| | 32 Winchester (32-20). |
| | 218 Bee (added in 1939). |
| STOCK | Plain walnut, not checkered, shotgun butt, pistol grip, checkered steel butt plate. |
| WEIGHT | About 6½ lbs. |
| SERIAL NUMBERS | M/65 rifles are serially numbered on underside of receiver. |
| | Numbered along with Model 1892s. |

The manufacture of the Model 65 was discontinued in 1947; about 5,704 were made.

The M/65 was an up-to-date rifle of the lever action type, but never had a large sale in the 25-20 Winchester and 32 Winchester (32-20) calibers due to the decreasing popularity of these calibers. M/65 rifles chambered for the 218 Bee cartridge had a very satisfactory sale.

The Model 65 rifle was followed by the Winchester Model 42 shotgun.

# MODEL 42 REPEATING SHOTGUN

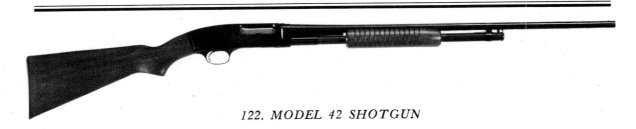

*122. MODEL 42 SHOTGUN*

Announcement of the new Winchester Model 42 hammerless slide action repeating shotgun, chambered for the 410 gauge, 3-inch shell, mentioned in price list of August 12, 1933, was an innovation. It was the first shotgun with this type of action ever developed especially for the 410 gauge shell.

Factory records show the first delivery of Model 42 shotguns to warehouse stock was made in May 1933.

## GENERAL SPECIFICATIONS OF THE M/42 SHOTGUN

| | |
|---|---|
| TYPE | Slide action repeating shotgun, hammerless, tubular magazine, takedown. |
| STYLES | Standard, Skeet Gun. |
| | Note: Trap Grade with full fancy wood and fancy checkering was furnished on each of the foregoing styles until this grade was dropped on January 1, 1940. After that date, M/42s with full fancy wood and fancy checkering were furnished on special order, but not under the name Trap Grade. |
| BARRELS | 28-inch and 26-inch, plain barrels. |
| | 28-inch and 26-inch, raised matted rib barrels (authorized on September 15, 1933). |
| | Ventilated rib barrels were never furnished on M/42 shotguns. |
| STANDARD CHOKES | Standard. |
| | Full choke. |
| | Modified choke. |
| | Skeet choke. |
| | Cylinder bore. |

Skeet Gun, No. 1 skeet choke.

No. 1 Skeet changed to No. 2 skeet choke (authorized on March 11, 1935).

Intermediate chokes were not furnished on M/42 shotguns.

CHAMBERS    Standard, 410 gauge, 3-inch shell.

Optional, 410 gauge, 2½-inch shell (authorized on March 11, 1935).

Skeet Gun, 410 gauge, 3-inch shell.

Optional, 410 gauge, 2½-inch (authorized on March 11, 1935).

Changed to 410 gauge, 2½-inch as standard equipment (authorized on May 6, 1940).

STOCKS    Standard: plain walnut, pistol grip, no checkering.

Skeet Gun: selected walnut, straight grip, checkered. Optional pistol grip (authorized on June 28, 1939). Changed to pistol grip as standard (authorized on May 6, 1940).

Hard rubber butt plate is standard on all M/42 shotguns.

SLIDE HANDLE    Standard style, round with circular grooves, no checkering.

On June 27, 1945, a new standard slide handle was authorized, of a different shape, slightly larger, nearly flat on the bottom side and with grooves on the side only. This new slide handle was put into use during 1947.

Skeet Gun, extension slide handle, fancy checkering.

MAGAZINE    Tubular magazine.

Capacity, 410 gauge 3-inch, 5 shells.

Capacity, 410 gauge 2½-inch, 6 shells.

Notes: By Presidential Proclamation, signed February 2, 1935, based on the recommendation of the U. S. Biological Survey, the capacity of any auto loading or repeating shotgun used in shooting migratory birds is specifically limited to three shots. This means only two shells in the magazine and one shell in the chamber. On February 22, 1935, a special shaped wood magazine plug was authorized to reduce the magazine capacity to two shells. One of these plugs included in each carton containing a M/42 shotgun after that date.

RECEIVER    Straight line matting on top of receiver.

WEIGHTS    Shotgun with 26-inch barrel—about 5⅞ lbs.

Shotgun with 28-inch barrel—about 6 lbs.

SERIAL NUMBERS    M/42 shotguns are serially numbered from 1 up, on underside of receiver and underside of receiver extension.

The M/42 was discontinued in 1963; about 159,353 were made.

Although the Model 42 in design and appearance closely resembles the Winchester Model 12, it was not a copy of this model but was in all respects a small, lightweight shotgun developed especially for the 410 gauge shell.

In 1955, Skeet and Deluxe versions were made available with Simmons ribs until the end of production in 1963.

The Model 42 shotgun was followed by the Winchester Model 67 Rifle.

# MODEL 67 RIM FIRE RIFLE

### 123. MODEL 67 RIFLE

### 124. MODEL 67 BOY'S RIFLE

Announcement of the Winchester Model 60 single shot rifle in 1931 marked the beginning of an intense rivalry between domestic firearms manufacturers to hold their position in this low priced, single shot rim fire rifle field. Competitors' models were revamped, longer barrels and many new features were added at a considerable increase in production cost. And several new and more expensive models were developed and placed on the market with selling prices scaled down to meet the low price competition.

Winchester revamped the Model 60, retaining the same mechanism and the same 27-inch round barrel that was used on the later production of the Model 60, and announced the new rifle as the Winchester Model 67 Single Shot rifle in the 1934 catalog. Later in 1937, at the request of Ad Topperwein, a Junior type rifle with a shorter stock and 20-inch barrel was added. That same year the standard type of Model 67 was offered for sale equipped with the then new Winchester 2¾- or 5-power telescope. These rifle barrels were equipped with telescope sight bases, the telescope and mounts being packed separately in the same carton with the rifle.

Factory records show the first delivery of Model 67 rifles to warehouse stock was made on April 19, 1934.

## GENERAL SPECIFICATIONS OF THE M/67 RIFLE

| | |
|---|---|
| TYPE | Bolt action single shot rifle, cocked by pulling rearward on the firing pin head, takedown. |
| STYLES | Sporting Rifle; Smooth Bore Rifle (authorized on September 9, 1936); Junior Rifle (authorized on August 8, 1937). |
| | Rifle with miniature target shot boring (authorized on April 24, 1940). |
| | Rifles with Winchester 2¾-power and 5-power (cross hair) telescopes were authorized on March 9, 1937. |
| | Rifles with Winchester P 2¾-power (post) telescopes were authorized on November 20, 1937. These rifles were equipped with telescope bases attached to the rifle barrel. Telescopes were not attached to the rifle but were packed separately in the same carton with the rifle. |
| BARRELS | Sporting Rifle, 27-inch, round. |
| | Smooth Bore Rifle, 27-inch, round. |
| | Junior Rifle, 20-inch, round. |
| | Rifle with miniature target boring, 24-inch, round. |
| CHAMBERS | Sporting Rifle and Junior Rifle. |
| | 22 Short, 22 Long, and 22 Long Rifle, interchangeably. |
| | 22 W.R.F. (authorized on June 17, 1935). |
| | 22 Long Shot and 22 Long Rifle shot smooth bore, interchangeably, authorized on September 9, 1936. |
| | 22 Long Rifle Shot (miniature target boring) was authorized on April 24, 1940. |
| STOCK | Plain walnut, pistol grip, finger groove in each side of forearm, stock changed to forearm without finger grooves in 1935. |
| | The latest style stock, longer, and of a different shape, was authorized on October 25, 1937. With this stock, the stock stud screw is flush with the bottom of the forearm. Composition butt plate. |
| CHROMIUM PLATING | The bolt, bolt handle, safety lock, and trigger are chromium plated. |
| COMPONENT PARTS | Changes to improve the extraction of the fired cartridges and effect a smoother closing of the bolt were authorized on January 8, 1938. The bolt retaining spring was omitted, and the bolt, sear, and extractor were changed. |
| WEIGHTS | Sporting Rifle, about 5 lbs. |
| | Junior Rifle, about 4½ lbs. |
| | 22 Long Rifle Shot, about 5¼ lbs. |
| SERIAL NUMBERS | M/67 rifles were not serially numbered for domestic sales, but were numbered for foreign export. Discontinued in 1963; about 383,587 were made. |

### Special Notes

Due principally to the difficulty of obtaining a sufficient supply of telescopes because of war conditions, the telescope equipped Model 67s were withdrawn from the market in 1942.

All other styles of Model 67 rifles were retained in the line. With the return to commercial production after World War II, they were again manufactured and sold in very large quantities, and held their own regardless of the many competitive models which were offered by nearly all manufacturers of firearms.

The Model 67 rifle was followed by the Winchester Model 68 rifle.

# MODEL 68 RIM FIRE RIFLE

*125. MODEL 68 RIFLE*

This new model was a companion rifle to the Model 67 and differed from it principally in sight equipment. It was first offered for sale in the Winchester 1934 catalog, listed as the Winchester Model 68 Single Shot Rifle.

Factory records show the first delivery of Model 68 rifles to warehouse stock was made on May 23, 1934.

## GENERAL SPECIFICATIONS OF THE M/68 RIFLE

| | |
|---|---|
| TYPE | Bolt action single shot rifle, cocked by pulling rearward on the firing pin head, takedown. |
| STYLES | Sporting Rifle. |
| | Rifles with Winchester 5-power telescopes were authorized on March 9, 1937. These rifles were equipped with telescope bases attached to the rifle barrel. Telescopes were not attached to the rifle but were packed separately in the same carton with the rifle. |
| BARRELS | 27-inch, round. |
| CHAMBERS | 22 Short, 22 Long, and 22 Long Rifle, interchangeably. |
| | 22 W.R.F. (authorized on June 17, 1935). |
| STOCK | Plain walnut, pistol grip, finger groove in each side of forearm. Stock changed to forearm without finger grooves in 1935. The latest style stock, longer, and of a different shape was authorized on October 25, 1937. With this stock, the stock stud screw is flush with the bottom of the forearm. Composition butt plate. |
| COMPONENT PARTS | Changes were authorized on January 8, 1939, to improve the extraction of the fired cartridge and effect a smoother closing of the bolt; the bolt retaining spring was omitted and the bolt, sear, and extractor were changed. |

WEIGHT         About 5 lbs.
SERIAL NUMBERS  M/68 rifles are not serially numbered.

The manufacture of M/68 rifles with Winchester 5-power scopes was discontinued in 1939.
   Manufacture of the standard Model 68 rifle was discontinued in 1946; about 100,730 were made.

### Special Note

The Winchester Model 68, due to its more expensive sights, sold at slightly higher prices than its companion rifle, the Winchester Model 67, and consequently had a considerably smaller volume of sale.
   The Model 68 rifle was followed by the Winchester Model 69 rifle.

# MODEL 69 REPEATING RIFLE

*126. MODEL 69A RIFLE*

In 1927, Winchester had developed and placed on the market two bolt action rim fire rifles of the detachable box magazine type, the Model 56 Sporting Rifle and the Model 57 Accuracy Rifle. Neither had been particularly successful. They were equipped with short barrels 22 inches in length and were considered too high in price to meet with general customer acceptance.

   Later, in response to insistent customer demand for a Winchester rifle of this same bolt action type, but of a more modern design, Winchester went to work on the development of a new model that could be used satisfactorily for both sporting and target work and be sold in the intermediate price class. This new rifle, listed as the Winchester Model 69, was first announced to the trade in the January 1, 1935, price list.

   Factory records show the first delivery of Model 69 rifles to warehouse stock was made on March 15, 1935.

## GENERAL SPECIFICATIONS OF THE M/69 RIFLE

TYPE    Bolt action repeating rifle, detachable box magazine, takedown.
STYLES  Sporting Rifle; Target Rifle, authorized on December 26, 1940; Match Rifle, authorized on December 26, 1940. These target and match rifles have a special shaped butt stock and were equipped with a 1-inch army type leather sling strap, changed in 1947 to a 1¼-inch sling strap.

Rifles with Winchester 2¾-power, P 2¾-power, and 5-power telescopes were authorized in 1937. These rifles were equipped with telescope bases attached to the rifle barrel. Telescopes were not attached to the rifle but were packed separately in the same carton with the rifle.

BARRELS    Standard Rifle, 25-inch, round, tapered, open rear sight and hooded front sight.
Standard Rifle, 25-inch, round, tapered, open sporting sights.
Target Rifle, 25-inch, round, tapered (22 Long Rifle).
Match Rifle, 25-inch, round, tapered (22 Long Rifle).
M/69 barrels were changed to a slightly heavier 25-inch round barrel (authorized on November 30, 1937).

CHAMBERS    22 Short, 22 Long, and 22 Long Rifle, interchangeably.

STOCK    Plain walnut, pistol grip.
Stock changed to a new sporting type with semi-beavertail forearm and pistol grip (authorized on October 25, 1937). With this stock the stock stud-screw is flush with the bottom of the forearm.
Composition butt plate.

MAGAZINE    Detachable box magazine.
22 Short, 5 cartridge capacity.
22 Long or 22 Long Rifle, 5 cartridge capacity.
Longer magazines, holding either ten 22 Long Rifle or ten 22 Short cartridges, were also furnished at extra cost.
Note: The Single Loading Adaptor which was developed for the M/52 rifle can also be used on this model. This Single Loading Adaptor is similar in appearance to the standard 5 shot 22 Long Rifle magazine except it has a flexible straight line cartridge guide affixed to the top of the magazine in place of the regular magazine follower.

COMPONENT PARTS    A rebounding lock was authorized on August 23, 1935, to make M/69 rifles acceptable by the Canadian Customs authorities for shipment into the Dominion of Canada.

COCKING MECHANISM    The first production of M/69 rifles was made with a mechanism that cocked the rifle by the closing motion of the bolt. This mechanism was changed to cock the rifle by the opening motion of the bolt (authorized on November 30, 1937). M/69 rifles of this later type are known as M/69 A rifles.

WEIGHT    About 5 lbs.

SERIAL NUMBERS    M/69 rifles are not serially numbered.

The manufacture of M/69 rifles with 2¾ power, P 2¾ power, and 5 power telescopes, was discontinued in 1941. All other styles were discontinued in 1963; about 355,363 were made.

## Special Note

The Winchester Model 69 is a modern rifle in all respects, and was furnished with either open sights or a peep sight combination for sporting use, also in two sight combinations for accuracy shooting. All Model 69 rifles are especially accurate and had a very satisfactory sale.

The Model 69 rifle was followed by the Winchester Model 71 rifle.

# MODEL 71 LEVER ACTION RIFLE

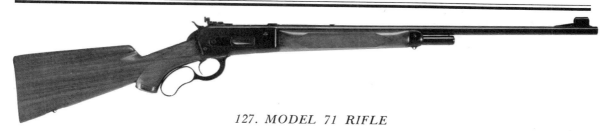

*127. MODEL 71 RIFLE*

The next development by Winchester was a revamping of the old Model 1886 Lever Action Repeater, having a visible hammer and a tubular magazine. This revamped model, listed as the Winchester Model 71 Lever Action Repeating Rifle, was first announced to the trade in the January 1, 1936, price list. The Model 71 is of the same basic design as the older Model 1886, with the parts somewhat simplified and strengthened to handle the 348 Winchester smokeless cartridge designed especially for this new model.

Factory records show the first delivery of Model 71 rifles to warehouse stock was made on November 2, 1935.

## GENERAL SPECIFICATIONS OF THE M/71 RIFLE

| | |
|---|---|
| TYPE | Lever action repeating rifle, tubular magazine, solid frame. |
| STYLES | Sporting rifles, with open sporting rear sight or with peep sight. These rifles had checkering, pistol grip stock with rubber grip cap and were equipped with a 1-inch army type leather sling strap with quick detachable swivels. This style of rifle with a 20-inch round barrel was added on January 14, 1937 (20-inch barrels were discontinued in 1947). |
| | Sporting rifles, with open sporting rear sight or with peep sight. These rifles are the same as the foregoing except they have no checkering, pistol grip cap, sling strap, or quick detachable swivels (authorized on January 6, 1936). This style of rifle with a 20-inch round barrel was added on January 14, 1937 (20-inch barrels were discontinued in 1947). |
| BARRELS | Rifle, 24-inch, round. |
| | Rifle, 20-inch, round (20-inch barrels were discontinued in 1947). |
| | Forged ramp on barrel for front sight base, front sight cover attached. |
| CHAMBER | 348 Winchester. |
| STOCK | Plain walnut, sporting type with semi-beavertail forearm. The stock was changed to the same type but with the comb carried forward approximately 1 inch (authorized on September 3, 1937). Steel butt plate, checkered. |
| MAGAZINE | Tubular magazine, 4 cartridge capacity. |
| COMPONENT PARTS | A safety located on the front end of the lower tang was authorized on September 3, 1937. |

WEIGHTS　　　　Rifle, 24-inch barrel—about 8 lbs.

Rifle, 20-inch barrel—about 7¾ lbs.

SERIAL NUMBERS　　M/71 rifles were serially numbered, on underside of receiver.

The Model 71 was discontinued in 1957; about 47,254 were made.

*Special Note*

This model has a remarkably fast and smooth working lever action, and in combination with the several styles and weights of bullets which were furnished in the 348 Winchester cartridge it made an ideal arm for large game shooting.

The Model 71 rifle was followed by the Winchester Model 37 shotgun.

# MODEL 37 SHOTGUN

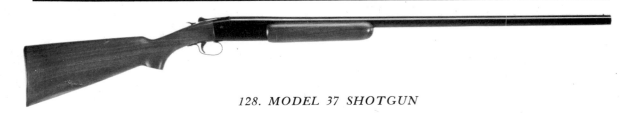

*128. MODEL 37 SHOTGUN*

In the January 2, 1936, catalog, Winchester announced the new Model 37 Single Shot Shotgun. This model was developed to meet competition of the various models having the standard visible hammer actions that had been manufactured for many years by several competitive firearms producers.

The Winchester Model 37 was of the top lever, breakdown type, having an automatic ejector and with a so-called semi-hammerless action.

Factory records show the first delivery of Model 37 shotguns to warehouse stock was made on February 10, 1936.

## GENERAL SPECIFICATIONS OF THE M/37 SHOTGUN

TYPE　　　　　Single shot, semi-hammerless, automatic ejector, breakdown, cocking lever.

STYLES　　　　Standard; Boy's Model (introduced 1958).

BARRELS　　　12 gauge, 32-inch, 30-inch, 28-inch, full choke.

AND CHOKES　16 gauge, 32-inch, 30-inch, 28-inch, full choke.

20 gauge, 32-inch, 30-inch, 28-inch, full choke.

28 gauge, 30-inch, 28-inch, full choke.

410 gauge, 28-inch, 26-inch, full choke.

BARRELS　　　M/37 shotguns were furnished with plain barrels only.

| | |
|---|---|
| CHOKES | Modified choke or cylinder bore was furnished at no extra charge on special order only. |
| CHAMBERS | 12 gauge, 2¾-inch shell. |
| | 16 gauge, 2¾-inch shell. |
| | 20 gauge, 2¾-inch shell. |
| | 28 gauge, 2⅞-inch shell. |
| | 410 gauge, 3-inch shell. |
| STOCK | Plain walnut, pistol grip, composition butt plate. |
| FOREARM | Plain walnut, semi-beavertail shape. |
| | Export style of forearm for export sale authorized on March 22, 1936. This forearm is slightly smaller and has more taper on the front portion. The export style of forearm was authorized for use on all M/37 shotguns on December 4, 1941, to become effective when stocks on hand of the older domestic shape were used up. |
| | This change was authorized in order that M/37s with one style of forearm could be used in filling orders for both domestic and export shipment. |
| COMPONENT PARTS | Top lever originally used on M/37 shotguns was made of sheet metal folded to shape. Changed to solid forging (authorized on September 25, 1936). |
| | A new design larger cocking lever was authorized on February 19, 1937. |
| WEIGHTS | 12 gauge, 30-inch barrel—about 6 lbs. |
| | 16 gauge, 28-inch barrel—about 6 lbs. |
| | 20 gauge, 28-inch barrel—about 5¾ lbs. |
| | 28 gauge, 28-inch barrel—about 5¾ lbs. |
| | 410 gauge, 26-inch barrel—about 5¾ lbs. |
| SERIAL NUMBERS | M/37 shotguns were not serially numbered. |

The M/37 shotgun was discontinued in 1963; about 1,015,554 were made.

## Special Note

The Winchester Model 37 Steelbuilt shotgun, as the name implies, is built of steel throughout, no castings of any kind being used in the construction. It is a very sturdy and well built arm and had a very satisfactory sale, both in this country and through export channels.

The Model 37 shotgun was followed by the Winchester Model 38 shotgun.

# MODEL 38 SHOTGUN

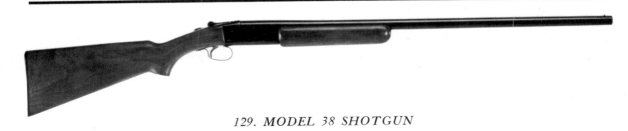

*129. MODEL 38 SHOTGUN*

Manufacture of the M/38 shotgun was authorized on November 18, 1936. It was designed to be made under the same general specifications as the M/37 except for such changes as were necessary to make the M/38 a full hammerless shotgun. This model was never offered for sale, as the authority for its manufacture was later canceled.

   Only a few sample guns of this model were produced for test purposes.

   The M/38 shotgun was followed by the Winchester Model 70 rifle.

# MODEL 70 BOLT ACTION RIFLE

*130. MODEL 70 RIFLE (PRE-1964)*

*131. MODEL 70 VARMINT RIFLE (CIRCA 1966)*

*132. MODEL 70 RIFLE (CIRCA 1966)*

*132A. MODEL 70 MAGNUM (CIRCA 1975)*

*132B. MODEL 70 MANNLICHER (CIRCA 1968)*

*132C. MODEL 70 INTERNATIONAL ARMY MATCH RIFLE (TYPE I, CIRCA 1970)*

*132D. MODEL 70 INTERNATIONAL ARMY MATCH RIFLE (TYPE II, CIRCA 1971)*

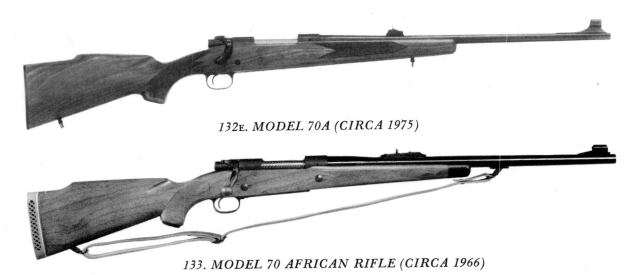

*132E. MODEL 70A (CIRCA 1975)*

*133. MODEL 70 AFRICAN RIFLE (CIRCA 1966)*

In order that the Winchester Model 54 bolt action rifle be kept up to date in all respects, work was started on a redesign program. The new model, to incorporate many new features and improvements, was given a new Winchester model number. This new arm was first announced in the January 1, 1937, price list as the Winchester Model 70 Bolt Action Rifle. Some of the more important changes incorporated in the model were:

> Hinged floor plate.
> New speed lock fully adjustable with short pull.
> New design safety, swings horizontally, does not interfere with telescope sight.
> Manually releasable bolt stop, independent of the sear and trigger.
> Adjustable sling swivel base for the Target, Bull gun, and National Match styles.
> Stock with less drop, fuller forearm, better checkering.
> Forged steel trigger guard.

The original authorization to manufacture M/70 rifles was dated December 29, 1934; however, factory records show the first delivery of this model to warehouse stock was on August 14, 1936.

## GENERAL SPECIFICATIONS OF THE M/70 RIFLE

| | |
|---|---|
| TYPE | Bolt action repeating rifle, non-detachable box magazine, solid frame. |
| STYLES | Standard Rifle, first listed in 1937. |
| | Super Grade Rifle, first listed in 1937. |
| | Target Rifle, first listed in 1937. |
| | National Match Rifle, first listed in 1937. |
| | Bull Gun, first listed in 1937. |
| | Featherweight Rifle, first listed in 1952. |
| | Varmint Rifle, first listed in 1955. |
| | African Rifle, first listed in 1956. |
| | Westerner Rifle, first listed in 1960. |
| | Alaskan Rifle, first listed in 1960. |

|  |  |
|---|---|
| | Mannlicher-style, first listed in 1969. |
| | International Army Match Rifle, first listed in 1970. |
| BARRELS | Standard Rifle, 24-inch, round. |
| | Standard Rifle, 20-inch, round (20-inch barrels were discontinued in 1947). |
| | Super Grade Rifle, 24-inch, round. |
| | National Match Rifle, 24-inch, round. |
| | Target Rifle, 24-inch, round, medium weight. |
| | Bull Gun, 28-inch, round, extra heavy. |
| | Barrels also varied in lengths according to caliber and styles. |
| | Exceptions: |
| | 220 Swift and 300 H & H Magnum barrels furnished only in 26-inch length. |
| | 375 H & H Magnum barrels were originally 24-inch length and of standard weight. These barrels were later changed to a slightly heavier barrel, 24-inch length. On February 8, 1937, authorization was given to again change these barrels to 25-inch length and of a different taper. This change was put into effect as factory stocks of the older style barrels were used up. |
| STOCKS | Standard Rifle. |
| | Monte Carlo. |
| | Super Grade. |
| | Target Types. |

| CHAMBERS | | |
|---|---|---|
| | 22 Hornet. | 7mm. |
| | 220 Swift. | 7mm Remington Magnum. |
| | 22-250 Remington. | 30-06. |
| | 222 Remington. | 300 H & H Magnum. |
| | 225 Winchester. | 300 Savage. |
| | 243 Winchester. | 300 Winchester Magnum. |
| | 25-06 Remington. | 308 Winchester. |
| | 250-3000 Savage. | 338 Winchester Magnum. |
| | 257 Roberts. | 35 Remington. |
| | 264 Winchester Magnum. | 358 Winchester. |
| | 270 Winchester. | 375 H & H Magnum. |
| | | 458 Winchester Magnum. |

Note: A few M/70 rifles chambered for 7.65mm and 9mm, also a few Sniper's rifles were furnished from leftover M/54 barrels.

|  |  |
|---|---|
| SIGHTS | M/70 rifles were furnished with any suitable sight combination. |
| WEIGHTS | Standard Rifle, 24-inch barrel—about 7¾ lbs. |
| | Standard Rifle, 20-inch barrel—about 7½ lbs. |
| | Featherweight Rifle, 22-inch barrel—about 6½ lbs. |
| | Super Grade Rifle, 24-inch barrel—about 8 lbs. |
| | Target Model Rifle—about 10½ lbs. |
| | National Match Rifle—about 7¾ lbs. |
| | Sniper's Match Rifle—about 12 lbs. |
| | Bull Gun—about 13 lbs. |
| | Other Model 70s varied in weight according to caliber and style. |
| SERIAL NUMBERS | M/70 rifles are serially numbered, forward end of receiver on right side. |

Winchester Model 70 rifles are still being manufactured and offered for sale in a wide range of chamberings adaptable for practically all kinds of game hunting, and in types for long-range accuracy shooting.

A new improved stock was introduced in 1966, the year of the Winchester Centennial. Features include: A higher Monte Carlo comb and redesigned cheek piece to provide quicker eye-alignment with either telescopic or iron sights, and to reduce recoil effect at the shooter's cheek when the rifle is fired. A cross bolt (two on magnum models) is incorporated to provide increased strength in areas where recoil stress is greatest. A new pattern of positive checkering, both functional and artistic, is adapted to this stock—Standard, Magnum, and Varmint models.

Because of demand among shooters, the popular 22-250 Remington and 222 Remington calibers were added to the Model 70 line in 1967 and 1969 respectively.

In addition, the company continued to improve the appearance and materials in the post-1964 design. In 1968, an anti-bind device that prevented over-rotating the bolt was introduced and a polished stainless-steel magazine follower and black chromed steel floor plate were substituted for the previous components. The stock was further modified to suit shooter's requests and recommendations.

Also in 1968, Winchester introduced its first Mannlicher-style short-barreled rifle in the following calibers: 243 Win., 270 Win., 30-06 Springfield and 308 Win. The new version featured a 19-inch barrel bedded in a full-length American walnut stock with Monte Carlo profile and raised cheek piece. The gun was not widely promoted by the company and was little known among the majority of shooters, but achieved a certain underground popularity among hunters who prized it as a good rifle for pack trips and hunting in the high country. It was last listed by the company in 1972.

The Model 70 International Army Match Rifle was introduced in 1970. The rifle contains a forearm rail that is equipped to accept all standard Model 70 accessories, and its butt plate assembly is vertically adjustable. With an overall length of 43½ inches, the rifle weighs 11 pounds and is offered in 308 Winchester caliber only. An improved, modified version of this model was introduced in 1971 that featured a revised stock configuration that more closely met the International Shooting Union's requirements for army match rifle competition.

In 1972, the company continued its program of upgrading the Model 70 rifle's appearance. The Model 70 for that year featured a totally new stock configuration, and deep cut checkering supplanted the pressed checkering that had less than adorned the line since 1965. Designed for both comfort and a sleek appearance, the stock was kiln-dried, sized and turned and then coated with a semi-gloss finish formulated to withstand all weather and hard-use conditions. The pistol grip has a new contour that is shorter, rounder and more defined. The new overall design included a black fore-end tip and a black pistol grip cap with white spacers, an improved cheek piece, a knurled bolt handle and a rear sight leaf with a white diamond. In addition, each of the new models was equipped with quick-detachable sling swivels for the first time. Essentially, this 1972 refinement of the post-1964 Model 70 is the gun as it is manufactured and sold by the company today (1975). A Model 70 Super Grade was also reintroduced in 1972, but was phased out and last listed in 1973. It was available in four calibers: 243 Win., 270 Win., 30-06 Springfield and 300 Win. Magnum.

The Model 70A, an economical version of the standard Model 70, was also introduced in 1972. This rifle was a conservative variation of the existing bolt action Model 70 system without a hinged floor plate or any of the extra refinements incorporated in the 1972 design change. There are no black fore-end tip and pistol grip cap with white spacers or detachable sling swivels, but the stock has deep cut checkering. As for the action, it has the same features and three-position safety associated with the standard Model 70 line. It is available in the following calibers: 222 Rem., 22-250 Rem., 243 Win., 270 Win., 30-06 Springfield, 308 Win., 264 Win. Magnum, 7mm Rem. Magnum and 300 Win. Magnum.

Model 70 barreled actions were first offered in the 1965 catalog.

As of January 20, 1975, approximately 1,180,463 Model 70 rifles of all types had been manufactured.

The Model 70 rifle was followed by the Winchester Model 697 rifle.

# MODEL 697 RIFLE

(Appearance similar to Model 69)

Winchester next turned its attention to additional models of the rim fire rifles equipped with telescopes. The telescopes used were of 2¾- and 5-power magnification, made by an outside manufacturer. They were almost identical to the telescopes Winchester had previously used on the M/67 and M/68 single shot rifles and on the M/69 repeater.

The Model 697 was similar to the standard Model 69 except for the following: no sight cuts in barrel; no iron sights; no ramp or sight cover. Telescope bases were attached to barrel.

Model 697 rifles were first announced to the trade in the Winchester January 2, 1937, price list.

Factory records show the first delivery of Model 697 rifles to warehouse stock was made in June 1937.

## GENERAL SPECIFICATIONS OF THE M/697 RIFLE

| | |
|---|---|
| TYPE | Bolt action repeating rifle, detachable box magazine, takedown. |
| STYLES | Sporting Rifle only. |
| | This rifle was equipped with telescope bases attached to the barrel for Winchester 2¾-power or 5-power telescopes. Telescopes were not attached to the rifle but were packed separately in the same carton with the rifle. |
| BARRELS | 25-inch, round only. |
| | Changed to a 25-inch, round barrel, slightly heavier (authorized on November 30, 1937). |
| CHAMBERS | 22 Short, 22 Long, and 22 Long Rifle, interchangeably. |
| STOCK | Plain walnut, pistol grip. |
| | Stock changed to a new sporting type with semi-beavertail forearm and pistol grip (authorized on October 25, 1937). With this stock the stock stud screw is flush with the bottom of the forearm. |
| | Composition butt plate. |

| | |
|---|---|
| MAGAZINE | Detachable box magazine. |
| | **Magazine, 22 Short, 5 cartridge capacity.** |
| | **Magazine, 22 Long or 22 Long Rifle, 5 cartridge capacity.** |
| | Longer magazines holding ten 22 Long Rifle cartridges or ten 22 Short cartridges were also furnished at extra cost. |
| | Note: The Single Loading Adaptor developed for the M/52 rifle could also be used on this model. It is similar in appearance to the standard 5-shot, 22 Long Rifle magazine, except it has a flexible straight line cartridge guide affixed to the top of the magazine in place of the regular magazine follower. |
| WEIGHT | About 5 lbs. |
| SERIAL NUMBERS | M/697 rifles were not serially numbered. |

The manufacture of this model was discontinued in 1941.

*Special Note*

M/697 rifles had a very small sale due principally to the unsatisfactory type of telescope mount used.

The Model 697 rifle was followed by the Winchester Model 677 rifle.

# MODEL 677 RIFLE

(Appearance similar to Model 67)

The Model 677 was similar to the standard Winchester Model 67 except for the following: no sight cuts in barrel; no iron sights. Telescope bases were attached to barrel.

The Model 677 was first announced in the Winchester January 2, 1937, price list.

Factory records show the first delivery of Model 677 Rifles to warehouse stock was made in July 1937.

## GENERAL SPECIFICATIONS OF THE M/677 RIFLE

| | |
|---|---|
| TYPE | Bolt action single shot rifle, cocked by pulling rearward on the firing pin head, takedown. |
| STYLES | Sporting Rifle only. |
| | These rifles were equipped with telescope bases attached to the barrel for Winchester 2¾-power or 5-power telescopes. Rifles with P 2¾-power (post) telescopes were authorized on November 20, 1937. Telescopes were not attached to the rifles, but were packed separately in the same carton with the rifle. |
| BARREL | 27-inch, round. |
| CHAMBERS | 22 Short, 22 Long, and 22 Long Rifle, interchangeably. |
| STOCK | Plain walnut, pistol grip. |

A new style stock, longer and of a different shape, was authorized on October 25, 1937. With this stock, the stock stud screw is flush with the bottom of the forearm.

Composition butt plate.

PLATING          Bolt, bolt handle, safety lock, and trigger were chromium plated.

WEIGHT           About 5 lbs.

SERIAL NUMBERS    The M/677 rifle was not serially numbered.

The manufacture of this model was discontinued in 1939. About 2,239 were made.

## Special Note

The M/677 Rifle had a very small sale due principally to the unsatisfactory type of telescope mount used.

The Model 677 rifle was followed by the Winchester Model 72 rifle.

# MODEL 72 REPEATING RIFLE

### 134. MODEL 72 RIFLE

For a number of years competitive manufacturers had been producing bolt action repeating rifles equipped with a tubular magazine and chambered for rim fire cartridges. On March 4, 1938, Winchester announced their first rifle of this type as the Model 72 Repeating Rifle.

Factory records show the first delivery of Model 72 rifles was made on April 18, 1938.

## GENERAL SPECIFICATIONS OF THE M/72 RIFLE

TYPE          Bolt action repeating rifle, tubular magazine, takedown, cocked by the opening movement of the bolt.

STYLES        Sporting Rifle, with either open rear sight or peep sight. Bases were attached to the barrel for use with Winchester 2¾-power or 5-power telescopes.

These rifles were furnished with or without standard iron sights attached.

Telescopes were not attached to the barrel but were packed separately in the same carton with the rifle.

CHAMBER     Standard Rifle, 22 Short, 22 Long, and 22 Long Rifle, interchangeably.

Gallery Special (22 Short only) authorized on February 10, 1939, discontinued in 1942.

| MAGAZINE | Tubular Magazine. |
| | Capacity, 22 Short, 20 cartridges. |
| | Capacity, 22 Long, 16 cartridges. |
| | Capacity, 22 Long Rifle, 15 cartridges. |
| BARRELS | 25-inch, round, tapered. |
| STOCK | Plain walnut, semi-beavertail, pistol grip. With this stock, the stock stud screw is flush with the bottom of the forearm. |
| | Composition butt plate. |
| WEIGHT | About 5¾ lbs. |
| SERIAL NUMBERS | M/72 rifles were not serially numbered. |

The manufacture of M/72 rifles with Winchester 2¾- and 5-power telescopes was discontinued in 1941.

Model 72 rifles in two styles of sight combinations, open sights, and a rear peep sight, were discontinued in 1959. About 161,412 were made.

*Special Note*

The Winchester Model 72 was a well designed, strongly constructed repeating rifle with a long tubular magazine holding an ample supply of cartridges, but its sale never reached a very satisfactory volume due principally to the many competitive models which had become well established prior to the announcement of the Winchester Model 72.

The Model 72 rifle was followed by the Winchester Model 75 rifle.

# MODEL 75 BOLT ACTION RIFLE

*135. MODEL 75 TARGET RIFLE*

*136. MODEL 75 SPORTING RIFLE*

Winchester developed the Model 75 bolt action repeater, with detachable box magazine, as a medium priced accuracy rifle for junior target shooters and others who could not afford to purchase the higher priced Winchester Model 52 accuracy rifle. It was announced in the March 4, 1939, price list, as the Winchester Model 75 Bolt Action Repeater.

Factory records show the first delivery of Model 75 rifles to warehouse stock was made on August 26, 1938.

## GENERAL SPECIFICATIONS OF THE M/75 RIFLE

| | |
|---|---|
| TYPE | Bolt action repeating rifle, detachable box magazine, solid frame. Cocked with the opening movement of the bolt. |
| STYLES | Target Rifle; Target Rifle with Winchester 8-power telescope; Target Rifle with various combinations of target sights. Sporting Rifle (authorized on February 2, 1939). The sporting rifles were furnished in two sight combinations. Open rear and bead front sight. Lyman 57E receiver sight and bead front sight. |
| BARRELS | Target Rifle, 28-inch, round, drilled and tapped for the standard Winchester M/52 combination sight bases. Target rifles furnished with Winchester 8-power telescopes have telescope bases attached to the barrel. Sporting Rifle, 24-inch, round with forged ramp on barrel for front sight base and with front sight cover. |
| CHAMBER | 22 Long Rifle. |
| MAGAZINE | Detachable box magazine, capacity, 22 Long Rifle, 5 cartridges. Longer magazine holding ten 22 Long Rifle cartridges was furnished at extra cost. Note: The Single Loading Adaptor developed for the M/52 rifle could also be used on this model. It is similar in appearance to the standard 5-shot, 22 Long Rifle magazine except it has a flexible straight line cartridge guide affixed to the top of the magazine in place of the regular magazine follower. |
| STOCK | Target Rifle. Plain walnut, target style with semi-beavertail forearm, not checkered, pistol grip, checkered steel butt plate. Equipped with a 1¼-inch army type leather sling strap and metal base adjustment swivel allowing various adjustments of the sling strap. Sporting Rifle. Selected walnut, sporting type, checkered, pistol grip with hard rubber grip cap, equipped with 1-inch swivel bows, checkered steel butt plate. |
| CHAMBER | 22 Long Rifle. |
| LOCK | Equipped with speed lock. |
| WEIGHT | Target Rifle—about 8½ lbs. Sporting Rifle—about 5¾ lbs. |
| SERIAL NUMBERS | M/75 rifles were serially numbered, forward end of receiver, right side. |

The M/75 Target rifle and the M/75 Sporting rifle were developed as medium priced companions of the Winchester M/52s. They are both excellent rifles and sold in satisfactory quantities. Discontinued in 1958; about 88,715 were made.

M/75 Target rifles, equipped with a special combination of sights and slight difference in the stock dimensions, were used by the United States Government for training troops during World War II.

The Model 75 rifle was followed by the Winchester Model 74 rifle.

# MODEL 74 AUTOMATIC (SELF-LOADING) RIFLE

*137. MODEL 74 RIFLE*

To meet a continued customer demand for a medium priced self-loading rifle chambered for 22 caliber rim fire cartridges, Winchester developed a new rifle of this type in 22 Short caliber. It was announced in the March 4, 1939, price list as the Winchester Model 74 Automatic (Self-Loading) Rifle.

Factory records show the first delivery of Model 74 rifles to warehouse stock was made on February 15, 1939, in 22 Short chambering only.

The 22 Long Rifle chambering was added in 1940.

## GENERAL SPECIFICATIONS OF THE M/74 RIFLE

TYPE
Automatic (self-loading) repeating rifle, tubular magazine in butt stock, take-down.

STYLES
Sporting Rifle, with open sporting rear sight or with elevating peep sight; Gallery Special (22 Short only). A steel shell deflector for this gallery rifle was authorized on April 26, 1939. This shell deflector is made of thin steel, rounded on the top to fit the receiver. The bottom part was shaped to cover the back and side portion of the ejection port, the ejected shell being deflected downward and forward. It is attached to the rifle by the use of a long pin to hold the slotted part of the deflector in position by spring tension. One of these shell deflectors was attached to all M/74 Gallery rifles as standard equipment.

Gallery rifles in two styles of chromium plated trimmings were also furnished on special order only at extra cost.

| BARRELS | 24-inch, round. |
| CHAMBER | 22 Short only (discontinued in 1952) or 22 Long Rifle only. |
| MAGAZINE | Tubular magazine in butt stock. |
| | Capacity, 22 Short, 20 cartridges. |
| | Capacity, 22 Long Rifle, 14 cartridges. |
| STOCK | Plain walnut, sporting type with semi-beavertail forearm, not checkered, pistol grip, checkered steel butt plate. |
| WEIGHT | About 6¼ lbs. |
| SERIAL NUMBERS | M/74 rifles are serially numbered from 1 up, on forward end of receiver, left side. |

M/74 rifles had a very large sale. Discontinued in 1955; about 406,574 were made.

*Special Notes*

The M/74 was designed as a medium priced high quality, self-loading (simple blowback) rifle to handle either standard velocity or Super Speed and Super-X 22 Short or 22 Long Rifle cartridges. With the type of mechanism used in the M/74 rifle, the trigger must be pulled and released for each shot.

One of the special features of this model is the bolt which is easily removable in one piece for cleaning or inspection.

The Model 74 rifle was followed by the Winchester Model 24 Shotgun.

# MODEL 24 DOUBLE BARREL SHOTGUN

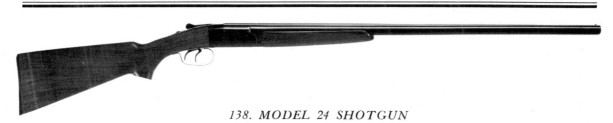

*138. MODEL 24 SHOTGUN*

Winchester's next development was a medium price class, double barrel, hammerless shotgun that could be sold in competition with other manufacturers' models that had been on the market for many years. This top lever, breakdown model, known as the Winchester Model 24 Double Barrel shotgun, was first announced in the January 2, 1940, price list.

Factory records show the first delivery of Model 24 shotguns to warehouse stock was made on April 21, 1939.

# GENERAL SPECIFICATIONS OF THE M/24 SHOTGUN

| | | |
|---|---|---|
| TYPE | Double barrel shotgun, hammerless, automatic ejectors, breakdown. | |
| STYLES | Standard only. | |

BARRELS

| | Right | Left |
|---|---|---|
| 12 gauge, 30-inch, | Mod. | Full |
| 12 gauge, 28-inch, | Mod. | Full |
| 12 gauge, 28-inch, | *Cyl. | Mod. |
| 12 gauge, 26-inch, | *Cyl. | Mod. |
| 16 gauge, 28-inch, | Mod. | Full |
| 16 gauge, 26-inch, | *Cyl. | Mod. |
| 20 gauge, 28-inch, | Mod. | Full |
| 20 gauge, 26-inch, | *Cyl. | Mod. |

*These chokes changed to improved cylinder and modified in 1947.

| | |
|---|---|
| TRIGGER | Double triggers only. |
| RIB | Raised matted rib only. |
| SAFETY | Automatic safety only. |
| CHAMBERS | 12 gauge, 2¾-inch. |
| | 16 gauge, 2¾-inch. |
| | 20 gauge, 2¾-inch. |
| STOCK | Plain walnut, pistol grip, semi-beavertail forearm, not checkered, checkered composition butt plate. |
| | Straight grip stocks furnished at no extra charge. |
| | Fancy walnut, checkered or not checkered, and stocks to customer's dimensions furnished at extra charge, on special order only. |
| WEIGHTS | 12 gauge, 30-inch barrel—about 7 lbs. 7 oz. |
| | 16 gauge, 28-inch barrel—about 6 lbs. 9 oz. |
| | 20 gauge, 28-inch barrel—about 6 lbs. 8 oz. |
| SERIAL NUMBERS | M/24 shotguns were serially numbered from 1 up, on underside of receiver, front of trigger guard. |

Discontinued in 1957; about 116,280 were made.

## Special Note

The M/24, a well constructed arm made of strong high quality steel throughout, was a very satisfactory arm in the medium price class.

The Model 24 was followed by the Winchester Model 40 shotgun.

# MODEL 40 AUTOMATIC
# (SELF-LOADING) SHOTGUN

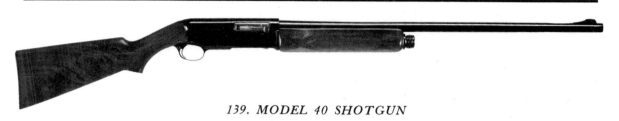

*139. MODEL 40 SHOTGUN*

The second Winchester shotgun of the self-loading, long recoil type was first announced in the January 2, 1940, price list.

Factory records show the first delivery of Model 40 shotguns to warehouse stock was made in January 1940.

## GENERAL SPECIFICATIONS OF THE M/40 SHOTGUN

| | |
|---|---|
| TYPE | Automatic (self-loading) repeating shotgun, hammerless, tubular magazine, takedown. |
| STYLES | Standard; Skeet Gun, with Cutts Compensator and skeet tube attached. |
| | 1 extra 705 full choke tube and a special wrench for attaching or removing the tube were included. |
| | A modified choke tube was substituted for the full choke tube when so ordered by the customer. |
| BARRELS | Standard. |
| AND CHOKES | 12 gauge, 30-inch, full choke. |
| | 12 gauge, 30-inch, modified choke. |
| | 12 gauge, 28-inch, full choke. |
| | 12 gauge, 28-inch, modified choke. |
| | The front bead sight and ramp was forged on the barrel. |
| | Any standard Winchester choke or bore was furnished on special order at no extra charge. |
| | Solid raised matted rib or ventilated rib barrels were not furnished on the M/40. |
| | Skeet Gun. |
| | Specially shaped barrel with shoulder forged on the muzzle end, threaded to fit the threading on the compensator body. |
| | No choke in barrel; barrel length with skeet tube attached, 24 inches. |
| CHAMBERS | 12 gauge, 2¾-inch shell only. |

| | |
|---|---|
| MAGAZINE | Tubular magazine, capacity 4 shells. |
| | Note: By Presidential Proclamation signed February 5, 1935, based on the recommendation of the United States Biological Survey, the capacity of any auto loading or repeating shotgun used in shooting migratory birds is specifically limited to three shots. This means only two shells in the magazine and one shell in the chamber. For this purpose a special shaped wood magazine plug was included in each carton containing a M/40 Shotgun. |
| STOCKS | Standard: Plain walnut, not checkered, pistol grip, hard rubber checkered butt plate. |
| | Skeet Gun: Selected walnut, checkered, pistol grip with hard rubber pistol grip cap, hard rubber checkered butt plate. |
| | Straight grip stocks of standard dimensions were furnished on both the Standard and Skeet Guns on special order at no extra charge. |
| | Straight or pistol grip stocks of special dimensions were furnished on special order only and at extra charge. |
| FOREARM | Standard, plain walnut, rock elm insert, semi-beavertail, not checkered. |
| | Skeet Gun, semi-beavertail, checkered. |
| SAFETY | Specially designed safety that can be locked off by rotating about one eighth of a turn by inserting a coin in the slot. Reversing this procedure returns the safety to normal. |
| WEIGHTS | Standard—about 8 lbs. |
| | Skeet Gun—about 8 lbs. |
| SERIAL NUMBERS | M/40 shotguns are serially numbered on underside of receiver. |

The M/40 was discontinued in 1941; about 12,000 were made.

### Special Note

At the time of production, the M/40 differed from most self-loading shotguns. It did not have the familiar hump or protrusion at the top rear of the receiver, but was of the so-called goose neck shape, curving gracefully down toward the tang, thus eliminating any optical interference when sighting the gun. However, certain weaknesses developed and its manufacture was discontinued.

The Model 40 was followed by the U. S. Rifle Cal. 30 M1.

# U.S. RIFLE CAL. 30 M1, GARAND-M 39

*140. U. S. RIFLE M-1 GARAND (M-39)*

The U. S. Rifle Cal. 30 M1 was developed by John C. Garand of the Springfield Armory, and was commonly known as the Garand Rifle. At the Winchester factory it was known as the Model 39. This rifle was manufactured by Winchester for the United States Government during World War II, with the first delivery made in 1940.

## GENERAL SPECIFICATIONS OF THE U. S. RIFLE CAL. 30 M1

| | |
|---|---|
| TYPE | Semi-automatic repeating rifle, gas operated, detachable clip magazine, solid frame. |
| STYLES | Standard style only. |
| BARREL | 24-inch, round, with bayonet attachment. |
| CHAMBER | 30-06 Springfield. |
| MAGAZINE | Detachable clip. Eight cartridges, staggered in a double row, held together by the steel clip. |
| STOCK | Plain walnut, military type (three piece), pistol grip, checkered steel butt plate. Butt plate changed in 1942 to checkered steel with a hinged cap for access to a recess in the stock holding a combination tool assembly. Equipped with three 1¼-inch sling swivel bows. |
| SIGHTS | Special military sights. |
| METAL PARTS | Parkerized finish. |
| WEIGHT | About 9¼ lbs. |
| SERIAL NUMBERS | U. S. Rifles Cal. 30 M1 were serially numbered, at top of receiver, near rear end. |

Discontinued in 1945; 513,582 were made.

### Special Note

The U. S. Rifle Cal. 30 M1 was manufactured for the United States Government only and was not listed in the Winchester catalog or price lists.

The U. S. Rifle Cal. 30 M1 was followed by the Winchester Model 30 rifle.

# MODEL 30 RIFLE

*141. MODEL 30 EXPERIMENTAL RIFLE*

The Winchester Model 30 rifle was authorized on September 25, 1941, and was developed by Winchester to compete with the U. S. Rifle Cal. 30 M1 (Garand Rifle). This model was a semi-automatic, detachable box magazine type and was chambered for the 30-06 Springfield service cartridge. Only a few rifles were made up for exhibition and test purposes.

# G30 R RIFLE

Two examples of a redesigned M/30 rifle, known as the Winchester G30 R semi-automatic, were made up in January 1943 for exhibition and test purposes. They were not listed in Winchester catalogs or price lists or offered for public sale.

The Winchester Model 30 rifle was followed by the U. S. Carbine Cal. 30 M1 (Model 31).

# U.S. CARBINE CAL. 30 M1

*142. U. S. CARBINE M-1 (M-31)*

This model was developed by the Winchester engineering staff. Officially called the U. S. Carbine Cal. 30 M1, it was commonly known in the Winchester factory as the M/31 (G3199M).

GENERAL SPECIFICATIONS OF THE U. S. CARBINE CAL. 30 M1

| | |
|---|---|
| TYPE | Semi-automatic repeating carbine, gas-operated, detachable box magazine, solid frame. |
| STYLE | Standard style only. |
| BARREL | 18-inch, round. |
| CHAMBER | U. S. Carbine Cal. 30 M1. |
| MAGAZINE | Detachable box magazine holding 15 cartridges, double row, staggered. |
| STOCK | Plain walnut, military type (two piece), pistol grip, checkered steel butt plate. |
| SLING STRAP | Equipped with 1-inch web sling strap held flat against the left-hand side of the carbine. The rear end of the strap is held by wrapping around a metal tube in a recess in the butt stock. This tube is removable and is used as an oil can. |
| SIGHTS | Special military sights. |
| METAL PARTS | Parkerized finish. |
| WEIGHT | About 4½ lbs. |
| SERIAL NUMBERS | Carbines 30 Cal. M1 are serially numbered, top of receiver near rear end. |

Discontinued in 1945; 818,059 were made.

## *Special Note*

The U. S. Carbine Cal. 30 M1 was manufactured for the United States Government during World War II and was not listed by Winchester in catalogs or price lists.

# U.S. CARBINE CAL. 30 M2

The U. S. Carbine Cal. 30 M2 was the U. S. Carbine Cal. 30 M1 with changes in the mechanism to also operate at full automatic. During the early part of 1945, a quantity of these carbines was manufactured for the United States Government only.

Winchester assigned their model number 32 (32M) to this arm.

# U.S. CARBINE CAL. 30 T3

*143. U.S. CARBINE T-3 (G33M)*

This carbine was similar to the U. S. Carbine Cal. 30 M1 except for slight changes in the receiver and stock, and had no rear sight attached, but included adjusting screws on the receiver for sight attachment.

A few of these carbines were made for the United States Government during the latter part of World War II.

Winchester assigned their model number 33 (G33M) to this arm.

# MODEL 77 RIFLE

*144. MODEL 77 EXPERIMENTAL RIFLE*

The Winchester Model 77 rifle was authorized on December 12, 1941, for development as a target practice rifle for the United States Marine Corps.

GENERAL SPECIFICATIONS OF THE M/77 RIFLE

| | |
|---|---|
| TYPE | Semi-automatic repeating rifle, detachable box magazine, solid frame. |
| STYLE | Target Rifle. |
| BARREL | 24-inch, round, heavy. |
| CHAMBER | 22 Long Rifle. |
| MAGAZINE | Detachable box magazine holding 8 cartridges. |
| STOCK | Military type. |
| SLING STRAP | Equipped with a 1¼-inch army type leather sling strap attached with 1¼-inch swivel bows. |
| SIGHTS | Target sights. |

Due to the pressure of other defense work, Winchester did not accept a contract for the manufacture of a quantity of these rifles. Only a few sample rifles were manufactured for exhibition and test purposes.

The Model 77 rifle was followed by the Winchester Model 43 Rifle.

# MODEL 43 REPEATING RIFLE

*145. MODEL 43 RIFLE*

Authorization for the development of a new bolt action repeating rifle with a detachable box magazine was given on May 31, 1944. This model was to be developed as a sort of a Junior Winchester Model 70, to handle the 218 Bee, 22 Hornet, 25-20 Winchester, and 32-20 Winchester cartridges.

Factory records show the first delivery of M/43 rifles to warehouse stock on February 4, 1949. This model was first listed in the Winchester January 14, 1949, price list.

## GENERAL SPECIFICATIONS OF THE M/43 RIFLE

| | |
|---|---|
| TYPE | Bolt action repeating rifle, detachable box magazine, solid frame. |
| STYLES | Standard Rifle, plain stock and forearm. |
| | Special Rifle, with checkered grip and forearm and pistol grip cap, was furnished either with open sporting rear sight or Lyman 57A micrometer receiver sight. Open rear sight rifles have receiver drilled and tapped for attaching Lyman 57A receiver sight. |
| BARRELS | 24-inch, round, tapered Winchester proof-steel barrel, crowned on the muzzle. Matted front sight ramp forged integral with barrel. |
| ACTION | Bolt action with speed lock. Positive twin extractors. Rifle cocks on opening motion of the bolt. |
| RECEIVER | Alloy steel. |
| BOLT | Twin locking lugs. Easy to operate pear-shaped handle. |
| SAFETY | Positive side lever safety. |
| MAGAZINE | Box type, flush with bottom of forearm. Capacity, 3 cartridges in 218 Bee, 22 Hornet, and 25-20 Winchester; 2 cartridges in 32-20 Winchester. Cartridge in chamber makes rifle either a 4 or 3 shot repeater. |
| STOCK | Standard Rifle, full pistol grip stock of genuine American walnut, no checkering. Full shaped forearm. 1-inch swivel bows attached. No sling strap. |
| SIGHTS | Standard rifle, Winchester 103 bead front on forged ramp sight base with removable sight cover and Winchester 22 open sporting rear. |
| WEIGHT | About 6 lbs. |
| SERIAL NUMBERS | Model 43 was serially numbered, first on left front of receiver, then right front of receiver. Discontinued in 1957; about 62,617 were made. |

The Special Rifle was available in two styles, bead front sight on forged ramp base with removable sight cover and Lyman 57A micrometer receiver sight, or with bead front sight on forged ramp base with sight cover and Winchester open sporting rear.

The Model 43 was the first postwar development in Winchester center fire rifles. It embodied the well-proved principles of the famous smooth, fast Winchester bolt action that adapted it to that highly popular sport known as pest and small game shooting.

The Model 43 rifle was announced simultaneously with the Winchester Model 47 rifle.

# MODEL 47 SINGLE SHOT RIFLE

*146. MODEL 47 RIFLE*

Authorization for the development of a new bolt action, single shot rifle was given on May 31, 1944. This rifle was chambered for 22 Short, 22 Long, and 22 Long Rifle cartridges, interchangeably.

Factory records show the first delivery of M/47 rifles to warehouse stock on July 13, 1948. This model was first listed in the Winchester January 14, 1949, price list.

## GENERAL SPECIFICATIONS OF THE M/47 RIFLE

| | |
|---|---|
| TYPE | Bolt action, single shot, takedown. |
| STYLES | Manufactured in two styles. One has a bead front sight and Winchester open sporting rear sight; the second a bead front sight on ramp with removable sight cover and receiver peep sight with adjustments for windage and elevation. |
| CALIBERS | 22 Short, 22 Long, and 22 Long Rifle rim fire, interchangeably. |
| BARREL | 25-inch, round, tapered and crowned on the muzzle. |
| ACTION | Bolt action, cocking on opening motion of the bolt. Speed lock. Positive twin extractors. Bolt, bolt handle, and trigger chrome-plated. |
| SAFETY | Side lever automatic type, operating on opening rearward movement of the bolt. Must be released manually before rifle can be fired. Forward motion of lever to firing position reveals red dot on receiver as warning signal. |
| STOCK | Ample size, pistol grip sporting type stock of genuine American walnut with superior finish. Checkered composition butt plate. |

| SIGHTS | Winchester No. 97 bead front on ramp with detachable sight cover, adjustments for windage and elevation. Or Winchester No. 75 bead front and Winchester No. 32 open sporting rear. |
|---|---|
| WEIGHT | Approximately 5¼ lbs. |
| SERIAL NUMBERS | M/47 rifles were not serially numbered. |

The manufacture of the M/47 was discontinued in 1954; about 43,123 were made.

The Model 47 rifle was followed by the Winchester Model 25 Repeating Shotgun.

# MODEL 25 REPEATING SHOTGUN

*147. MODEL 25 SHOTGUN*

The Model 25 was authorized on December 30, 1947, and first delivery was made to warehouse stock on March 17, 1949.

This model was first listed in the February 2, 1950, price list.

## GENERAL SPECIFICATIONS OF THE M/25 SHOTGUN

| TYPE | Slide action, hammerless, solid frame. |
|---|---|
| STYLES | Made in 12 gauge only in combinations of barrel length and chokes. |
| BARRELS | Furnished in 28-inch length with full or modified choke; 26-inch length with improved cylinder. |
| SIGHTS | Winchester No. 81A bead front. |
| CHAMBER | 12 gauge, 2¾-inch shells. |
| ACTION | Slide action. |
| SAFETY | Positive cross lock safety operating horizontally across front of trigger guard. |
| STOCK | Pistol grip stock and well-formed slide handle of genuine American walnut. |
| MAGAZINE | Capacity, 4 rolled crimp shells, 5 folded crimp shells, with 1 shell in chamber. Furnished with wooden magazine plug to reduce magazine capacity to 2 shells. |
| WEIGHT | Approximately 8 lbs. with 28-inch barrel. |
| SERIAL NUMBERS | The Model 25 was serially numbered on the underside of receiver. |

Discontinued in 1954; about 87,937 were made.

The Model 25 shotgun was followed by the Winchester Model 50 Automatic (Self-Loading) Shotgun.

# MODEL 50 AUTOMATIC
# (SELF-LOADING) SHOTGUN

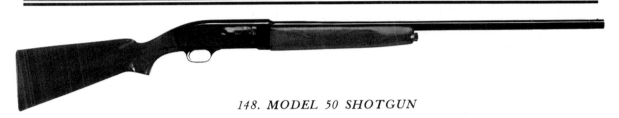

### 148. MODEL 50 SHOTGUN

The third Winchester shotgun of the self-loading type was introduced as the Model 50 in 1954. Model number "50" was authorized on July 1, 1947, to cover a new design of self-loading shotgun.

The first Model 50 was sent to the warehouse April 15, 1954. Model 50, serial number "1,001" was shipped May 19, 1954. The first receiver on that gun, number 1,001, was scrapped and a second receiver numbered 1,781 replaced it. Serial numbers started with number 1,000. Mr. J. M. Olin received the Model 50 bearing that number.

## GENERAL SPECIFICATIONS OF THE M/50 SHOTGUN

| | |
|---|---|
| TYPE | Automatic (self-loading) recoil operated, non-recoiling barrel, repeating shotgun, hammerless, tubular magazine, takedown. |
| STYLES | Standard Field Gun. |
| | Field Gun with Winchester special ventilated rib barrel. |
| | Skeet Gun, standard weight with Winchester special ventilated rib. |
| | Made in 12 and 20 gauges. The 12 gauge was available in Field, Skeet, and Trap styles; 20 gauge in Field and Skeet styles. |
| | Pigeon Grade, with deluxe features was made on special order, in 12 or 20 gauge. |
| | Trap Gun, Monte Carlo stock only. Standard weight, with Winchester special ventilated rib. |
| | Featherweight (made in the same styles as above, except the Trap Gun). |
| | Pigeon Grade, standard weight or featherweight. The Pigeon grade was available as: |
| |     Field Gun with plain barrel. |
| |     Field Gun with Winchester special ventilated rib. |
| |     Skeet Gun with Winchester special ventilated rib. |
| |     Trap Gun with Winchester special ventilated rib and Monte Carlo stock. |
| BARRELS | *Standard Gun, plain barrel.* |
| | 12 gauge, 30-inch, full choke; 28-inch, full or modified choke; 26-inch, imp. cylinder or Winchester skeet choke. |

20 gauge, 28-inch, full or modified choke; 26-inch, imp. cylinder or Winchester skeet choke (all available early in 1956).

*Standard Gun, Winchester special ventilated rib.*

12 gauge, 30-inch, full choke; 28-inch, full or modified choke; 26-inch, imp. cylinder choke.

20 gauge, 28-inch, full choke; 28-inch, modified choke; 26-inch, imp. cylinder choke.

*Skeet Gun, Winchester special ventilated rib.*

12 gauge, 26-inch, Winchester skeet choke.

20 gauge, 26-inch, Winchester skeet choke (available early 1956).

*Trap Gun.*

12 gauge, 30-inch, full choke.

*Featherweight Field Gun with plain barrel or ventilated rib barrel, first listed in 1958.*

12 gauge, 30-inch, full choke; 28-inch, full or modified choke; 26-inch, imp. cylinder choke.

20 gauge, 28-inch, full or modified choke; 26-inch, imp. cylinder choke.

*Featherweight Skeet Gun.*

12 or 20 gauge, 26-inch, Winchester skeet choke.

Pigeon Grade available with any combination of the above listed barrel lengths or chokes in 12 or 20 gauge.

All barrels were of Winchester proof steel.

| | |
|---|---|
| CHAMBERS | Chambered for regular field or high-velocity long range loads, including 2¾-inch magnum, without any adjustment. |
| EXTRA BARRELS | Interchangeable barrels for the Model 50 were available in a variety of lengths and chokes. These barrels were easily installed, no tools, no factory-fitting necessary. |
| SIGHTS | Bead front sight of shotgun type. |
| STOCKS | Pistol grip stock and forearm of American walnut. Hand checkered. Fluted comb. Composition butt plate. |
| MAGAZINE | Tube below barrel. Capacity 2 shells. With one shell in chamber, gun has total capacity of three shots. Magazine loads and unloads from bottom of receiver. Ejects from side. |
| SAFETY | Cross bolt safety at forward part of trigger guard. |
| WEIGHTS | 12 gauge, approximately 7¾ lbs. |
| | 20 gauge, approximately 6¾ lbs. |
| | Featherweight, 12 gauge, less than 7 lbs. |
| SERIAL NUMBERS | M/50 shotguns were serially numbered starting with number 1,000, located on forward underside of receiver. |

This model was discontinued in December 1961, with about 196,402 made.

### Special Notes

The Winchester Model 50 works on the short recoil principle. When the gun is fired, the barrel remains fixed and rigid with the receiver. The floating chamber moves back a fraction of an inch, about 1/10 inch, and starts the action on its way to the rear. The bolt continues to the rear, activated by its own momentum. During this motion the empty shell is extracted and ejected and a loaded shell is lifted in line with the chamber. On the return or closing motion of the bolt, the loaded shell is seated in the chamber with the action locked and cocked behind it.

Receiver, barrel, breech bolt, and other critical metal parts were machined from Winchester proof steel, a chrome molybdenum alloy steel famous for its strength and toughness.

The receiver was milled from a solid block; barrel was bored from a solid bar. There are no metal stampings in the Model 50.

The Model 50 shotgun was followed by the Model 77 rifle.

# MODEL 77 AUTOMATIC (SELF-LOADING) RIFLE

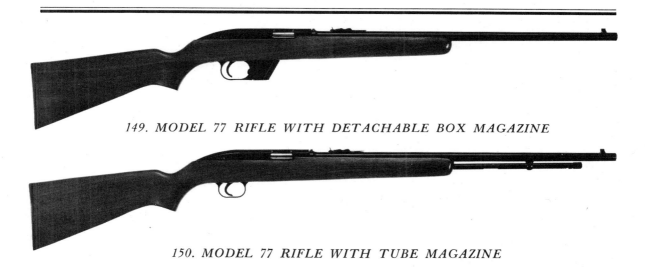

*149. MODEL 77 RIFLE WITH DETACHABLE BOX MAGAZINE*

*150. MODEL 77 RIFLE WITH TUBE MAGAZINE*

The Model 77 Winchester is a semi-automatic rim fire rifle made to operate on the blowback principle.

The first Model 77 was delivered to warehouse stock about April 21, 1955. Serial number 1,001 was shipped May 13, 1955. It was first listed in the Winchester catalog for 1955.

## GENERAL SPECIFICATIONS OF THE M/77 RIFLE

TYPE          Automatic (self-loading).
STYLE         Standard only.
BARREL        22-inch round, tapered, crowned at muzzle.
ACTION        Semi-automatic (self-loading). First cartridge is manually loaded by pulling

[ 147 ]

|                  | back and sharply releasing operating knob on left side. Rifle can then fire as fast as the trigger can be pulled. |
|------------------|---|
| MAGAZINES        | Detachable box magazine holds eight 22 Long Rifle cartridges. |
|                  | Tubular magazine holds fifteen 22 Long Rifle cartridges. |
|                  | Extra 8-shot clip or box magazines available at additional charge. |
| CHAMBER          | 22 Long Rifle, designed for all 22 Long Rifle cartridges, except low-velocity match ammunition. (In catalog for December 1955 and after, the phrase "except low-velocity match ammunition" does not appear.) |
| SAFETY           | Side lever safety on the right side of the receiver directly blocks the trigger when in the "safe" position. |
| SIGHTS           | Winchester number 75 bead front and number 32B sporting rear sight. Receiver grooved for easy attachment of scope mount. |
| STOCK            | Walnut sporting type pistol grip stock. Semi-beavertail forearm. Checkered composition butt plate. |
| WEIGHT           | About 5½ lbs. |
| SERIAL NUMBERS   | The Model 77 rifles are serially numbered from 1,001 up; located on front right side of receiver. |

Box magazine model discontinued in 1962 and the tubular magazine model in 1963. Number manufactured was about 217,180.

*Special Notes*

The trigger guard was made of nylon. The receiver is totally enclosed except for the ejection port on right side.

The Model 77 rifle was announced simultaneously with the Winchester Model 88 rifle.

# MODEL 88 RIFLE

*151. MODEL 88 RIFLE*

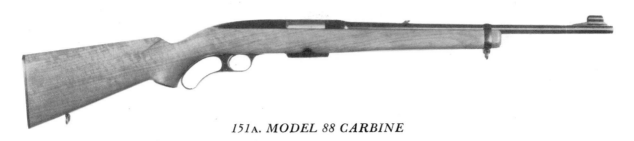

## 151A. MODEL 88 CARBINE

Designed to handle cartridges ballistically comparable to the 30-06 Springfield, usually used in bolt action, semi-automatic, or automatic type rifles.

First listed in catalog for 1955. Received in warehouse May 9, 1955. Serial number 4 was the first one shipped on May 18, 1955.

### GENERAL SPECIFICATIONS OF THE M/88 RIFLE

| | |
|---|---|
| TYPE | Lever action repeating rifle, hammerless, detachable box magazine, solid frame. |
| STYLE | Sporting rifle and carbine (introduced in 1968). |
| BARREL | Tapered 22-inch barrel; 19-inch barrel (carbine). |
| ACTION | Hammerless lever action, short lever stroke 60° arc, rotary head locking bolt, triple locking lugs, side ejection. Receiver drilled and tapped for receiver sights and scope mounts. |
| MAGAZINE | Detachable box magazine, holds four cartridges. Locking latches at front and rear. Extra magazines available. In 1956 these magazines were listed as holding five cartridges; in 1957 reverted back to 4 cartridges. The magazine for the 284 caliber cartridge holds 3 cartridges. |
| CHAMBERS | 308 Winchester (available 1955). |
| | 243 Winchester (available 1956). |
| | 358 Winchester (available 1956; last listed in 1962). |
| | 284 Winchester (available 1963). |
| SAFETY | Cross lock safety located in front portion of trigger guard. Red warning indicator shows when in "fire" position. |
| SIGHTS | Winchester No. 103C bead front sight on ramp with removable sight cover. Lyman No. 16A, adjustable, folding leaf rear sight. |
| STOCK | One piece pistol grip, walnut, checkered grip and forearm. Nylon cap on pistol grip and nylon butt plate. |
| WEIGHT | About 6½ lbs. |
| SERIAL NUMBERS | Serially numbered from 1 up, located left front of receiver. |

The Model 88 was offered in carbine style with a 19-inch barrel in 1968. It was initially offered in three calibers: 243 Win., 284 Win. and 308 Win. It had an overall length of 39½ inches and had all the features standard on the rifle version. By 1971, the Model 88 carbine was listed in 243 Win. and 308 Win. calibers only.

In 1973 both rifle and carbine models were listed for 243 Win. and 308 Win. only. The Model 88 was last listed in 1973 and approximately 283,913 were manufactured. It should be noted that the Model 88 had a number of checkering designs, both cut and pressed, throughout the years.

The Model 88 rifle was followed by the Winchester Model 55 rifle.

# MODEL 55 RIM FIRE RIFLE

*152. MODEL 55 RIFLE*

Introduced in 1957. First listed in the 1958 catalog.

GENERAL SPECIFICATIONS OF THE M/55 RIFLE

| | |
|---|---|
| TYPE | Top loading single shot automatic. |
| STYLE | Sporting rifle. |
| BARREL | 22-inch. |
| CHAMBER | 22 Short, Long, and Long Rifle, interchangeably. |
| STOCK | One piece, pistol grip. |
| SIGHTS | Open sporting sights. |
| SERIAL NUMBERS | The Model 55 Rim Fire Rifles were not serially numbered. |

Discontinued in 1961; approximately 45,060 were manufactured.

### *Special Note*

The Model 55 Single Shot automatic was the second Winchester to be called the Model 55. The first Model 55 was a lever action repeating center fire rifle made from 1924 to 1932. It was a modern version of the Model 1894 rifle.

The Model 55 rifle was followed by the Winchester Model 59 shotgun.

# MODEL 59 AUTOMATIC (SELF-LOADING) SHOTGUN

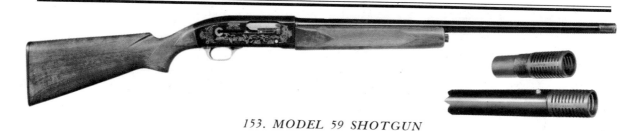

*153. MODEL 59 SHOTGUN*

The fourth Winchester shotgun of the self-loading type was introduced as the Model 59 in 1959. First listed in catalog for 1960.

## GENERAL SPECIFICATIONS OF THE M/59 SHOTGUN

| | |
|---|---|
| TYPE | Automatic, self-loading, recoil operated, non-recoiling barrel, repeating shotgun. Hammerless, tubular magazine, takedown. |
| STYLES | Standard Field Gun. |
| | Pigeon Grade was first listed in 1962 catalog. Made with hand finished and hand checkered stock of selected walnut. Hand finished internal parts and engine turned bolt and carrier. |
| BARREL | 12 gauge patented "Win-Lite" barrel of steel and glass fibers. 500 miles of glass fiber are wound around, fused, and bonded to a thin steel liner. The finished barrel was colored gun blue. Available in 30-inch, 28-inch, and 26-inch lengths. Full, modified, or improved cylinder chokes. Instantly interchangeable barrels, without tools or factory fitting. |
| | In 1961, the Winchester "Versalite" choke was first listed. This gave a choice of full, modified, or improved cylinder patterns from the same barrel, by changing choke tubes. Also reduced recoil. |
| MAGAZINE | Total capacity 3 shots (2 plus one in chamber). Magazine loads and unloads from bottom of receiver. |
| RECEIVER | High strength aluminum alloy, inscribed with hunting scenes and with the trigger guard and carrier release button in a gold color. |
| CHAMBERS | Chambered for all 2¾-inch shells, 12 gauge. Regular, field loads, or super long range loads, including magnums; without adjustment. |
| SIGHTS | Bead front sight of shotgun type. |
| STOCK | Checkered pistol grip and forearm of American walnut. Composition butt plate, fluted comb. |
| SAFETY | Positive crosslock located in upper front of trigger guard. Shows red indicator when in "Fire" position. |

[ 151 ]

| WEIGHT | About 6½ lbs. |
|---|---|
| SERIAL NUMBERS | M/59 shotguns were serially numbered from 1 up, located on bottom front of receiver. Discontinued 1965. |

### Special Note

The Winchester Model 59 works on the short recoil principle. When the gun is fired, the barrel remains fixed and rigid with the receiver. The floating chamber moves back a fraction of an inch, about 1/10 inch, and starts the action on its way to the rear. The bolt continues to the rear, activated by its own momentum. During this motion the empty shell is extracted and ejected and a loaded shell is lifted in line with the chamber. On the return or closing motion of the bolt, the loaded shell is seated in the chamber with the action locked and cocked behind it.

It should be noted that a small number of experimental Model 59 shotguns were made in both 20 gauge and, more significantly from a historical standpoint, in a special 14 gauge based on a revolutionary short aluminum shotshell produced by the Winchester-Western shotshell facility in East Alton. These last guns were used for a season at Nilo Farms and their performance was carefully evaluated. Although there was great interest in the program and both shotshells and shotguns performed in a satisfactory manner, the project was dropped because of the almost insurmountable problems involved in educating both distributor and consumer to a new gauge and shotshell length combined with a new aluminum case. There were probably individual guns — both in 20 and 14 gauge — that have found their way into private hands, and they must be considered extreme rarities. Occasionally, small amounts of the experimental aluminum 14 gauge ammunition is encountered, but it is increasingly rare. A total of 82,085 Model 59 shotguns of all types were manufactured.

The Model 59 shotgun was followed by the M14 Springfield rifle.

# MILITARY RIFLE, 7.62mm, M14 SPRINGFIELD

*154. M-14*

Adoption of this new rifle to replace four current U. S. Army shoulder weapons rounded out a program for a new weapons system, long planned and partly consummated recently with the adoption of the M60 General Purpose Machine Gun. Both the new rifle and the new machine gun fire the 7.62mm NATO cartridge, which is common to our NATO allies. The M14 was introduced in August 1960.

GENERAL SPECIFICATIONS OF THE M14 SPRINGFIELD

| | |
|---|---|
| TYPE | Military, gas operated. Made in semi-automatic action only, also with a selector for semi-automatic or full automatic fire. |
| STYLE | Military. |
| BARREL | 22-inch length. |
| MAGAZINE | 20-round capacity. |
| SIGHTS | Adjustable military. |
| CHAMBER | 7.62mm Nato (308). |
| STOCK | Military, two piece. |
| WEIGHT | Empty, less sling—8.7 lbs. |
| SERIAL NUMBERS | The M14 was serially numbered, located top rear of receiver. |

Discontinued in June 1963; about 356,501 were made.
The Model 14 rifle was followed by the Winchester Model 100 rifle.

# MODEL 100 AUTOMATIC (SELF-LOADING) RIFLE

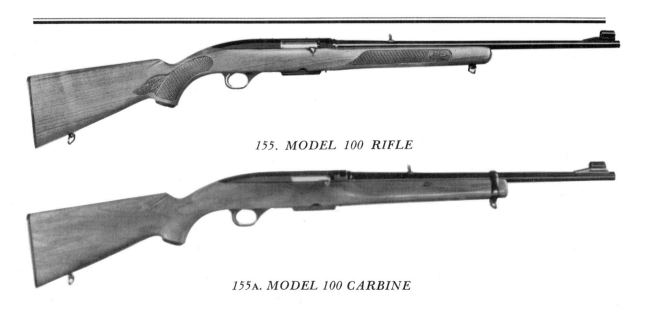

*155. MODEL 100 RIFLE*

*155A. MODEL 100 CARBINE*

[ 153 ]

The Model 100 was especially designed to fill the need for an accurate, dependable automatic hunting rifle. Introduced in 1960, it was first listed in the 1961 catalog.

The Model 100 was offered in carbine style with a 19-inch barrel in 1967. It was initially offered in three calibers: 243 Win., 284 Win. and 308 Win. It had an overall length of 39½ inches and incorporated all the features standard on the rifle version. By 1971, the Model 100 carbine was listed in 243 Win. and 308 Win. calibers only.

In 1973 both rifle and carbine models were listed in 243 Win. and 308 Win. calibers only. The Model 100 was last listed in 1973 and approximately 262,838 were manufactured. It should be noted that the Model 100 had a number of checkering designs, both cut and pressed, throughout the years.

## GENERAL SPECIFICATIONS OF THE M/100 RIFLE

| | |
|---|---|
| TYPE | Gas operated, automatic (self-loading) rifle. |
| STYLE | Sporting Rifle only. |
| BARREL | 22-inch, round. |
| ACTION | Hammerless, autoloading, rotary headlocking bolt, triple locking lugs, side ejection. Receiver drilled and tapped for receiver sights and scope mounts. |
| MAGAZINE | Detachable box magazine holds 4 cartridges and one in the chamber. Total 5 cartridges. (In caliber 284, the magazine holds 3 cartridges.) |
| SAFETY | Cross bolt in forward section of trigger guard. Red indicator when in "Fire" position. |
| SIGHTS | Hooded bead front sight and folding leaf rear sight. |
| CHAMBERS | 243 Winchester, 308 Winchester, 284 Winchester (first listed in 1963 catalog). |
| STOCK | One piece American walnut, checkered pistol grip. Fitted with 1-inch sling swivels. |
| WEIGHT | About 7½ lbs. |
| SERIAL NUMBERS | The Model 100 is serially numbered, at left front of receiver. |

The Model 100 rifle was followed by the Winchester Model 200 Series rifles.

# 200 SERIES, 22 RIM FIRE RIFLES

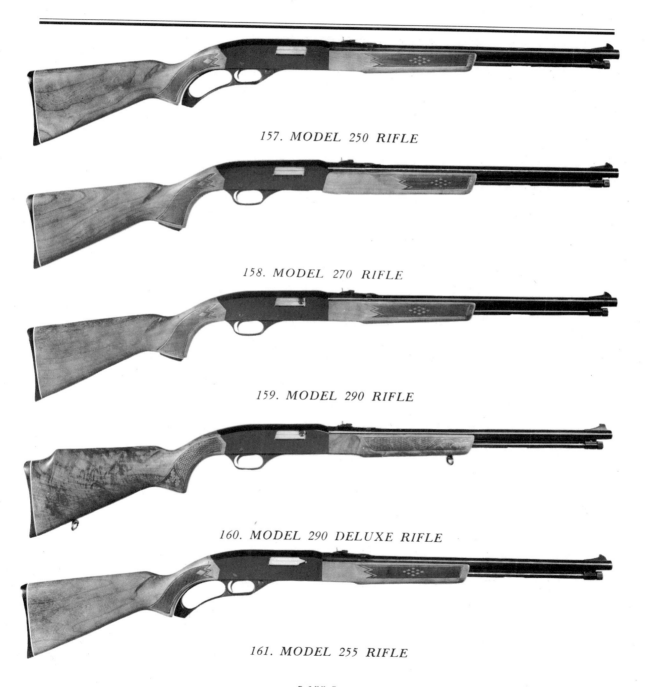

157. MODEL 250 RIFLE

158. MODEL 270 RIFLE

159. MODEL 290 RIFLE

160. MODEL 290 DELUXE RIFLE

161. MODEL 255 RIFLE

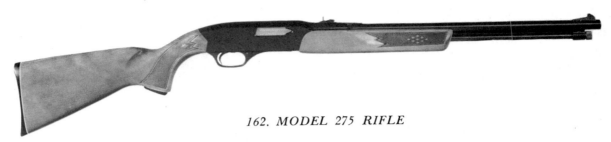

*162. MODEL 275 RIFLE*

The 200 Series of 22 rim fire rifles—Model 250 Lever Action, Model 270 Slide Action, Model 290 automatic (self-loading)—was announced in 1963. The family was increased in 1964 with the introduction of the Model 255 Lever Action Magnum and the Model 275 Slide Action Magnum, both built for the 22 Winchester Magnum Rimfire cartridge.

In 1965 the 200 Series Deluxe was announced, with all five models being available in this custom quality.

Styling changes were announced for 1966 in all three of the standard 200 Series basic action types—the addition of positive, decorative checkering at the pistol grip and forearm, and a white spacer between the stock and butt plate.

## GENERAL SPECIFICATIONS OF THE 200 SERIES RIM FIRE RIFLES

| | |
|---|---|
| TYPE | Model 250, lever action; Model 270, slide action; Model 290, Automatic (self-loading). |
| STYLES | Standard and Deluxe. |
| BARREL | 20½-inch only. |
| MAGAZINE | Tubular. Capacity, 21 Short, 17 Long, 15 Long Rifle cartridges. |
| CHAMBER | 22 rim fire, Short, Long, and Long Rifle, interchangeably. |
| STOCK | Model 250, walnut finish. Model 270, walnut finish, forearm also available of weatherproof, high impact Cycolac (discontinued in 1965). Model 290, walnut finish wood. |
| SIGHTS | Front, square post on streamlined ramp; rear, square notch, adjustable for windage and elevation. |
| RECEIVER | High-strength aluminum alloy, grooved for tip-off scope mounts. |
| SAFETY | Cross lock, located on front of trigger guard. |
| WEIGHT | About 5 lbs. |

## MODELS 255 and 275

| | |
|---|---|
| TYPE | Model 255, lever action. Model 275, slide action. |
| STYLES | Standard and Deluxe. |
| CHAMBER | 22 Winchester Magnum Rimfire. |
| MAGAZINE | Capacity: 11 cartridges, 22 Winchester Magnum Rimfire only. |
| SERIAL NUMBERS | Start with 50,000, located on bottom front of receiver. |

*Special Note*

The 200 Series Deluxe rifles, announced in 1965, include all five models. Features include: high-gloss Monte Carlo selected walnut stocks with fluted combs, cheek pieces, basket weave checkering, white spacers between butt plate and stock, sling swivels on all models except slide action.

In 1971, the Model 290 was dropped from the list in 22 Short, but remains in 22 Long and 22 Long Rifle (interchangeable in same gun) to date of this publication (1975). The Model 255 and Model 275 Magnum rifles were also not listed for 1971 and dropped from the line with these final production figures: 55,310 (M/255) and 47,657 (M/275). In 1972, the Model 250 Deluxe was not listed.

In 1973, the Models 290, 270 and 250 were listed in standard grade only; the Deluxe versions of the Models 290 and 270 had been dropped. In 1974, the standard Models 270 and 250 were dropped from the line, leaving only the Model 290. The total number of Model 250 lever action rifles of all types (both standard and deluxe) made was 191,264; the total of all Model 270 slide action rifles of all types (both standard and deluxe) was 112,716.

At this date (1975), only the Model 290 and Model 190 (an economical version of the Model 290) remain in the line as representative of this "family line" of the first post-1964 rim fire rifles. A total of 1,699,422 rifles of both versions have been manufactured as of January 23, 1975.

The Model 200 Series rifles were followed by the Winchester Model 101 over-and-under shotgun.

# MODEL 101 OVER-AND-UNDER SHOTGUN

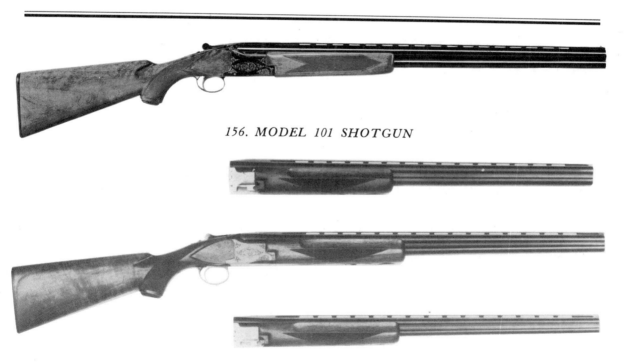

*156. MODEL 101 SHOTGUN*

*156A. MODEL 101 SHOTGUN IN 410 WITH 28 AND 20 GAUGE BARRELS*

*156B. MODEL 101 SINGLE BARREL SHOTGUN*

*156C. MODEL 101 SHOTGUN, TRAP SET*

*156D. MODEL 101 PIGEON GRADE TRAP GUN*

During recent years, the over-and-under type shotgun has become increasingly popular among shooters for field shooting as well as for skeet and trap. Winchester developed a high grade gun of this kind, announced in 1963 as the Model 101 Field Gun with Ventilated Rib, in 12 gauge. 20 gauge added in 1966. Since then a variety of styles has been introduced.

## GENERAL SPECIFICATIONS OF THE M/101 OVER-AND-UNDER SHOTGUN

TYPE — Over-and-under double barrel shotgun, hammerless, breakdown, ventilated rib, automatic ejectors, single selective trigger.

STYLES — Field Gun; Magnum Field Gun, available June 1966 (12 gauge only); Skeet Gun; Trap Gun, Monte Carlo stock; Trap Gun, regular stock; Pigeon Grade Trap Gun; Triple Barreled Skeet Set (.410, 28 and 20 gauge on same frame, cased); Single Barrel Trap Gun; Combination Single Barrel and Double Barrel Trap Gun on same frame, cased.

[ 158 ]

| | |
|---|---|
| BARRELS | Field Gun, 30-inch, full and full choke; 30-inch modified and full choke; (12 gauge only); 28-inch, modified and full choke; 26-inch, improved cylinder and modified choke; 26½-inch, improved cylinder and modified choke (20, 28 and .410 gauge only).<br>Magnum Field Gun, 30-inch full and full choke (12 gauge only).<br>Skeet Gun, 26-inch, Skeet 1 and Skeet 2 (12 gauge only).<br>Trap Gun, 30-inch, full and full choke (12 gauge only).<br>Skeet Gun, 26½-inch, Skeet 1 and Skeet 2 (20 gauge only).<br>Skeet Gun, 28-inch, Skeet 1 and Skeet 2 (all gauges).<br>Skeet Set, 28-inch, Skeet I and Skeet 2 (20, 28 and .410 on same frame).<br>Single Barrel Trap Gun, 34-inch full, 32-inch full and 32-inch improved-modified choke barrels with ventilated rib. (Also available as part of trap combination with set of double barrels, 32-inch choked improved-modified and full, on same frame). |
| GAUGE | 12 gauge, 2¾-inch shells, except Magnum Field Gun which has 3-inch chambers.<br>20 gauge, standard chambers handle 2¾ and 3-inch shells.<br>28 gauge, standard 2¾-inch shells.<br>.410 gauge, 2½-inch chamber in skeet version; 3-inch chamber in field gun. |
| RECEIVER | Machined from solid block of high strength Winchester proof steel, hand engraved. All visible internal surfaces engine turned. |
| STOCK | Walnut, fluted comb, pistol grip and beavertail forearm checkered. |
| SAFETY | Barrel selector serves as the manual safety. |
| TRIGGER | Single selective trigger only. |
| SIGHTS | Field Gun, metal front; Skeet and Trap Guns, metal front and middle. |
| WEIGHT | 30-inch barrel—7¾ lbs. (12 gauge only).<br>28-inch barrel—7⅝ lbs. (12 gauge only).<br>26-inch barrel—7½ lbs. (12 gauge only).<br>20 gauge versions—6½ lbs.<br>28 gauge versions—6¼ lbs.<br>.410 gauge versions—6¼ lbs. |
| SERIAL NUMBERS | Serially numbered from 1 up, located on upper tang. |

*Special Notes*

In 1967, a Model 101 Trap Gun with Monte Carlo stock was made available with a full and improved-modified choke combination. A magnum model field gun in both 12 and 20 gauge was introduced that would take either 3-inch magnum or 2¾-inch standard shells. (Indeed, it is not commonly known, but *all* 20 gauge Model 101 shotguns are chambered for 3-inch shells — even the skeet versions.) The skeet version in 20 gauge (with 26½-inch barrels) was also brought out in 1967.

The company introduced .410 and 28 gauge Model 101 guns in 1968. Both were offered in either field or skeet guns — or in a special combination skeet set featuring .410, 28 gauge and 20 gauge with three sets of barrels designed and furnished with one stocked frame with case. The .410 field gun was chambered for 3-inch shells; the skeet model came with 2½-inch chambers. The 28 gauge was chambered with standard 2¾-inch chambers in both skeet and field styles. Extra barrels of different gauge were also available.

Also, in 1968, a single barrel trap gun, modified to fit a conventional Model 101 action and frame, was first listed in the United States. The new gun was offered with a choice of 34-inch full choke, 32-inch full choke or 32-inch improved-modified choke barrels, complete with ventilated rib. The single barrel Model 101 was also offered in three different combination sets. One set consisted of a complete 34-inch full choke single barrel Model 101 trap gun plus an extra set of interchangeable over-and-under barrels with forearm. A second combination set duplicated the first except for barrel lengths. The single barrel was 32 inches long, and the over-and-under barrels 30 inches long. The third combination consisted of a 32-inch full choke single barrel Model 101 trap gun plus two extra sets of interchangeable barrels each equipped with individual forearms. The first set of extra barrels was a 32-inch single barrel choked improved-modified and the second was a set of 32-inch over-and-under barrels choked improved-modified and full. The set included a fitted trunk case.

In 1971, the 28-inch barrel versions of the 12 and 20 gauge skeet models were dropped from the list. The single barrel trap gun with full choke was retained, but the improved-modified version was dropped. The number of interchangeable trap set combinations was reduced from three to two choices: the one including the 34-inch barrel was eliminated.

In 1972 and 1973, the trap line of the Model 101 was further reduced while the skeet and field line remained unchanged. Both 30-inch and 32-inch full and full choked Model 101 Trap guns with Monte Carlo stocks were dropped in 1972. The following year, all of the single barrel individual guns and combination trap sets were struck from the list.

Finally, in 1974, Winchester completed this phase of its reorganization of the Model 101 trap line by dropping all of its previous regular trap line and introducing one Pigeon Grade Trap Gun in either regular or Monte Carlo versions in improved-modified and full choke with either a 30-inch or 32-inch set of barrels. This new Pigeon Grade Trap Gun features a finely detailed, hand engraved, satin-finished receiver and a fancy grade French walnut stock and forearm with special hand checkering.

The 1975 Winchester catalog lists the following Model 101 specifications:

## MODEL 101 SPECIFICATIONS

| Model | Gauge | Chamber | Choke | Length Barrel (in inches) | Length Overall (in inches) | Nominal Length of Pull | Nominal Drop at Comb | Nominal Drop at Heel Monte Carlo | Pitch Down | Sights | Nominal Weight (lbs.) |
|---|---|---|---|---|---|---|---|---|---|---|---|
| 101 Pigeon Grade Trap | 12 | 2¾" | IM & F | 30", 32" | 47⅛", 49⅛" | 14⅜" | 1⅜" | 1⅞" | — | WB, F & M | 8¼ |
| Field | 12 | 2¾" | IC & M | 26" | 42¾" | 14" | 1½" | 2½" | — | MBF | 7¼ |
| Field | 12 | 2¾" | M & F | 28" | 44¾" | 14" | 1½" | 2½" | — | MBF | 7½ |
| Field | 12 | 2¾" | M & F | 30" | 46¾" | 14" | 1½" | 2½" | — | MBF | 7¾ |
| Field | 20 | 3" | IC & M | 26½" | 43¼" | 14" | 1½" | 2½" | — | MBF | 6½ |
| Field | 20 | 3" | M & F | 28" | 44¾" | 14" | 1½" | 2½" | — | MBF | 6½ |
| Field | 28 | 2¾" | IC & M | 26½" | 43¼" | 14" | 1½" | 2½" | — | MBF | 6¼ |
| Field | 28 | 2¾" | M & F | 28" | 44¾" | 14" | 1½" | 2½" | — | MBF | 6⅜ |
| Field | 410 | 3" | IC & M | 26½" | 43¼" | 14" | 1½" | 2½" | — | MBF | 6¼ |
| Field | 410 | 3" | M & F | 28" | 44¾" | 14" | 1½" | 2½" | — | MBF | 6⅜ |
| Field Magnum | 12 | 3" | M&F, F&F | 30" | 46¾" | 14" | 1½" | 2½" | 2" | MB, F & M | 7¾ |
| Skeet | 12 | 2¾" | S & S | 26" | 42¾" | 14" | 1½" | 2½" | 2" | MB, F & M | 7¼ |
| Skeet | 20 | 3" | S & S | 26½" | 43¼" | 14" | 1½" | 2½" | 2" | MB, F & M | 6½ |
| Skeet | 28 | 2¾" | S & S | 28" | 42¾" | 14" | 1½" | 2½" | 2" | MB, F & M | 6⅜ |
| Skeet | 410 | 2½" | S & S | 28" | 42¾" | 14" | 1½" | 2½" | 2" | MB, F & M | 6⅜ |
| Skeet Set | 20 | 2¾" | S & S | 28" | 42¾" | 14" | 1½" | 2½" | 2" | MB, F & M | 6½ |
| Interchangeable | 28 | 2¾" | S & S | 28" | 42¾" | 14" | 1½" | 2½" | 2" | MB, F & M | 6½ |
| Double Barrels | 410 | 2½" | S & S | 28" | 42¾" | 14" | 1½" | 2½" | 2" | MB, F & M | 6½ |

MBF—Metal Bead Front; WB—White Bead; MB, F & M—Metal Bead Front and Middle; F & F—Full and Full; IC & M—Improved Cylinder and Modified; IM & F—Improved Modified and Full; M & F—Modified and Full; F—Full; S & S—Skeet and Skeet.

The Model 101 shotgun was followed by the Winchester Model 1200 shotgun.

# MODEL 1200 SLIDE ACTION
# SHOTGUN

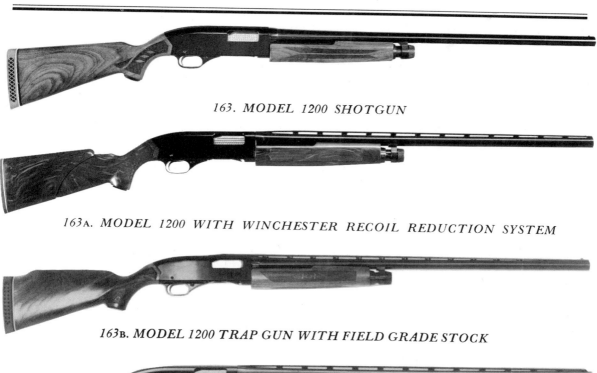

*163. MODEL 1200 SHOTGUN*

*163A. MODEL 1200 WITH WINCHESTER RECOIL REDUCTION SYSTEM*

*163B. MODEL 1200 TRAP GUN WITH FIELD GRADE STOCK*

*163C. MODEL 1200 WITH WINCHOKE*

*163D. WINCHOKE AND SPANNER WRENCH*

In line with the Winchester program of continued improvement in firearms, work was started to develop a slide action shotgun of modern design, utilizing the latest advancements in metallurgy.

The Winchester Model 1200 slide action shotgun, in Standard Grade, was introduced in 1964. This all-new gun has a rifle-type, head-locking, rotating bolt with four lugs that lock into the barrel extension. This new design eliminates stress and strain to the gun's receiver during firing.

## GENERAL SPECIFICATIONS OF THE M/1200 SLIDE ACTION SHOTGUN

TYPE
: 5-shot, slide action shotgun. Front locking rotating bolt is enhanced with engine turning.

STYLES
: Field Gun, plain barrel.
Field Gun, ventilated rib.
Magnum Field Gun, plain barrel.
Magnum Field Gun, ventilated rib.
Deer Gun, rifle type sights.
Trap Gun, regular comb, ventilated rib, deluxe checkering.
Trap Gun, Monte Carlo comb, ventilated rib, deluxe checkering.
Skeet Gun, ventilated rib, deluxe checkering.

BARRELS
: 12 gauge: 30-inch, full choke; 28-inch, full or modified choke; 26-inch, improved cylinder or skeet bore; 22-inch, special bore for Deer Gun. 30-inch, full choke, designed to handle both 3-inch magnum and all 2¾-inch shells interchangeably in Magnum Field Gun (added in 1966).
16 gauge: 28-inch, full or modified choke; 26-inch, improved cylinder choke.
20 gauge: 28-inch full or modified choke; 26-inch, improved cylinder or skeet bore. 28-inch, full choke, designed to handle both 3-inch magnum and all 2¾-inch shells interchangeably in Magnum Field Gun. Barrels within a gauge are interchangeable, excepting 3-inch magnums.

MAGAZINE
: 4 shells, plus one in the chamber. (Factory installed removable plug limits magazine capacity to two shells.)

| | |
|---|---|
| RECEIVER | Rust proof, high strength aluminum alloy. Direct unloading from magazine. |
| STOCKS | Checkered American walnut, fluted comb, pistol grip and Winchester recoil pad. Trap and Skeet Guns have deluxe checkering. |
| SAFETY | Positive cross lock. Located in upper front end of trigger guard. |
| SIGHTS | Field Guns, metal bead front; Trap and Skeet Guns, metal bead middle and red bead front; Deer Gun, rifle type front and rear. |
| WEIGHTS | Field Gun—6¼ to 7 lbs., depending on gauge and barrel length. |
| | Field Gun, ventilated rib—6½ to 7¼ lbs., depending on gauge and barrel length. |
| | Magnum Field Gun, 12 gauge—about 7¾ lbs.; 20 gauge—about 7⅜ lbs. |
| | Magnum Field Gun, ventilated rib, 12 gauge—about 7⅞ lbs.; 20 gauge—about 7⅝ lbs. |
| | Deer Gun—about 6½ lbs. |
| | Trap Gun, 12 gauge only, regular stock—about 8¼ lbs. |
| | Trap Gun, 12 gauge only, Monte Carlo comb—about 8¼ lbs. |
| | Skeet Gun, 12 gauge—about 7½ lbs.; 20 gauge—about 7¼ lbs. |
| SERIAL NUMBERS | Serially numbered from 100,000 up, located on bottom front of receiver. As of January 23, 1975, serial number 909,489 had been reached. |

## Special Notes

Model 1200 shotguns in 12 gauge Field, Magnum Field, Trap and Skeet models were made available in 1966 with the new Winchester Recoil Reduction System which reduces apparent recoil by 78 per cent. This system was last listed in the 1970 catalog.

The Model 1200 Deer Gun was discontinued in 1974. A Model 1200 Riot Gun was dropped the same year.

In 1969, the company introduced the Winchoke, a quickly interchangeable choke system, for both the Model 1200 and the Model 1400 shotguns. The Winchoke was a variation of the Versalite choke pioneered by the company for its revolutionary glass-barreled Model 59 autoloading shotgun back in 1961. Available in improved cylinder, modified and full chokes, the Winchoke tubes screw into the specially adapted gun muzzle and are tightened with the spanner wrench provided. The tubes present no unsightly bulge or obstruction in the line of sight but are contained with the barrel itself. The Winchoke system was expanded to both the Model 1200 and 1400 trap lines in 1971, so that the trap shooter had the versatility and flexibility of three shotguns in one.

The 16 gauge was dropped from the line in 1973. Both trap and skeet models were dropped from the line in 1974, and since that date only 12 and 20 gauge guns (available with either 28-inch plain or ventilated ribs and Winchoke as an option) have been listed. Both gauges are available in magnum versions with 3-inch chambers.

# MODEL 1400 AUTOMATIC SHOTGUN

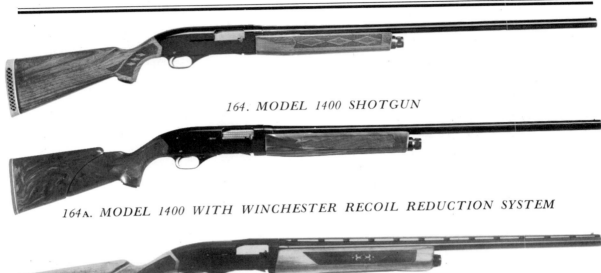

*164. MODEL 1400 SHOTGUN*

*164A. MODEL 1400 WITH WINCHESTER RECOIL REDUCTION SYSTEM*

*164B. MODEL 1400 MARK II*

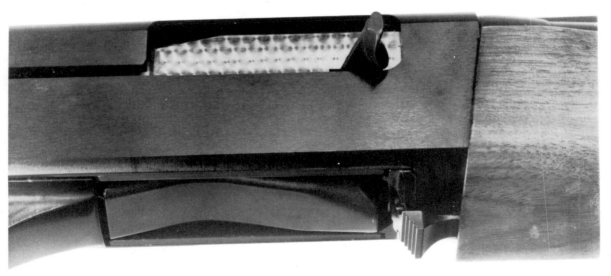

*164C. MODEL 1400 MARK II LOADING SYSTEM*

## 164D. MODEL 1400 MARK II, LEFT-HANDED VERSION

The Winchester Model 1400 Automatic (self-loading) shotgun was announced with the Model 1200 Slide Action shotgun in 1964. It has similar rotating, bolt-head, locking lugs, but the mechanism is gas operated to extract, eject, and chamber a fresh shell automatically when the gun is fired.

## GENERAL SPECIFICATIONS OF THE M/1400 AUTOMATIC SHOTGUN

| | |
|---|---|
| TYPE | 3-shot, gas operated shotgun. Self compensation valve in the gas chamber automatically adjusts for standard or magnum loads. |
| STYLES | Field Gun, plain barrel. |
| | Field Gun, ventilated rib. |
| | Deer Gun, rifle type sights. |
| | Trap Gun, regular stock, ventilated rib, deluxe checkering. |
| | Trap Gun, Monte Carlo comb, ventilated rib, deluxe checkering. |
| | Skeet Gun, ventilated rib, deluxe checkering. |
| BARRELS | 12 gauge: 30-inch, full choke; 28-inch, full or modified choke; 26-inch, improved cylinder or skeet bore; 22-inch, special bore for Deer Gun. |
| | 16 gauge: 28-inch, full or modified choke; 26-inch, improved cylinder choke. |
| | 20 gauge: 28-inch, full or modified choke; 26-inch, improved cylinder or skeet bore. |
| | Barrels within a gauge are interchangeable. |
| MAGAZINE | Two 2¾-inch shells, plus one in the chamber. |
| RECEIVER | Rust proof, high strength aluminum alloy. Direct unloading from magazine. |
| STOCKS | Checkered American walnut, fluted comb, pistol grip and Winchester recoil pad. Trap and Skeet Guns have deluxe checkering. |
| SAFETY | Positive cross lock, located in upper front of trigger guard. |
| SIGHTS | Field Guns, metal bead front; Trap and Skeet Guns, metal bead middle and red bead front. Deer Gun, rifle type front and rear. |
| WEIGHT | Field Gun—6¼ to 7 lbs., depending on gauge and barrel length. |
| | Field Gun, ventilated rib—6½ to 7¼ lbs., depending on gauge and barrel length. |
| | Deer Gun—about 6½ lbs. |
| | Trap Gun, 12 gauge only, regular stock—about 8¼ lbs. |
| | Trap Gun, 12 gauge only, Monte Carlo comb—about 8¼ lbs. |
| | Skeet Gun, 12 gauge—about 7½ lbs.; 20 gauge—about 7¼ lbs. |
| SERIAL NUMBERS | Serially numbered from 100,000 up, located on bottom front of receiver. As of January 23, 1975, serial number 726,790 had been reached. |

The Model 1400 shotgun was followed by the Wyoming Diamond Jubilee Commemorative Carbine in 1964.

### Special Note

Model 1400 shotguns in 12 gauge Field, Trap and Skeet models were made available in 1966 with the new Winchester Recoil Reduction System which reduces apparent recoil by 78 per cent. This Recoil Reduction System was last listed in the 1970 catalog.

In 1968, Winchester took heed of the widespread resistance of sportsmen-consumers to the loading system of its Model 1400 semi-automatic shotgun and introduced a new push-button carrier release designed to speed and simplify the loading and unloading process. Situated on the bottom of the receiver at the base of the forearm, the new carrier release is serrated to provide positive non-slip thumbing. With the gun's action open, the first shell dropped in can be chambered quickly at a touch of the release button as opposed to the old method which required the shooter to stick his finger into the magazine hole to close the action. The new version was designated the Model 1400 Mark II.

In the same year, Winchester also brought out left-handed versions in 12 gauge field, skeet and trap Model 1400 Mark II shotguns. As noted in the immediately previous section on the Model 1200 slide action shotgun, the Winchoke, a quickly interchangeable choke system, was introduced for the Model 1400 as well. Please refer to that section for further details and illustration of the Winchoke. The Winchoke was available on 12, 16 and 20 gauge field guns and on the left-handed 12 gauge field gun.

In 1970, trap and skeet guns were offered with field grade stocks at reduced prices.

In 1971, the Winchoke system was extended to the Model 1400 Trap Gun with Monte Carlo stock. The left-handed models were last listed in 1972 and dropped for 1973. The 16 gauge Model 1400 line was also dropped for 1973. The Deer Gun was dropped in 1974.

As of 1974 and to date (1975), the Model 1400 is carried in 12 and 20 gauge field grade only in either 28-inch plain or ventilated rib barreled versions (with Winchoke option). The trap and skeet grades were dropped from the catalog in 1974.

# WYOMING DIAMOND JUBILEE COMMEMORATIVE CARBINE (1964)
*See Commemorative section*

# CENTENNIAL '66 CARBINE AND RIFLE

*See Commemorative section*

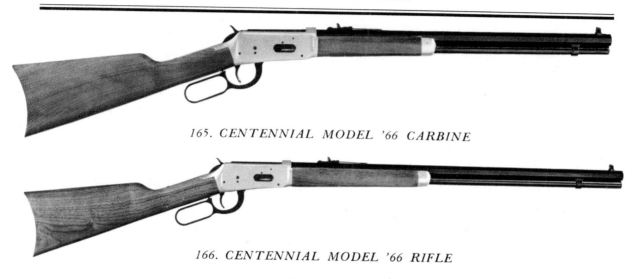

*165. CENTENNIAL MODEL '66 CARBINE*

*166. CENTENNIAL MODEL '66 RIFLE*

# NEBRASKA CENTENNIAL CARBINE (1966)

*See Commemorative section*

# MODEL 670 BOLT ACTION
# CARBINE AND RIFLE

*167. MODEL 670 RIFLE*

The Winchester Model 670 was introduced in 1966 with three versions available—Carbine, Sporting Rifle, and Magnum Sporting Rifle—and in seven center fire calibers. The M/670 was designed to fill the needs of outdoorsmen seeking a dependable bolt action arm for hard day-in-day-out use, combining accuracy with style and economy. It features: recessed bolt face to completely enclose and support the cartridge head for ultimate safety; free-floating barrel for best accuracy; wide serrated trigger with greater finger bearing surface for improved trigger control. Red indicator shows when the rifle is cocked. Two-position safety locks the firing pin when in the safe (rear) position, but not the bolt, to allow safe removal of cartridges from the magazine. The safety is off when pushed fully forward.

## GENERAL SPECIFICATIONS OF THE M/670

| | |
|---|---|
| TYPE | Bolt action repeating rifle, non-detachable box magazine. |
| STYLES | Sporting Rifle. |
| | Carbine. |
| BARRELS | Sporting Rifle, 22-inch, round. |
| | Magnum Rifle, 24-inch, round. |
| | Carbine, 19-inch, round. |
| MAGAZINE CAPACITY | Sporting Rifle and Carbine, 4 cartridges, plus one in the chamber. |
| | Magnum Rifle, 3 cartridges, plus one in the chamber. |
| CHAMBERS | Sporting Rifle, 225, 243, 270, and 308 Winchester, and 30-06 Springfield. |
| | Magnum Rifle, 264 and 300 Winchester Magnum; 7mm Remington Magnum. |
| | Carbine, 243 Winchester, 270 Winchester, and 30-06 Springfield. |
| STOCK | High-comb Monte Carlo for precise aiming with scope or iron sights. Checkering at pistol grip and forearm, walnut finish. |
| SIGHTS | Scope-high, open, adjustable rear, and bead on ramp front. |
| | Both detach easily from barrel for scope mounting. |
| WEIGHTS | Sporting Rifle—about 7 lbs. |
| | Magnum Rifle—about 7¼ lbs. |

Carbine—about 6¾ lbs.

SERIAL NUMBERS    M/670 rifles are serially numbered from 100,000 up, located at forward end of receiver on right side. As of January 20, 1975, serial number 196,440 had been reached.

The Model 670 rifle was announced simultaneously with the Winchester Centennial '66 center fire rifle and the Model 190, 22 caliber, rim fire rifle.

### *Special Notes*

In 1967, the 7mm Remington Magnum was added for the Model 670 Magnum sporting rifle line. By 1969, the 7mm Remington Magnum and 308 Winchester were no longer listed. In 1970, the Model 670 carbine was dropped and the Model 670 rifle was listed chambered for 243 and 270 Winchester and 30-06 Springfield only. In 1971 it was listed in 243 and 30-06 only.

Winchester announced a renovated Model 670 in 1972 that incorporated the following improvements: the same stock configuration as the redesigned 1972 Model 70 and a totally new checkering pattern on dark, solid American hardwood; for the first time, a cheek piece and Winchester's exclusive three-position Model 70-type safety; a rear sight leaf with white diamond.

The gun was not listed in 1974, but the 1975 catalog features the Model 670 equipped with a 4-power Weaver scope as a special package. Again, it is available in 243 Winchester and 30-06 Springfield only.

# MODEL 190 AUTOMATIC (SELF-LOADING) 22 RIM FIRE RIFLE AND CARBINE

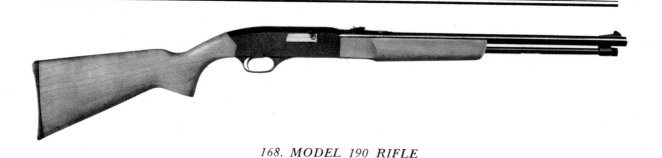

*168. MODEL 190 RIFLE*

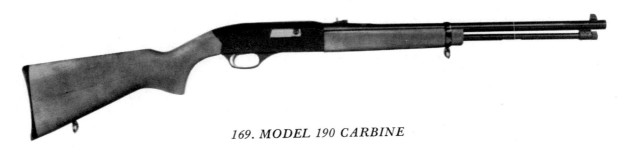

### 169. MODEL 190 CARBINE

The Model 190 Automatic 22 rim fire rifle was designed as a rugged, man-size sporter, somewhat similar to the Model 290—an economy model for the discriminating shooter.

## GENERAL SPECIFICATIONS OF THE M/190 AUTOMATIC 22 RIM FIRE RIFLE

| | |
|---|---|
| TYPE | Automatic (self-loading). |
| STYLE | Standard Rifle. |
| MAGAZINE | Tubular. Capacity, 21 Short, 17 Long, or 15 Long Rifle. |
| CHAMBER | 22 rim fire, Short, Long, and Long Rifle interchangeably. |
| STOCK | Walnut finish. |
| SIGHTS | Front, square post on streamlined ramp; rear, square notch. |
| RECEIVER | High-strength aluminum alloy, grooved for tip-off scope mounts. |
| SAFETY | Cross lock, located on front end of trigger guard. |
| WEIGHT | About 5 lbs. |
| SERIAL NUMBERS | M/190 rifles are serially numbered with the 200 Series, located on the bottom front of the receiver. |

### Special Note

In 1967, the company produced a carbine version of the Model 190 rifle. The Model 190 carbine was similar to the rifle version except it featured a 20½-inch barrel and a traditional Western-style barrel band with sling swivels. It was dropped from the 1973 catalog. The Model 190 has not been listed in 22 Short since 1970. Since 1973, the Model 190 rifle has been listed as available with a 4-power Weaver scope only.

# MODEL 121 SINGLE SHOT
# BOLT ACTION 22 RIM FIRE RIFLE

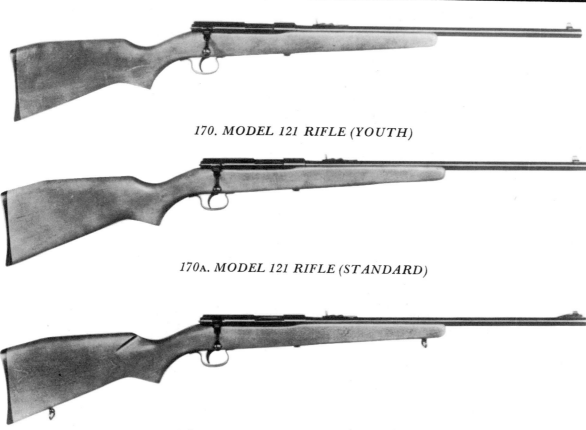

*170. MODEL 121 RIFLE (YOUTH)*

*170A. MODEL 121 RIFLE (STANDARD)*

*170B. MODEL 121 RIFLE (DELUXE)*

The Model 121 Single Shot 22 rim fire rifle was designed to provide beginning and young shooters with a bolt action system that would provide a safe, efficient and reliable first firearm. In addition to handling one cartridge at a time, the rifle has a safety catch that automatically engages itself in the "safe" position each time the bolt handle is raised. The rifle cannot be discharged after each loading until the safety has been manually depressed. Three different versions of the basic model were available. The Youth model offers a short butt stock for the younger shooter; the Standard has a stock of conventional length for the average man-sized youngster or adult. In addition, a third, Deluxe, version has a standard length stock with the extra features of a Monte Carlo, fluted comb and sling swivels. The Deluxe rifle also has a special trigger mechanism and a ramped bead post front sight. The Model 121, in all styles, handles 22 Short, Long or Long Rifle cartridges interchangeably. It was introduced in 1967 as part of a matched family of 22 rim fire rifles.

## GENERAL SPECIFICATIONS OF THE M/121 SINGLE SHOT BOLT ACTION 22 RIM FIRE RIFLE

| | |
|---|---|
| TYPE | Single Shot bolt action. |
| STYLE | Youth, Standard and Deluxe versions (Youth version 1¼ inches shorter). |
| MAGAZINE | None (one round in chamber maximum loading). |
| CHAMBER | 22 rim fire; Short, Long and Long Rifle interchangeably. |
| STOCK | Walnut finish American hardwood; one piece modified Monte Carlo. |
| SIGHTS | Bead-post front and open rear (Deluxe version has bead post front ramped and dovetailed; adjustable open rear sight). All M/121 rifles are grooved for telescopic sight mounts. |
| RECEIVER | Steel. |
| BARREL | Winchester Proof Steel, 20¾-inch, round, 1-in-16-inch twist. |
| WEIGHT | 5 lbs. |
| SAFETY | Engages automatically when bolt is lifted for loading. |
| SERIAL NUMBERS | The Model 121 rifles had no serial numbers. |

The Model 121 rim fire rifle was last listed in the 1972 catalog and was dropped from the line for 1973. A total of 72,561 were made.

The Model 121 was followed by the Model 131 repeating, clip loading, bolt action 22 rim fire rifle.

# MODEL 131 REPEATING (CLIP LOADING) BOLT ACTION 22 RIM FIRE RIFLE

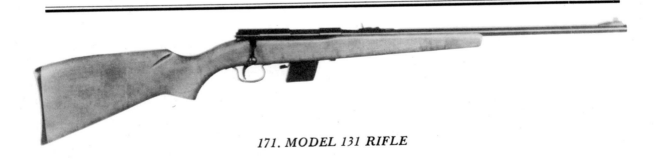

*171. MODEL 131 RIFLE*

The Model 131 repeating, clip loading, bolt action 22 rim fire rifle was introduced in 1967 simultaneously with the Model 121 single shot rifle. It was part of a contemplated family of 22 standard and magnum rim fire rifles the company planned to introduce in 1967. Essentially, the Model 131 rifle is a modified version of the Model 121 with a clip loading feature to make it a repeater. A companion 22 magnum rim fire rifle, the Model 135, was announced, but never produced.

## GENERAL SPECIFICATIONS OF THE M/131 REPEATING CLIP LOADING BOLT ACTION 22 RIM FIRE RIFLE

| | |
|---|---|
| TYPE | Repeating, clip loading, bolt action. |
| STYLE | Standard only. |
| MAGAZINE | Clip; capacity seven; Short, Long and Long Rifle interchangeably. |
| CHAMBER | 22 rim fire; Short, Long and Long Rifle interchangeably. |
| STOCK | Walnut finish American hardwood. |
| SIGHTS | Bead-post front and open rear. Receiver grooved for telescopic sights. |
| RECEIVER | Steel. |
| BARREL | Winchester Proof Steel, 20¾-inch, round, 1-in-16-inch twist. |
| WEIGHT | 5 lbs. |

The Model 131 rim fire rifle was last listed in the 1972 catalog and dropped from the line for 1973. A total of 16,371 were made. It was followed by the Model 141 repeating, tubular magazine, bolt action 22 rim fire rifle, which was announced simultaneously with the Model 121 and Model 131.

# MODEL 141 REPEATING (TUBULAR MAGAZINE) BOLT ACTION 22 RIM FIRE RIFLE

*172. MODEL 141 RIFLE*

The Model 141 repeating, tubular magazine, bolt action 22 rim fire rifle was introduced in 1967 simultaneously with the Model 121 and Model 131 rim fire rifles. It was also part of a contemplated family of 22 standard and magnum rim fire rifles the company planned to introduce in 1967. Essentially, the Model 141 is a modified version of the Model 121 with a tubular magazine in the butt stock to make it a repeater. A companion 22 magnum rim fire rifle, the Model 145, was announced but never produced.

## GENERAL SPECIFICATIONS OF THE M/141 REPEATING TUBULAR MAGAZINE BOLT ACTION 22 RIM FIRE RIFLE

| | |
|---|---|
| TYPE | Repeating, tubular magazine, bolt action. |
| STYLE | Standard only. |
| MAGAZINE | Tubular; butt loading; 19 Shorts, 15 Longs or 13 Long Rifles. (Cartridges may be mixed interchangeably with varying capacity.) |
| CHAMBER | 22 rim fire; Short, Long and Long Rifle interchangeably. |
| STOCK | Walnut finish American hardwood. |
| SIGHTS | Bead-post front and open rear. Receiver grooved for telescopic sights. |
| RECEIVER | Steel. |
| BARREL | Winchester Proof Steel, 20¾-inch, round, 1-in-16-inch twist. |
| WEIGHT | 5 lbs. |

The Model 141 rim fire rifle was last listed in the 1972 catalog and dropped from the line in 1973. A total of 16,592 were made. The Models 121, 131 and 141 were followed in 1967 by the introduction of the Model 150 lever action, repeating, 22 rim fire rifle.

# MODEL 150 REPEATING
# LEVER ACTION 22 RIM FIRE CARBINE

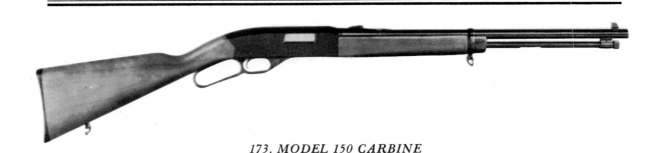

*173. MODEL 150 CARBINE*

The Model 150 repeating, lever action, 22 rim fire carbine was introduced in 1967 and is a modification of the standard lever action Model 250 rifle. It was designed for those shooters who like firearms with a typically western straight grip stock and styling. It also came equipped with sling swivels, which were not standard on the Model 250.

GENERAL SPECIFICATIONS OF THE M/150 REPEATING LEVER ACTION 22 RIM FIRE CARBINE

| | |
|---|---|
| TYPE | Repeating, lever action. |
| STYLE | Standard carbine only. |
| MAGAZINE | Tubular magazine below barrel; 21 Shorts, 17 Longs or 15 Long Rifles (cartridges may be mixed interchangeably with varying capacity). |
| CHAMBER | 22 rim fire, Short, Long and Long Rifle interchangeably. |
| STOCK | Walnut finish American hardwood. |
| SIGHTS | Adjustable rear; bead-post front. Receiver grooved for telescopic sights. |
| RECEIVER | High strength aluminum alloy. |
| SAFETY | Cross bolt safety in front of trigger guard. |
| BARREL | Winchester Proof Steel, 20½-inch, round. |
| SERIAL NUMBER | Located on bottom front of receiver. |
| WEIGHT | About 5 lbs. |

The Model 150 rim fire carbine was last listed in the 1973 catalog and dropped from the line in 1974. A total of 47,436 were made. The Model 150 was followed by the Canadian '67 Centennial Commemorative Carbine and Rifle.

# CANADIAN '67 CENTENNIAL CARBINE AND RIFLE (1967)

*See Commemorative section*

# ALASKA PURCHASE CENTENNIAL COMMEMORATIVE CARBINE (1967)

*See Commemorative section*

# ILLINOIS SESQUICENTENNIAL CARBINE (1968)

*See Commemorative section*

# BUFFALO BILL CARBINE AND RIFLE (1968)

*See Commemorative section*

## WEAVER ACQUISITION

"NEW YORK, March 28, 1968 — Olin Mathieson Chemical Corporation will acquire W. R. Weaver Company, El Paso, Tex., the world's largest producer of telescopic sights for firearms, under terms of an agreement reached between the two companies today. The announcement was made by Gordon Grand, president of Olin and William R. Weaver, president and founder of Weaver."

# MODEL 370 SHOTGUN

*174. MODEL 370 SHOTGUN*

The Model 370 single shot shotgun was introduced by the company in 1968 as a replacement for the old Model 37, which had been dropped from the line in 1964. The Model 370 is a single barrel, break-open type, single shot shotgun with an automatic ejector. The gun's traditional exposed hammer, serrated for positive thumbing, has a rebound safety position. It was produced in Winchester's Canadian plant in Cobourg, Ontario, and is similar to the old Cooey single shot shotgun famous throughout the Dominion for years.

## GENERAL SPECIFICATIONS OF THE M/370 SINGLE SHOT SHOTGUN

| | |
|---|---|
| TYPE | Single shot, hammer, breakdown gun. (Note: The action release lever swings to either side for right- or left-hand shooting convenience.) |
| GAUGE AND CHAMBER | 12 gauge, 3-inch chamber. |
| | 16 gauge, 2¾-inch chamber. |
| | 20 gauge, 3-inch chamber. |
| | 28 gauge, 2¾-inch chamber. |
| | .410 bore, 3-inch chamber. |
| BARREL | 12 gauge, 30-, 32- or 36-inch. |
| | 16 gauge, 30- or 32-inch. |
| | 20 gauge, 28-inch (except Youth Model, 26-inch). |
| | 28 gauge, 28-inch. |
| | .410 bore, 26-inch. |
| CHOKE | All barrels full choke only. (Exception: A Youth Model was introduced in 1969 that offered a 20 gauge with improved modified choke.) |
| SIGHTS | Brass bead front sight only. |
| EJECTOR | Automatic. |
| STOCK | Walnut finish, American hardwood. Pistol grip. Stock and forearm. Black, non-skid butt plate. |
| WEIGHT | 12, 16, 20 and 28 gauges, about 6 lbs.; .410 bore, 5 lbs. |

The Model 370 was also brought out in a special Youth Model in 1969 in both 20 gauge and .410 bore, with 26-inch barrels and with a 12½-inch pull from trigger to butt. The stock also featured a rubber recoil pad rather than the standard butt plate. The Model 370 was last listed in 1972 and dropped from the line in 1973. A total of 221,578 were made. The Model 370 was followed by the Golden Spike and Theodore Roosevelt Commemorative Models in 1969.

# GOLDEN SPIKE CARBINE (1969)

*See Commemorative section*

# THEODORE ROOSEVELT CARBINE AND RIFLE (1969)

*See Commemorative section*

# MODEL 770 BOLT ACTION RIFLE

*175. MODEL 770 BOLT ACTION RIFLE*

The Model 770 Bolt Action Rifle was introduced in 1969 in both standard and magnum sporting rifles, and in nine calibers. Designed for sportsmen who wanted a bolt action rifle with the features long associated with the Model 70, but at an economical price, the Model 770 was planned to fill a gap somewhere between the popular, higher priced Model 70 and the Model 670, a basic and inexpensive bolt action rifle marketed by Winchester from 1964.

GENERAL SPECIFICATIONS OF THE MODEL 770 BOLT ACTION SPORTING RIFLE

| | |
|---|---|
| TYPE | Light weight, bolt action, center fire, repeating rifle. |
| STYLES | Standard and Magnum Sporting Rifles. |
| BARRELS | Standard, 22-inch, round; Magnum, 24-inch, round. |
| MAGAZINE | Non-detachable box magazine. |
| | Capacity — four cartridges in all Standard calibers. |
| | — three cartridges in Magnum calibers. |
| | *Exception: In 1969, the 222 Remington rifles took three cartridges only; in 1970, this model was modified to take four cartridges as well. |
| CHAMBERS | Standard, 222 Remington, 22-250 Remington, 243 and 270 Winchester, 30-06 Springfield, 308 Winchester. |
| | Magnum, 264 Winchester Magnum, 7mm Remington Magnum, 300 Winchester Magnum. |
| SAFETY | Three position safety. Red cocking lever. |
| SIGHTS | Adjustable open rear and bead front on ramp. |
| STOCK | Walnut stock with Monte Carlo. Checkered undercut cheek piece. Pistol grip with cap. Composition butt plate on Standard models; rubber recoil pads on Magnum rifles. |
| WEIGHT | 7⅛ lbs. (7¼ lbs. for 300 Magnum version). |
| SERIAL NUMBER | Located on front of receiver on right side. |

The Model 770 was last listed in 1971 and dropped from the line in 1972. A total of 20,938 were manufactured.

The Model 770 was followed by the Cowboy Commemorative Carbine.

# COWBOY COMMEMORATIVE CARBINE (1970)
*See Commemorative section*

# LONE STAR COMMEMORATIVE CARBINE AND RIFLE (1970)

*See Commemorative section*

# WINCHESTER AIR GUNS (1970)
### Models   363, 416, 422, 423, 425, 427, 435, and 450

*See section on Winchester Air Guns*

# NATIONAL RIFLE ASSOCIATION CENTENNIAL MUSKET AND RIFLE (1971)

*See Commemorative section*

# MODEL 310 SINGLE SHOT
# BOLT ACTION 22 RIM FIRE RIFLE

*176. MODEL 310 RIFLE*

The Model 310 Single Shot bolt action 22 rim fire rifle was introduced in 1971. Designed as a rim fire cosmetic copy of the famous Model 70 bolt action center fire sporting rifle, the Model 310 featured a streamlined bolt action styling associated with more expensive big game rifles: a satin-finished American walnut stock with Monte Carlo and fluted combs combined with a checkered pistol grip and forearm. The Model 310 incorporated an excellent action designed and tested in Australia before introduction in the United States.

## GENERAL SPECIFICATIONS OF THE MODEL 310 SINGLE SHOT BOLT ACTION 22 RIM FIRE RIFLE

| | |
|---|---|
| TYPE | Single shot bolt action. |
| STYLE | Standard only (no Youth or Deluxe versions). Overall length, 39½ inches. |
| MAGAZINE | None (one round in chamber maximum loading). |
| CHAMBER | 22 rim fire: Short, Long and Long Rifle interchangeably. |
| STOCK | One piece, satin-finished American walnut; Monte Carlo; checkered pistol grip and forearm. Sling swivels. 13½-inch pull. |
| SIGHTS | Ramped bead-post front; adjustable open rear. Receiver grooved for telescopic sights and drilled and tapped for optional micrometer rear sights. |
| RECEIVER | Steel. |
| BARREL | Winchester Proof Steel, 22-inch, round. |
| WEIGHT | Approximately 5⅝ lbs. |
| SAFETY | Positive safety lever on right side of receiver. Quick release. |
| SERIAL NUMBER | Located on right side of receiver. |

The Model 310 rim fire rifle was last listed in the 1974 catalog and was dropped from the line in 1975. A total of 13,544 were manufactured.

The Model 310 was introduced simultaneously with the Model 320, which follows.

# MODEL 320 REPEATING (CLIP LOADING) BOLT ACTION 22 RIM FIRE RIFLE

*177. MODEL 320 RIFLE*

The Model 320 repeating, clip loading, bolt action 22 rim fire rifle was introduced in 1971 simultaneously with the Model 310 single shot rifle. Essentially, the Model 320 rifle is a modified version of the Model 310 with a clip loading feature to make it a repeater. A companion 22 Magnum rim fire rifle, the Model 325, was announced, but never produced.

## GENERAL SPECIFICATIONS OF THE MODEL 320 CLIP LOADING REPEATING 22 RIM FIRE RIFLE

| | |
|---|---|
| TYPE | Repeating, clip loading, bolt action. |
| STYLE | Standard only. |
| MAGAZINE | Clip; capacity five; Short, Long or Long Rifle interchangeably. Extra clips were available in both 5-shot and 10-shot capacity at additional cost. |
| CHAMBER | 22 rim fire; Short, Long and Long Rifle interchangeably. |
| STOCK | One piece, satin-finished American walnut; Monte Carlo; checkered pistol grip and forearm. Sling swivels. 13½-inch pull. |
| SIGHTS | Ramped bead-post front; adjustable open rear. Receiver grooved for telescopic sights and drilled and tapped for optional micrometer rear sights. |
| RECEIVER | Steel. |
| BARREL | Winchester Proof Steel, 22-inch, round. |
| WEIGHT | Approximately 5⅝ lbs. |
| SAFETY | Positive safety lever on right side of receiver. Quick release. |
| SERIAL NUMBER | Located on right side of receiver. |

The Model 320 repeating rim fire rifle was last listed in the 1974 catalog.

The Model 320 was followed by the Model 9422 lever action rim fire.

# MODEL 9422 REPEATING
# LEVER ACTION 22 RIM FIRE
# AND 22 MAGNUM RIM FIRE RIFLE

*178. MODEL 9422*

The Model 9422 Lever Action repeating rifle was introduced in both 22 rim fire and 22 Magnum rim fire versions in 1972. Designed in the image of the renowned Winchester Model 94 30-30 center fire deer rifle, the new rifle was brought out in response to the longstanding request of legions of Model 94 admirers. The gun represented a reaffirmed commitment on Winchester's part to a quality image. No expense was spared on design, quality control and production. It rapidly became one of the most popular Winchester rifles of this century.

## GENERAL SPECIFICATIONS OF THE MODEL 9422 LEVER ACTION RIM FIRE RIFLES

| | |
|---|---|
| TYPE | Repeating, lever action. |
| STYLE | Standard and Magnum. Carbines. |
| MAGAZINE | Tubular; capacity: Standard, 21 Shorts, 17 Longs or 15 Long Rifles; Magnum: 11 cartridges. |
| CHAMBER | 22 rim fire: Short, Long or Long Rifle interchangeably. 22 Magnum rim fire: Magnum only. |
| STOCK | Satin-finished, American walnut. Two piece. |
| SIGHTS | Front ramp, dovetail sight bead and hood; adjustable semi-buckhorn rear sight. Receivers grooved for telescopic mounts. (Note: The Model 9422 has side ejection and presents no hindrance to 'scopes.) |
| RECEIVER | Machined forged-steel receiver houses an all-steel action operated by an improved finger lever of forged steel. |
| BARREL | Winchester Proof Steel, 20½-inch, round. |
| WEIGHT | Approximately 6¼ lbs. in both versions. |
| SAFETY | Half-cock traditional lever action type. |
| SERIAL NUMBER | Located on bottom of receiver toward forearm. |

A total of 173,837 Model 9422 lever action rifles of both types had been manufactured as of January 20, 1975.

The Model 9422 was followed by the Model 37A single shot shotgun.

[ 183 ]

# MODEL 37A SINGLE SHOT SHOTGUN

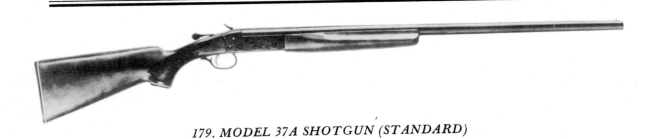

*179. MODEL 37A SHOTGUN (STANDARD)*

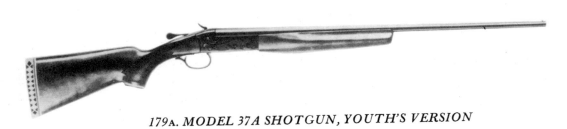

*179A. MODEL 37A SHOTGUN, YOUTH'S VERSION*

The Model 37A single shot shotgun was introduced by the company in 1973 as a replacement for the Model 370, which was last listed in the 1972 catalog. Essentially, the Model 37A is an upgraded version of the Model 370 and differs only in cosmetic features that were incorporated in the renovated model for consumer attraction. Those features include a roll-engraved receiver, a gold-plated trigger and a new checkering pattern on the pistol grip and the bottom of the forearm combined with white spacers between pistol grip cap and butt plate. The gun has a newly designed concave hammer spur for quick non-slip cocking.

## GENERAL SPECIFICATIONS OF THE M/37A SINGLE SHOT SHOTGUN

| | |
|---|---|
| TYPE | Single shot, hammer, breakdown gun. (Note: The action release lever swings to either side for right- or left-handed shooting convenience.) |
| STYLE | Standard and Youth models. |
| GAUGE AND CHAMBER | 12 gauge, 3-inch chamber. |
| | 16 gauge, 2¾-inch chamber. |
| | 20 gauge, 3-inch chamber. |
| | 28 gauge, 2¾-inch chamber. |
| | .410 bore, 3-inch chamber. |
| BARREL | 12 gauge, 30-, 32- or 36-inch. |
| | 16 gauge, 30-inch. |
| | 20 gauge, 28-inch (youth gun, 26-inch). |

|  | 28 gauge, 28-inch. |
|  | .410 bore, 26-inch. |
| CHOKE | All barrels full choke only on Standard models. The 20 gauge Youth gun has improved modified choke. |
| SIGHTS | Brass bead front sight only. |
| EJECTOR | Automatic. |
| STOCK | Walnut finish, American hardwood. Two piece. Pistol grip cap with white spacer. Butt plate with white spacer. Forearm grooved for hand hold. Checkering on pistol grip and bottom of forearm. Youth stock has 12½-inch pull. |
| WEIGHT | About 6 lbs. except for .410 bore, 5½ lbs. |

The Model 37A continues in the line in 1975. A total of 209,191 have been manufactured in Winchester's Canadian plant in Cobourg, Ontario.

The Model 37A was followed by the Texas Ranger Commemorative rifle.

---

# THE TEXAS RANGER COMMEMORATIVE RIFLE (1973)

*See Commemorative section*

---

# SUPER-X MODEL 1 AUTOLOADING SHOTGUN

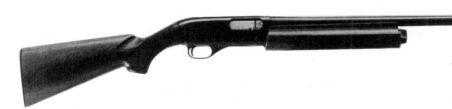

*180. SUPER-X MODEL 1 FIELD GUN*

*180A. SUPER-X MODEL 1 TRAP GUN*

*180B. SUPER-X MODEL 1 SKEET GUN*

The Super-X Model 1 Autoloading shotgun was introduced in 1974 after five years of extensive research and design development. It was designed to incorporate the reliability, durability and quality workmanship of the famous Winchester Model 12 pump gun in a semi-automatic shotgun. The Super-X Model 1 is a gas-operated repeater with all metal parts of machined steel matched to a barrel and barrel extension of the same manganese-chrome-moly steel used in the production of Model 12 barrels.

Machined from a solid block of alloy steel, the receiver houses a unique, three-piece, straight line bolt with rear lock up, designed to operate on a straight plane, level with the barrel. Since the bolt is always flush against the shell head when fired, the distortion that often results to the shell head with a swing-up type of bolt is eliminated.

The heart of the Super-X Model 1 is its newly engineered, self-compensating gas operation system. In lieu of the action bars common to most semi-automatic shotguns, the Super-X Model 1 employs a machined steel rod of short-stroke design to operate its action. This patented design, which effectively utilizes more of the gas energy to work the gun's action, substantially reduces recoil in the new autoloader. Entirely self-compensating, the gas system makes any adjustment for either high or low base loads unnecessary.

Speedy and simplified loading is also one of the significant features of the Super-X Model 1, which has a five-round capacity with factory-installed plug removed and one round in the chamber. After loading a round in the chamber, the magazine can be filled by depressing the carrier release button and inserting shells through the bottom of the receiver. When the steel carrier is pushed upward into the receiver, and the carrier release button is released, the carrier will lock in the upward position for ease of loading. Then, a touch of the release button will drop the carrier down into the locked position, where it remains until the gun is fired. The carrier then unlocks, feeds another shell and locks again, thus assuring more positive feeding and less possibility of jamming.

The gun's one-piece trigger guard, milled from a solid forging of the same steel alloy as the receiver, contains a cross-bolt safety conveniently located up front for fast, easy access. The safety is reversible for left-handed shooters.

Both the stock and forearm are of high-grade American walnut, with real cut checkering that is functional as well as ornamental. The rich, dark finish of the wood is still another feature of the Super-X Model 1 preferred by a majority of the shooters who contributed to the gun's design.

The new Winchester Super-X Model 1 is available initially in 12 gauge, with 2¾-inch chamber, in three different versions — Field, Trap and Skeet guns.

## GENERAL SPECIFICATIONS OF THE SUPER-X MODEL 1 AUTOLOADING SHOTGUN

| | |
|---|---|
| TYPE | Gas-operated, autoloading shotgun. |
| STYLE | Field, Trap and Skeet models. |
| GAUGE | 12 gauge only as of 1975. |
| CHAMBER | 2¾-inch only as of 1975. |
| BARREL | Field: 26-, 28- and 30-inch, plain or ventilated rib. |
| | Trap: 30-inch, ventilated rib. |
| | Skeet: 26-inch, ventilated rib. |
| CHOKE | Field: Improved cylinder (26-inch); modified or full (28-inch); full (30-inch). |
| | Trap: Modified or full in either Monte Carlo or regular versions. |
| | Skeet: Skeet. |
| SIGHTS | Field Plain: metal bead front only. |
| | Field, Trap and Skeet Ventilated Rib: metal bead front and middle. Deer gun has iron sights adapted for rifle-type aiming. |
| SAFETY | Cross-bolt shotgun type, reversible for left-handed shooters. |
| MAGAZINE | Tubular, under barrel. Capacity: four with one in chamber. |
| | (Note: All Super-X Model 1 shotguns have a factory-installed plug.) |
| STOCK | Satin-finished, American walnut. Cut checkering. Trap gun has black rubber recoil pad with white spacer. Field and skeet guns have traditional Winchester Repeating Arms butt plate. |
| SERIAL NUMBER | On left side of receiver. |

As of January 20, 1975, a total of 34,801 Super-X Model 1 shotguns had been manufactured.

The Super-X Model 1 shotgun was followed by the Model 490 Automatic 22 rim fire rifle.

# MODEL 490 REPEATING (AUTOLOADING) 22 RIM FIRE RIFLE

*181. MODEL 490 RIFLE*

The Model 430 repeating, Autoloading, 22 rim fire rifle was introduced by Winchester in its 1974 catalog. It was designed and engineered as a high-quality rim fire rifle with center fire styling in Winchester's Canadian plant in Cobourg, Ontario. Actual production and delivery of Model 490 rifles did not take place until 1975.

## GENERAL SPECIFICATIONS OF THE M/490 REPEATING AUTOLOADING 22 RIM FIRE RIFLE

| | |
|---|---|
| TYPE | Repeating, clip loading, semi-automatic. |
| STYLE | Standard only. |
| MAGAZINE | Clip (box) holds five cartridges. Ten and 15 shot clips also available. |
| CHAMBER | 22 Long Rifle only. |
| STOCK | Satin-finished American walnut. Cut checkering. |
| SIGHTS | Folding leaf sporting rear; hooded front on ramp. Receiver grooved for tip-off telescopic sight mounts. |
| SAFETY | Cross bolt. |
| RECEIVER | Steel. Blued steel cocking handle acts as open action lock. |
| BARREL | Winchester Proof Steel, 22-inch, round. |
| WEIGHT | 6 lbs. |

The Model 490 was the last firearm introduced by Winchester in its domestic United States market in 1975 and, hence, the final entry in this fourth edition of *The History of Winchester Firearms*. The last sections of this book will cover a number of items, however, including two commemoratives (one for Canada and one for other International markets) and two double barrel Winchesters produced in Spain for areas outside of the United States — all introduced and produced in 1975.

# WINCHESTER PRECISION
# AIR RIFLES AND PISTOLS

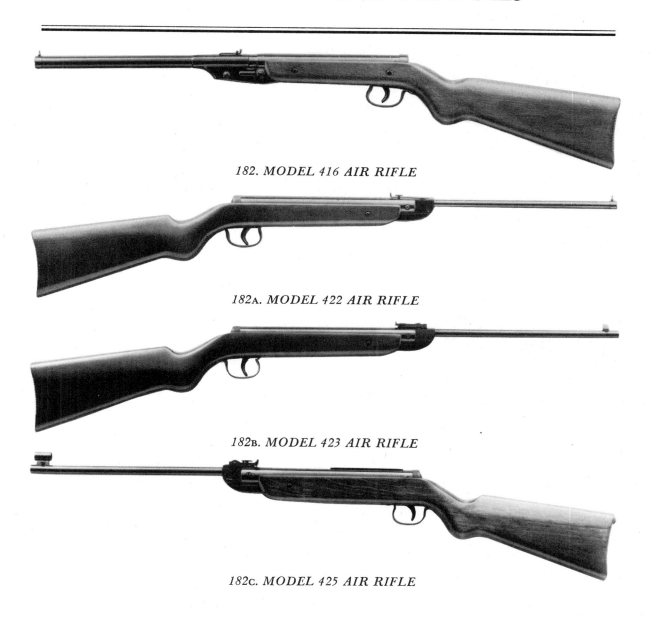

*182. MODEL 416 AIR RIFLE*

*182A. MODEL 422 AIR RIFLE*

*182B. MODEL 423 AIR RIFLE*

*182C. MODEL 425 AIR RIFLE*

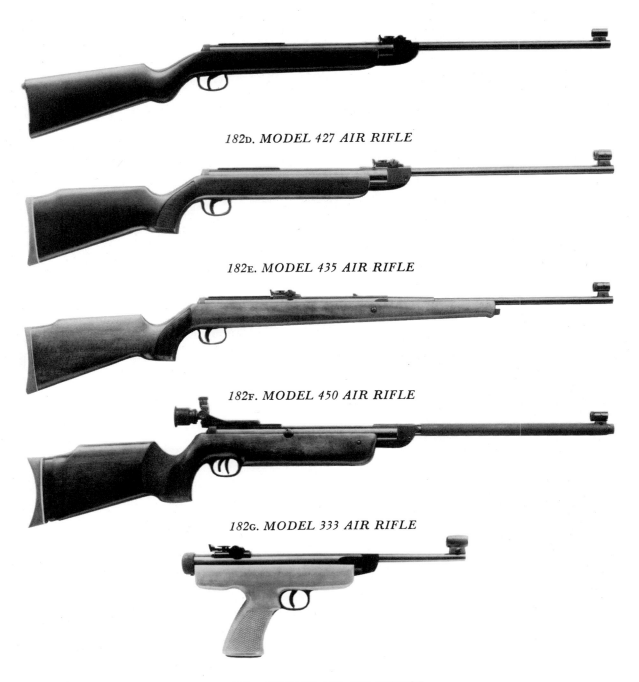

*182d. MODEL 427 AIR RIFLE*

*182e. MODEL 435 AIR RIFLE*

*182f. MODEL 450 AIR RIFLE*

*182g. MODEL 333 AIR RIFLE*

*182h. MODEL 353 AIR PISTOL*

*1821. MODEL 363 AIR PISTOL*

*General Background*

In a significant innovation in its product line, the Winchester-Western Division of the then Olin Mathieson Chemical Corporation announced the introduction in 1969 of a whole new series of Winchester Precision Air Rifles and Pistols.

Designed to fill a longstanding void between powder-burning firearms and BB guns, the new line, comprising 10 different models, included eight rifles and two pistols, all of single-shot type, scientifically engineered and precision built for long-lasting reliability, exceptional power and optimum accuracy.

Winchester cited the absence of both recoil and noise — the two most common deterrents to would-be shooters — as appealing and definitely significant attributes of the air gun. Additionally, because the air gun lends itself to safe, convenient and practicable indoor or backyard target range use, it makes an ideal instrument by which to encourage recreational shooting as an increasingly popular family-oriented pastime.

Toward this goal, the new line of Winchester Precision Air Rifles and Pistols encompassed the broadest possible range of price, preference and utility. From the Model 416 rifle, with an initial suggested list price of $15.95, right up to the Model 333 rifle, which retailed in 1969 for $169.95, there was a shoulder gun or pistol to accommodate the needs and tastes of every shooter, beginner or expert, youth or adult.

The new line incorporated numerous features seldom found in air guns. With the exception of the Model 416, all of the new guns were fitted with rifled steel barrels for ultimate precision accuracy. Double pull type triggers, adjustable rear sights and stocks designed for functional ruggedness as well as esthetic appearance were standard features of every model.

Six of the eight rifles were offered in the popular 177 caliber; the remaining two were chambered in the larger 22 caliber. Both were well-suited for small game or target shooting. One pistol, the Model 363, came in 177 caliber and the other, the Model 353, was offered in choice of 177 or 22 calibers.

All of the Winchester Precision Air Rifles and Pistols were of the single-shot type and, with one exception, had a hinged break-open barrel. Compressed air, generated by an easy-cocking but powerful mainspring, is the power source for the Winchester Precision Air Rifles and Pistols. The cocking of most models is accomplished simply by breaking open the barrel and applying gentle downward pressure to engage the trigger mechanism. One rifle, the Model 450, has a special short-stroke lever built into the bottom of its forearm to effect the cocking operation.

Although Winchester Precision Air Rifles and Pistols will adequately handle standard quality lead pellets, consistent maximum accuracy could always be ensured with Winchester Regular or Match Pellets. Precise manufacturing and high quality control standards guarantee the requisite uniformity of size and weight of these pellets, designed expressly for use in Winchester Precision Air guns.

Manufactured in West Germany, to exacting Winchester specifications, the line of Winchester Precision Air Rifles and Pistols was last listed in the 1974 catalog and dropped in 1975. A total of 19,259 were made through 1973.

## I. GENERAL SPECIFICATIONS OF THE WINCHESTER PRECISION AIR RIFLES

The shoulder guns available ran the full gamut from the lightweight, modestly priced Model 416, designed for the youthful beginner, to the hefty, competition-weight Model 333, scientifically engineered for the sophisticated demands of the most serious competitive target shooter.

Leading off the eight different rifles in the line was the Model 416. The Winchester Model 416 Precision Air Rifle is of appropriate weight (2¾ pounds) and overall length (33 inches) to fit the youthful physique. Its hinged break-open barrel, which fires the popular 177 caliber pellet, requires only gentle downward pressure to cock. It is equipped with bead-post front and adjustable rear sights, as well as double pull type trigger.

The Model 422 constituted a step up for the older child or the adult novice. With an overall length of 36 inches and a comfortable weight of 3¾ pounds, the Model 422 has a hinged barrel of rifled steel, bored for the 177 caliber pellet. A bead-post front and adjustable screw rear sight and double pull type trigger combine to give reliable accuracy at medium ranges.

Third in the new line was the Model 423, a slightly heavier (4 pounds) 177 caliber air rifle of 36-inch overall length. Its hinged rifled steel barrel is fitted with ramped blade front and adjustable rear sights, and it has a double pull type trigger.

Designed for the more advanced shooter, the Model 425, a solid 5-pound rifle with overall length of 38 inches, was next. Bored for the higher density 22 caliber pellet, the hinged, break-open barrel of rifled steel easily cocks a powerful mainspring that delivers a muzzle velocity of 543 f.p.s. With adjustable double pull type trigger and hooded front and adjustable micrometer rear sights, the Model 425 also has a dovetail base to permit the mounting of a telescopic sight.

The Model 427 was another 22 caliber air rifle for both target shooter and small game hunter. With a weight of 6 pounds, this 42-inch long man-size shoulder gun features a hinged, rifled steel barrel that accurately speeds its 22 caliber pellets toward the target at 660 f.p.s. muzzle velocity. Moderate downward pressure cocks its extra-strong mainspring while its more sophisticated sights — an adjustable micrometer rear and a hooded front — combine with adjustable double pull trigger to produce consistently excellent accuracy. Provision for scope mounting is provided by a dovetail base.

The Model 435 was for the serious competitive target shooter. It has a precision rifled steel hinged barrel, with interchangeable front sight assembly and finely adjustable micrometer rear sight, and a dovetail base for the mounting of a scope. A stock equipped with cheek piece and rubber butt pad plus an adjustable double pull trigger and positive pistol grip checkering are standard features of this 177 caliber rifle.

Number seven in the new line of Winchester Precision Air Rifles was the Model 450, which most aptly might be termed the graduate shooter's air rifle. Its main features are a fixed barrel of rifled steel and a special cocking lever action. The latter, located under the forearm of the one-piece stock, cocks an extra powerful mainspring which delivers the gun's 177 caliber pellet at a muzzle velocity of 693 f.p.s. An interchangeable front sight assembly — including bead, blade, ring and pointed post sight inserts — was supplied with each gun. The Model 450 was fitted with finely adjustable micrometer rear sight for precise windage and elevation corrections. Both front and rear sights were fully detachable to give a more streamlined appearance when scope is mounted on the dovetail base. A cheek piece, finely checkered pistol grip and rubber butt plate were standard features.

Finally, at the top of the new air rifle line was the Model 333. Recoil — almost imperceptible in all of the new Winchester Precision Air Gun line — is totally eliminated in the Model 333, by means of the gun's specially designed double piston action. Throughout the entire shooting sequence, during and after let-off, the gun rests motionless in the shooter's hands. A two-stage trigger adjustable for weight, pre-travel and sear-off is also equipped with a safety that automatically locks the trigger when the barrel is open.

The gun's precision rifled steel hinged barrel came with a special corrosion-resistant glare-proof sleeve and the most sophisticated sighting equipment. Complementing the precision adjustable diopter rear sight and rubber eye piece was an interchangeable front sight assembly, complete with bead, blade, ring and pointed post inserts. The Model 333 has a Walnut match-type stock with cheek piece and Monte Carlo profile, as well as finely detailed hand checkering and stippling. A side locking lever with red indicator instantly shows that the gun is cocked, locked and ready for the next shot. Offered in 177 caliber, the competition quality air rifle provides superlative accuracy, measurable in one-hole shot groups.

### WINCHESTER PRECISION AIR RIFLE SPECIFICATIONS

| Rifle Model | Overall Length | Weight | Caliber | Barrel | Muzzle Velocity feet/sec. |
|---|---|---|---|---|---|
| 416 | 33" | 2¾ lbs. | 177 | Smooth | 363 |
| 422 | 36" | 3¾ lbs. | 177 | Rifled | 480 |
| 423 | 36" | 4 lbs. | 177 | Rifled | 480 |
| 425 | 38" | 5 lbs. | 22 | Rifled | 543 |
| 427 | 42" | 6 lbs. | 22 | Rifled | 660 |
| 435 | 44" | 6½ lbs. | 177 | Rifled | 693 |
| 450 | 44½" | 7¾ lbs. | 177 | Rifled | 693 |
| 333 | 43¼" | 9½ lbs. | 177 | Rifled | 576 |

## II. GENERAL SPECIFICATIONS OF THE WINCHESTER PRECISION AIR PISTOLS

Like their long gun counterparts, the Winchester Precision Air Pistols are virtually noise and recoil free, relying on compressed air generated by a powerful mainspring for their source of power.

The first of two air pistols available was the Model 353, a rugged and reliable pistol combining short-range power with consistently excellent accuracy. Gentle downward pressure on the gun's hinged break-open barrel cocks the mainspring for each shot. The precision rifled steel barrel is fitted with a detachable bead front sight with hood and a micrometer rear sight. Additional features include an adjustable double pull trigger and a match grade stock of ultra-tough plastic with detailed pistol grip checkering and stippled thumb rest. Available in a choice of two calibers, the popular 177 and the larger 22, the Model 353 scales slightly under 2¾ pounds and has an overall length of 16 inches.

The second pistol in the new line, the Model 363, was designed expressly for the top accuracy needs of the competitive target shooter. The specially engineered double piston action completely eliminates all trace of recoil and enables the gun to remain motionless in the shooter's hand during and after the shot. The hinged barrel of precision rifled steel is bored for the 177 caliber pellet. An adjustable double pull type trigger, interchangeable front sight assembly, with bead, blade, ring and pointed post inserts, plus a finely adjustable micrometer rear sight are standard features. Sure grip checkering and comfortable stippled two-inch thumb rest are provided on the pistol's match grade stock of super-strong composition plastic. With an overall length of 16 inches, the Model 363 weighs an even 3 pounds.

| Pistol Model | Overall Length | Weight | Caliber | Barrel | Muzzle Velocity feet/sec. |
|---|---|---|---|---|---|
| 353 | 16″ | 2 lbs., 11 oz. | 177 & 22 | Rifled | 378 |
| 363 | 16″ | 3 lbs. | 177 | Rifled | 378 |

*Special Note*

As previously mentioned, the Winchester Precision Air Rifles and Pistols were dropped from the line in 1975. As of this publication, stocks of most of the ten models offered are still in channels of distribution to dealer outlets and it is anticipated that those wishing to obtain one of these highly desirable little Winchesters should have little trouble in doing so for some time.

# WINCHESTER COMMEMORATIVES DOMESTIC ISSUES (UNITED STATES)

The Winchester Commemorative firearms program is perhaps unique in both company and industry history. While the commemorative firearm idea was undoubtedly pioneered by the Colt Patent Firearms Company some twenty-odd years ago, that primarily handgun firm had neither the market nor the capacity to make large quantities of any one model in any one year. Winchester had both the basic chassis — the Model 94 lever action repeating rifle — upon which to build a variety of individual commemorative versions and also the factory capacity to make very large quantities of that model. As it turned out — and as Winchester could barely believe — over 100,000 units of two different models were made and over half a million commemoratives of all types (domestic and foreign) were made from 1966 to 1975.

While Winchester had made a very limited commemorative edition (only 1,500 guns) for the Wyoming Jubilee Commission in 1964 on special order, the company had made no serious plans for any nationally promoted and distributed commemorative model. As the company's hundredth anniversary approached, however, some of Winchester's marketing people began thinking in terms of some sort of special firearm to mark that important date in 1966. First thoughts were directed toward an exact replica of the Model 1866, "The First Winchester," but production proved impractical in the domestic plant and the company was reluctant to have its centennial commemorative made overseas. It is interesting to note that a replica Model 1866 was made in Italy and marketed here in the United States to capitalize on Winchester's birthday celebration, but it in no way can be considered a genuine Winchester, let alone an authentic Winchester commemorative. The same applies to other pseudo-Winchesters — Model 1873s and others — that have been dumped on the domestic market over the years.

Winchester decided that it would take the existing Model 94 action — possibly the most famous sporting firearm ever made — and refine it into a Centennial '66 Model in two versions — a carbine and a full-length rifle. The company anticipated that they might sell 20,000 or so guns during the year. They were very mistaken. As soon as the word on the new Winchesters spread throughout the country after the national announcement in January 1966, the orders literally deluged the company and a complete reevaluation of the production and marketing capacity had to be made. By the end of the National Sporting Goods Show in February, it was obvious that Winchester's potential production for the calendar year was sold out and orders would have to be allocated. At this time, management made a crucial decision to limit the Model '66 production to only those guns that could be made during that centennial year and not to yield to the temptation to keep the factory machinery running into 1967 and beyond until all the orders were filled. No one will ever know how many Model '66 rifles and carbines could have been sold. An independent — and highly respected — market research firm surveyed the market at the time and came back with the astounding projection of more than a million units that might have been sold in the United States alone. It was the beginning of an unusual and exciting era in Winchester's history.

# WYOMING DIAMOND JUBILEE CARBINE

*183. WYOMING DIAMOND JUBILEE CARBINE, RIGHT SIDE (1964)*

*183A. WYOMING DIAMOND JUBILEE CARBINE, LEFT SIDE*

The Wyoming Diamond Jubilee Carbine is the first — and perhaps the rarest — Winchester commemorative firearm. Authorized by the Wyoming Jubilee Commission in 1964 on a royalty basis, the gun was distributed through Billings Hardware Company exclusively. Although the original suggested retail price was only $99.95, premium prices were paid for the Wyoming Commemorative from the first as only 1,500 firearms were authorized and sold. The Wyoming Diamond Jubilee Carbine commands prices in excess of $500 in the present market.

## GENERAL SPECIFICATIONS OF THE WYOMING DIAMOND JUBILEE CARBINE

| | |
|---|---|
| TYPE | Lever action, repeating, center fire Model 94. |
| STYLE | Carbine only. |
| CALIBER | 30-30 only. |
| MAGAZINE | Tubular, under barrel; capacity, 6 cartridges. Full length. Magazine plug blued. |
| BARREL | 20-inch, round. Barrel bands blued. |
| RECEIVER | Receiver case-hardened and roll-engraved. |
| MEDALLION | Gold-plated medallion embedded in stock. |
| SIGHTS | Hooded ramp front; open rear. |
| BUTT PLATE | Standard Model 94 type. |
| WEIGHT | Approximately 6¾ lbs. |
| SERIAL NUMBER | Numbered from 1 up, located on the front underside of the receiver. A total of 1,500 were made in the New Haven plant. |

# CENTENNIAL '66 CARBINE AND RIFLE

*184. CENTENNIAL MODEL '66 CARBINE (1966)*

*184A. CENTENNIAL MODEL '66 RIFLE*

The limited edition, Centennial '66, 30-30 Winchester caliber, in both carbine and rifle form, was announced in January 1966. It is a commemorative arm to celebrate the 100th anniversary of the Model 1866 repeating rifle, the first firearm to bear the Winchester name.

Although having the appearance of its history-making ancestors—blued octagon barrel, shiny golden receiver, crescent-shaped solid brass butt plate, and the traditional saddle ring which is decorative as well as functional—the Centennial '66 is a modern sporting rifle, combining the cumulative improvements made in the basic lever action design with modern metallurgy and modern production methods.

The Centennial '66 is decorated with commemorative inscriptions, "WINCHESTER CEN-TENNIAL '66" on the gold plated upper tang, and "A CENTURY OF LEADERSHIP 1866-1966" along the blued, octagon barrel.

## GENERAL SPECIFICATIONS OF THE CENTENNIAL '66

| | |
|---|---|
| TYPE | Lever action repeating rifle. |
| STYLES | Sporting Rifle and Carbine. |
| BARRELS | Sporting Rifle, 26-inch, octagon. |
| | Carbine, 20-inch, octagon. |
| MAGAZINE | Tubular, full length. |
| | Magazine capacities: |
| | Sporting Rifle, 8 cartridges, plus one in the chamber. |
| | Carbine, 6 cartridges, plus one in the chamber. |
| CHAMBER | 30-30 Winchester. |
| RECEIVER | Gold plated. |
| STOCKS | Rifle type butt, straight grip, stock and forearm of American walnut with high-gloss finish. |
| SIGHTS | Buckhorn rear, post front. |
| WEIGHTS | Sporting Rifle—about 8 lbs. |
| | Carbine—about 7 lbs. |
| SERIAL NUMBERS | Centennial '66s are serially numbered from 1 up, located on the underside of the receiver near the forward end. A total of 102,039 were made in New Haven. |

# NEBRASKA CENTENNIAL CARBINE

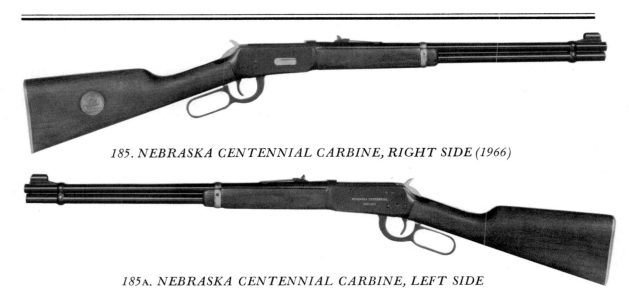

*185. NEBRASKA CENTENNIAL CARBINE, RIGHT SIDE (1966)*

*185A. NEBRASKA CENTENNIAL CARBINE, LEFT SIDE*

The Nebraska Centennial Carbine was authorized by the Nebraska Centennial Commission in 1966 and was distributed in that state only. Distribution was concurrent with the marketing of the Centennial '66 commemoratives nationally and very little attention — outside of Nebraska — was devoted to this limited edition firearm. Since only 2,500 were made, the "Nebraskan" is one of the more sought-after Winchester commemoratives.

## GENERAL SPECIFICATIONS OF THE NEBRASKA CENTENNIAL CARBINE

| | |
|---|---|
| TYPE | Lever action, repeating, center fire Model 94. |
| STYLE | Carbine only. |
| CALIBER | 30-30 only. |
| MAGAZINE | Tubular, under barrel; capacity, 6 cartridges. Magazine plug blued. **Full** length. |
| BARREL | 20-inch, round. One barrel band blued and one gold-plated. |
| RECEIVER | Blued. "NEBRASKA CENTENNIAL 1867-1967" engraved and gold-filled on left hand side. Hammer and spring cover gold-plated. |
| MEDALLION | Gold-plated medallion embedded in stock. |
| SIGHTS | Hooded ramp front; open rear. |
| BUTT PLATE | Gold-plated. |
| WEIGHT | Approximately 6¾ lbs. |
| SERIAL NUMBER | Numbered from 1 up, located on the front underside of the receiver. A total of 2,500 were made in the New Haven plant. |

# CANADIAN '67 CENTENNIAL
# RIFLE AND CARBINE

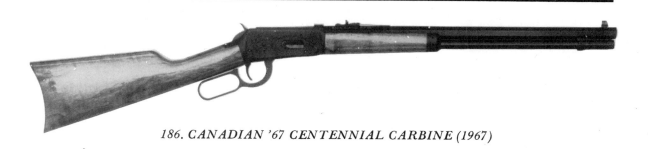

*186. CANADIAN '67 CENTENNIAL CARBINE (1967)*

*186A. CANADIAN '67 CENTENNIAL, CLOSE-UP OF LEFT SIDE OF RECEIVER*

*186B. CANADIAN '67 CENTENNIAL, CLOSE-UP OF BARREL ENGRAVING*

The Canadian '67 Centennial Rifle and Carbine models were issued during 1967, the hundredth anniversary of the establishment of Dominion status for Canada. While primarily distributed in the United States, a large number were also sold in Canada. The Canadian set was a follow-up on the successful Centennial '66 campaign of the previous year.

## GENERAL SPECIFICATIONS OF THE CANADIAN '67 CENTENNIAL RIFLE AND CARBINE

| | |
|---|---|
| TYPE | Lever action, repeating, center fire Model 94. |
| STYLE | Rifle and carbine. |
| BARRELS | Sporting rifle, 26-inch octagon. |
| | Carbine, 20-inch octagon. |
| MAGAZINE | Tubular, full length. Magazine capacities: sporting rifle, 8 cartridges; carbine, 6 cartridges. |
| CHAMBER | 30-30 Winchester. |
| RECEIVER | Black chrome and roll engraved with a maple leaf motif — five leaves to a side — symbolizing the 10 provinces of Canada. An additional maple leaf, larger than the rest, is centered on the left side of the receiver and symbolizes the nation's two northern territories. |
| STOCKS | Rifle type butt, straight grip, stock and forearm of American walnut. |
| SIGHTS | Dovetail bead post front; buckhorn rear. |
| WEIGHTS | Sporting rifle, about 8 lbs. |
| | Carbine, about 7 lbs. |
| SERIAL NUMBERS | Canadian '67s are serially numbered from 1 up, located on the underside of the receiver near the forward end. A total of 90,301 were made in the New Haven plant. |

# ALASKA PURCHASE
# CENTENNIAL CARBINE

*187. ALASKA PURCHASE CENTENNIAL CARBINE (1967)*

In commemoration of the 1967 celebration of the Alaskan Purchase Centennial, Winchester issued a limited edition of specially engraved rifles to be sold only through outlets in the 49th state. The firearm was authorized by the Purchase Centennial Commission.

This firearm — called the Alaska Purchase Centennial Rifle — was designed and manufactured to emphasize the part Winchester played over the last century in the settling of America's final frontier — from the days when the skeptics glanced northward and shuddered at "Seward's Icebox," up to 1967 when Alaska stood proudly alone as the largest and most naturally lucrative state in the U. S.

Winchester lever-action rifles and carbines became standard equipment for all Alaskans because of their light weight, mechanical dependability and accuracy.

While other firearm actions froze under the sub-zero temperatures the Winchesters kept firing — providing food and, in many cases, saving lives.

The Alaska Purchase Centennial, consequently, is patterned after Winchester's most famous lever-action — the Model 94 — with some distinctive embellishments to help tell the Alaska-Winchester story.

The receiver is engraved in traditional 19th-century filigree and is treated to give an "antique" appeal. Centered in the stock is the official Alaskan Purchase Centennial Medallion with the official totem-pole symbol of the state.

Since only 1,500 "Alaskans" were made in the New Haven plant, this model ranks with the "Wyoming" as one of the two rarest Winchester commemoratives.

## GENERAL SPECIFICATIONS OF THE ALASKA PURCHASE CENTENNIAL CARBINE

| | |
|---|---|
| TYPE | Lever action, repeating, center fire Model 94. |
| STYLE | Carbine only. |
| BARREL | 20-inch, round. Barrel bands blued. |
| MAGAZINE | Tubular, full length. Capacity, 6 cartridges. |
| CHAMBER | 30-30 only. |
| RECEIVER | Case-hardened "Antique" and roll-engraved with scroll. |

| | |
|---|---|
| STOCKS | American walnut. Straight grip, stock and forearm. |
| SIGHTS | Hooded ramp front; open rear. |
| WEIGHT | Approximately 6¾ lbs. |
| MEDALLION | "Totem" gold-plated medallion embedded in stock. |
| SERIAL NUMBER | Alaskan Centennial carbines are serially numbered from 1 up, located on the front underside of the receiver. A total of 1,500 were manufactured at the New Haven plant. |

# ILLINOIS SESQUICENTENNIAL CARBINE

*188. ILLINOIS SESQUICENTENNIAL CARBINE, DETAILS (1968)*

In commemoration of the 150th anniversary of the admission of the 21st state to join the Union, Winchester issued a limited edition of an official Illinois Sesquicentennial Model 94 carbine.

The traditional lever action 30-30 Winchester firearm was sanctioned by the Illinois Sesquicentennial Commission and, unlike other Winchester State Commemoratives, was offered through retail outlets throughout the entire country instead of just within the state concerned.

Winchester lever action rifles were standard equipment for Illinois farmers and settlers moving west with the opening of the last frontier after the Civil War. Winchester-Western has had a long association with Illinois, and all of the division's sporting ammunition — center and rim fire cartridges and shotshells — are made at East Alton, the birthplace of the old Western Cartridge Company.

The Illinois Sesquicentennial is patterned after Winchester's most famous lever action — the Model 94 — with some embellishments to underline the Illinois celebration. The receiver is engraved with the words "Land of Lincoln" and a profile of Illinois' most famous son.

A gold-colored inscription on the barrel, "Illinois Sesquicentennial 1818-1968," is complemented by a gold-plated metal butt plate, trigger, loading gate and saddle ring. The rifle also features an official souvenir medallion embedded in its American walnut stock.

| | |
|---|---|
| TYPE | Lever action, repeating, center fire Model 94. |
| STYLE | Carbine only. |
| BARREL | 20-inch, round. "Illinois Sesquicentennial 1818-1968" inscribed. |
| MAGAZINE | Tubular, full length. Capacity, 6 cartridges. |
| CHAMBER | 30-30 only. |
| RECEIVER | Roll-engraved with profile of Lincoln on left side and inscription "Land of Lincoln." |
| STOCKS | American walnut. Straight grip, stock and forearm. |
| SIGHTS | Hooded ramp front; open rear. |
| WEIGHT | Approximately 6¾ lbs. |
| MEDALLION | Gold-plated souvenir medallion embedded in stock. |
| SERIAL NUMBER | Illinois carbines are serially numbered from 1 up, located on the front underside of the receiver. A total of 37,468 were made in New Haven. |

# BUFFALO BILL
# RIFLE AND CARBINE

*189. BUFFALO BILL RIFLE (1968)*

*189A. BUFFALO BILL CARBINE*

The Winchester Buffalo Bill Commemorative Rifle and Carbine Model was introduced by Winchester in 1968.

"I have been using and have thoroughly tested your latest improved rifle. Allow me to say that I have tried and used nearly every kind of a gun made in the United States, and for general hunting, or Indian fighting, I pronounce your improved Winchester the Boss. Believe me, that you have the most complete rifle now made," Col. Cody stated in a letter to the old Winchester Repeating Arms Company from Fort McPherson, Nebraska, dated 1874.

The only firearm authorized by the Buffalo Bill Memorial Association, the new commemorative provided a royalty to the association for each unit sold through normal channels of distribution. In addition, the first 300 rifles were customized as special presentation models and these low serial numbered firearms were donated to the association for their fund-raising purposes.

The Buffalo Bill Museum houses perhaps the most extensive collection of Western artifacts in the world. Part of the Buffalo Bill Historical Center, which includes the Whitney Gallery of Western Art, the museum is another addition to the complex for which future plans include the building of a Plains Indian Museum.

Col. William F. (Buffalo Bill) Cody was born February 26, 1846, in Scott County, Iowa, and died January 10, 1917, in Denver, Colo. A man of many talents, Col. Cody achieved fame as a sportsman, Indian scout, marksman, guide, hunter, Pony Express rider, and superb showman. His storybook exploits on the western frontier earned him the respect of his contemporaries — both red and white — as well as a permanent place in the hearts of peoples everywhere who admire rugged individualism and pioneer spirit.

## GENERAL SPECIFICATIONS OF THE BUFFALO BILL COMMEMORATIVE RIFLE AND CARBINE

| | |
|---|---|
| TYPE | Lever action, repeating, center fire Model 94. |
| STYLE | Rifle and carbine. |
| BARRELS | Sporting rifle, 26-inch, octagon. |
| | Carbine, 20-inch, octagon. |
| MAGAZINE | Tubular, full length. Magazine capacities: sporting rifle, 8 cartridges; carbine, 6 cartridges. |
| CHAMBER | 30-30 Winchester. |
| RECEIVER | Black chromed. Roll-engraved with the name "Buffalo Bill" in old-fashioned script and the famous TE brand of his ranch. Elaborate scroll work further embellishes the receiver. |
| STOCK | American walnut. Straight grip, stock and forearm. |
| MEDALLION | Silver-plated medallion embedded in stock. |
| SIGHTS | Bead-post front; semi-buckhorn rear. |
| WEIGHTS | Sporting rifle, about 8 lbs. |
| | Carbine, about 7 lbs. |
| SERIAL NUMBER | Buffalo Bill rifles and carbines are serially numbered from "BB 1" up, located on front underside of receiver. A total of 112,923 Buffalo Bill models were made by the New Haven plant. |

The butt plate, saddle ring assembly, trigger, spring cover, hammer and forearm cap were all nickel-plated. The barrel and tang are inscribed respectively "Buffalo Bill Commemorative" and, in the Colonel's script, "W. F. Cody — Chief of Scouts." The Buffalo Bill Commemorative was the most popular of all Winchester commemoratives after the Centennial '66 and more guns of this model have been sold than of any other commemorative to this date. It is doubtful that any commemorative firearm of any manufacture will ever achieve the widespread distribution and sale that the Buffalo Bill did in 1968. Winchester contributed royalties totaling $573,835 to the Buffalo Bill Memorial Association, enabling them to expand their Historical Center in Cody, Wyo.

# GOLDEN SPIKE CARBINE

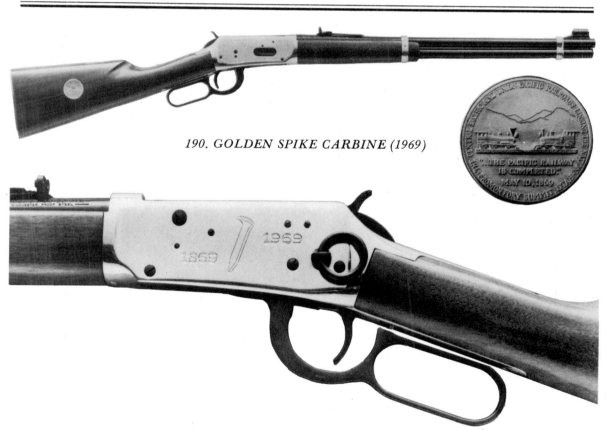

*190. GOLDEN SPIKE CARBINE (1969)*

*190A. GOLDEN SPIKE CARBINE, CLOSE-UP OF LEFT SIDE OF RECEIVER*

When the symbolic "Golden Spike" clanged under the ceremonial mallet at Promontory Summit, Utah, on May 10, 1969, more history than meets the eye was celebrated.

The occasion that marked the wedding of the railroads a century ago simultaneously honored the "gun that won the West" and the role it played in the building of the nation's first Transcontinental Railroad.

In commemoration of the Centennial celebration of that momentous event in American history, Winchester-Western announced the production of a special limited edition "Golden Spike" carbine for sale during 1969.

Like the Winchester repeaters that were ever present a century ago, providing sustenance and protection for the crews at end of track, the "Golden Spike" commemorative was of venerable lever action design. Its 20-inch round barrel is fully encircled by twin barrel bands plated in yellow gold. The gun's matching yellow gold receiver, engraved with decorative scrolled border on the right side, is inscribed on the off side with a railroad spike flanked by the dates 1869 and 1969.

The barrel carries an identifying "Golden Spike Commemorative" inscription and the upper tang bears the legend: "Oceans United By Rail."

## GENERAL SPECIFICATIONS OF THE GOLDEN SPIKE CARBINE

| | |
|---|---|
| TYPE | Lever action, repeating, center fire carbine. |
| BARREL | 20-inch, round. Gold-plated barrel bands. |
| MAGAZINE | Tubular, full length. Capacity, 6 cartridges. |
| CHAMBER | 30-30 Winchester. |
| RECEIVER | Gold-plated. |
| STOCK | Satin-finished American walnut. Straight grip and fluted comb. |
| SIGHTS | Hooded front and semi-buckhorn rear. |
| WEIGHT | Approximately 7 lbs. |
| MEDALLION | Struck by the United States Mint, the special Centennial medallion depicts the meeting of the engines of the Central Pacific and the Union Pacific Railroads at Promontory Summit, Utah, on May 10, 1869. It is embedded in the stock. |
| SERIAL NUMBERS | Golden Spike Carbines are serially numbered from 1 up, located on the front underside of the receiver. A total of approximately 70,000 were made in the New Haven plant. |

### Special Note

The Golden Spike Carbine was authorized by the Golden Spike Centennial Celebration Commission, the Union Pacific Railroad and the Southern Pacific Company.

# THEODORE ROOSEVELT
# COMMEMORATIVE
# RIFLE AND CARBINE

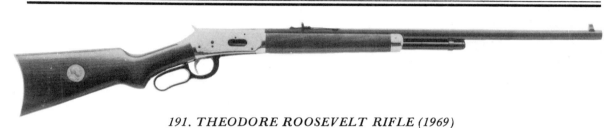

*191. THEODORE ROOSEVELT RIFLE (1969)*

*191A. THEODORE ROOSEVELT CARBINE*

*191B. THEODORE ROOSEVELT COMMEMORATIVE,*
*CLOSE-UP OF BOTH SIDES OF RECEIVER*

[ 207 ]

*191c. THEODORE ROOSEVELT COMMEMORATIVE MEDALLION*

*191*ᴅ. *THEODORE ROOSEVELT WITH WINCHESTER MODEL 1886*

In tribute to Theodore Roosevelt — soldier, statesman, author, naturalist, hunter, conservationist, President and "Sportsman of the Century" — Winchester issued the Theodore Roosevelt Commemorative Model 94, in both rifle and carbine styles, in 1969.

The only firearm authorized by the Theodore Roosevelt Association, the new limited edition commemorative provided a royalty to the association for each unit sold through normal channels of distribution. The funds accrued were used by the association in a manner consistent with Roosevelt's conservationist ideals. A total of $244,935 was paid to the association.

Designed expressly in honor of the 50th anniversary of T. R.'s death, the traditional 30-30 caliber lever action repeating firearm is distinctively patterned along the lines of one of his favorite game guns: the Winchester Model 1886.

## GENERAL SPECIFICATIONS OF THE THEODORE ROOSEVELT COMMEMORATIVE RIFLE AND CARBINE

| | |
|---|---|
| TYPE | Lever action, repeating, center fire Model 94. |
| STYLES | Rifle and carbine. |
| BARRELS | Sporting rifle, 26-inch, octagon. |
| | Carbine, 20-inch, octagon. |
| MAGAZINE | Tubular, full length for carbine, half-magazine for rifle. |
| | Magazine capacities: sporting rifle, 6 cartridges; carbine, 6 cartridges. |
| CHAMBER | 30-30 Winchester. |
| RECEIVER | White gold-plated. Roll-engraved with decorative scrolled border on right side and spread-winged American eagle between the inscription "26th President" and the dates "1901-1909," signifying Theodore Roosevelt's presidential term in office, on the left side. |
| STOCKS | Satin-finished American walnut. Half-pistol grip. |
| SIGHTS | Bead-post front and sporting open rear. |
| WEIGHTS | Sporting rifle, approximately 7½ lbs. |
| | Carbine, approximately 7 lbs. |
| MEDALLION | Struck from an original designed by J. E. Fraser in 1920, the medallion shows a bas-relief profile of the President and the dates of his birth and death in Roman numerals. The medallion is embedded in the stock. |
| SERIAL NUMBERS | Theodore Roosevelt Commemoratives are serially numbered from "TR 1" on up, located on the front underside of the receiver. A total of 52,386 "TR" commemoratives were made in the New Haven plant. |

*Special Note*

The gun's upper tang bears an engraved reproduction of Theodore Roosevelt's signature.

# COWBOY COMMEMORATIVE
# CARBINE

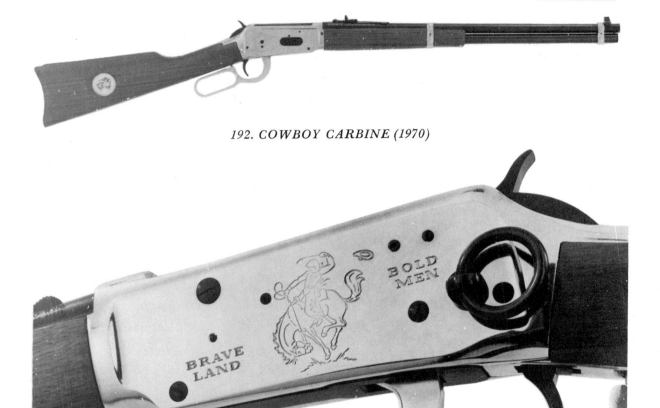

*192. COWBOY CARBINE (1970)*

*192A. COWBOY CARBINE, CLOSE-UP OF LEFT SIDE OF RECEIVER*

In tribute to one of the most colorful and admired symbols of the Western frontier — the American cowboy — Winchester introduced a new commemorative lever action carbine to be offered for sale as a limited edition firearm in 1970.

Authorized by the National Cowboy Hall of Fame, the Winchester Cowboy Commemorative Model 94 was announced at the Hall of Fame during ceremonies preceding the opening of the week-long National Rodeo Finals Championships in December 1969. Simultaneously unveiled were the famous western art and memorabilia of the Charles S. Schreyvogel studio collection.

"No one group of Americans has ever been more symbolic of this great nation, the fiber of its people, its spirit, history, traditions and growth than has the American Cowboy," said a Winchester spokesman. "To people the world over, the cowboy is America . . . both real and legendary, past and present, and always free. It is with pride and a sense of appropriateness that Winchester-Western — makers of 'the gun that won the West' — introduces this commemorative lever action carbine to honor the cowboy."

In addition, a special custom-made issue, limited in number, was produced for sale exclusively by the Cowboy Hall of Fame. Priced at $1,000 each, the custom Cowboy Commemorative Carbine features an extra-fancy selected American walnut stock with fine line hand checkering. Each gun came with its own velvet-lined mahogany presentation case, large cowboy medallion and parchment certificate recording the owner's name and the gun's serial number. Profit from the sale of these custom-made firearms enabled the Cowboy Hall to purchase the Schreyvogel studio collection, reportedly valued in six figures, for permanent exhibition.

Each Cowboy Commemorative purchaser became eligible for a free lifetime membership in the Winchester Club of the National Cowboy Hall of Fame. Purchasers also had an opportunity to buy reproductions of two famous works of western art: "Worked Over," a painting by Charles M. Russell, and "The Last Drop," a celebrated bronze by Charles Schreyvogel.

The National Cowboy Hall of Fame, situated on a site overlooking the old Chisholm Trail, houses extensive exhibits of western art, frontier lore and other artifacts of our nation's rich western heritage. Dedicated in 1965, the Cowboy Hall is a nonprofit organization supported by donations from its members and trustees. Honorary members include the governors of the seventeen Western states, prominent citizens from all parts of the nation, and celebrities of the entertainment world.

## GENERAL SPECIFICATIONS OF THE COWBOY COMMEMORATIVE CARBINE

| | |
|---|---|
| TYPE | Lever action, repeating, center fire Model 94. |
| STYLE | Carbine only. |
| BARREL | 20-inch, round. Nickel-plated barrel bands. |
| MAGAZINE | Tubular, full length. Capacity, 6 cartridges. |
| CHAMBER | 30-30 only. |
| RECEIVER | Nickel-plated and roll-engraved with inscription: "Brave Land — Bold Men" and "Bronco Rider" on left side; right side has engraved coiled lariat and spurs. |
| STOCK | Satin-finished American walnut. Extended forearm and straight grip. |
| SIGHTS | Dovetail front; adjustable semi-buckhorn rear. |
| WEIGHT | Approximately 7 lbs. |
| MEDALLION | Nickel-plated bucking bronco and cowboy medallion embedded in stock. |
| SERIAL NUMBER | Cowboy Commemoratives are serially numbered from "CB 1" on up, located on front underside of receiver. A total of 27,549 "Cowboys" were manufactured in the New Haven plant. |

# LONE STAR
# COMMEMORATIVE MODEL 94
# RIFLE AND CARBINE

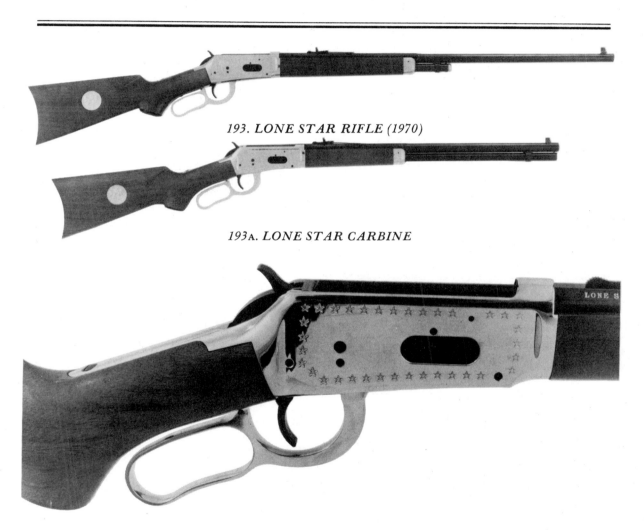

*193. LONE STAR RIFLE (1970)*

*193A. LONE STAR CARBINE*

*193B. LONE STAR COMMEMORATIVE, CLOSE-UP OF RIGHT SIDE OF RECEIVER*

*193c. LONE STAR COMMEMORATIVE, CLOSE-UP OF LEFT SIDE OF RECEIVER*

*193d. LONE STAR COMMEMORATIVE, CLOSE-UP OF MEDALLION*

In December 1845, the independent Republic of Texas became the 28th state admitted to the Union. To honor this great state, and the men who made Texas history, Winchester announced in January 1970 the latest in the series of commemorative firearms — the Lone Star Commemorative Model 94 Rifle and Carbine.

Patterned after the early Winchester lever action repeaters carried by the frontiersmen who pioneered and settled the nation's western states, the Lone Star firearms commemorated two important dates in Texas history: the 125th anniversary of its annexation to the United States and the 100th anniversary of its readmittance into the Union, following the War between the States.

Sale of the Texas commemoratives, which were issued in limited edition, provided a royalty of $90,385 to Game Conservation International, popularly known as Game Coin, for use in conservation research and to provide more game for the sportsmen of Texas.

## GENERAL SPECIFICATIONS OF THE LONE STAR COMMEMORATIVE MODEL 1894 RIFLE AND CARBINE

| | |
|---|---|
| TYPE | Lever action, repeating, center fire Model 94. |
| STYLES | Sporting rifle and carbine. |
| BARRELS | Sporting rifle, 26-inch, half-round, half-octagon (first use). Carbine, 20-inch, half-round, half-octagon. |
| MAGAZINE | Tubular: rifle, half-length; carbine, full length. Capacity, 6 cartridges both. |
| CHAMBER | 30-30 Winchester only. |
| RECEIVER | Gold-plated. The left side of the receiver is engraved with a large star and the dates 1845 and 1970, while both sides are engraved with a border of stars. |
| STOCKS | Satin-finished American walnut. Half-pistol grip and fluted comb. |
| SIGHTS | Bead-post front and semi-buckhorn rear. |
| WEIGHTS | Sporting rifle, about 7½ lbs. Carbine, about 7 lbs. |
| MEDALLION | A gold-plated medallion, embedded in the stock, bears the faces of five outstanding Texans — Sam Houston, Stephen F. Austin, Col. William Barret Travis, Jim Bowie and Davy Crockett. |
| SERIAL NUMBERS | Lone Star Commemoratives are serially numbered from "LS 1" on up, located on the front underside of the receiver. A total of 38,385 "Lone Stars" were made in the New Haven plant. |

# NRA CENTENNIAL MODEL 94 MUSKET AND RIFLE

*194. NRA CENTENNIAL MUSKET (1971)*

*194*A*. NRA CENTENNIAL RIFLE*

A century of dedicated service to the American rifleman — symbolic backbone of the nation's founding and perpetuation — marked the celebration in 1971 of the 100th anniversary of the National Rifle Association. The NRA, a million-plus-member organization, was founded in New York State on November 17, 1871.

In double tribute to that organization, its members past and present, and to the American rifleman of all time, Winchester issued two NRA Centennial commemorative firearms as limited edition models during 1971.

The first of the new commemoratives, the Winchester NRA Centennial Model 94 Musket, closely resembles the original Winchester Model 1895 NRA Musket, a military-style lever action firearm that was designed to meet requirements for match competition shooting under NRA rules at the turn of the century.

The second new commemorative, the Winchester NRA Centennial Model 94 Rifle, also is a lever action 30-30 caliber firearm. Distinctively different in appearance from the musket, the rifle is reminiscent of the earlier Winchester Model 64, formerly a highly popular rifle for deer hunting.

The NRA Commemoratives are unique in that the musket version is the only commemorative of that type that has been produced to date by Winchester and, secondly, they are the only commemoratives that have been carried and marketed more than one year by the company. They are listed in both the 1971 and the 1972 catalogs.

[ 216 ]

## GENERAL SPECIFICATIONS OF THE NRA CENTENNIAL MUSKET AND RIFLE

| | |
|---|---|
| TYPE | Lever action, repeating, center fire Model 94. |
| STYLE | Musket and rifle. |
| BARRELS | Musket, 26-inch, tapered, round. |
| | Rifle, 24-inch, tapered, round. |
| MAGAZINE | Tubular |
| | Musket, full length; capacity, 7 cartridges. |
| | Sporting rifle, half-length; capacity, 5 cartridges. |
| CHAMBER | 30-30 Winchester. |
| RECEIVER | Black chromed. The left side of the receiver is inscribed with the letters "NRA" encircled by a plain scrollwork design, flanked by the dates 1871-1971. Adorning the right side of the receiver are two additional scrollwork patterns of similarly plain design. |
| STOCKS | Satin-finished American walnut. Musket forearm extends to front of barrel. Rifle has traditional half-forearm. Musket has straight grip; rifle has semi-pistol grip. |
| SIGHTS | Musket, blade front and calibrated folding leaf rear. |
| | Rifle, bead-post front and adjustable semi-buckhorn rear. |
| WEIGHTS | Musket, about 7⅛ lbs. |
| | Rifle, about 6⅝ lbs. |
| MEDALLION | The NRA Seal, struck on a special silver-colored medallion, is set into the right side of each commemorative's stock. |
| SERIAL NUMBER | NRA Commemoratives are serial numbered from "NRA 1" on up, located on the front underside of the receiver. A total of 47,380 "NRAs" were made in the New Haven plant. |

# TEXAS RANGER COMMEMORATIVE MODEL 94 RIFLE

*195. TEXAS RANGER RIFLE (1973)*

[ 217 ]

One of the nation's most renowned law enforcement services, the Texas Rangers, celebrated its 150th anniversary in 1973 and Winchester honored this outstanding group of Texans by issuing a limited edition of 5,000 Texas Ranger Commemorative Model 94 rifles.

These firearms, sanctioned by the Texas Ranger Commemorative Commission, were available only in the State of Texas. The first 150 Texas Ranger Commemorative rifles, bearing serial numbers 1 through 150, were special-edition models and were sold only through the Texas Ranger Association. The remaining 4,850 models were available at regular Texas retail outlets.

During the early part of the 19th century, Stephen F. Austin began the colonization of the vast territory that was to ultimately become the nation's 28th state. Early settlers to this land, however, were constantly plagued by thieves and murderers who pillaged their property and wiped out entire families. There was no regular army to combat them and, in fact, no defense against them. Consequently, in 1823, the people of Texas banded together and formed the organization that has been the guardian of Texas law and order for the past 150 years.

## GENERAL SPECIFICATIONS OF THE TEXAS RANGER COMMEMORATIVE MODEL 94 RIFLE

| | |
|---|---|
| TYPE | Lever action, repeating, center fire Model 94. |
| STYLE | Carbine only. |
| BARREL | 20-inch, round. |
| MAGAZINE | Tubular, full length. Capacity, 6 cartridges. |
| CHAMBER | 30-30 only. |
| RECEIVER | Plain. |
| STOCK | Semi-fancy American walnut. Square comb and curved butt plate. |
| SIGHTS | Curved post front and semi-buckhorn rear. |
| WEIGHT | Approximately 7 lbs. |
| MEDALLION | A facsimile of the famous "Texas Ranger Star" is embedded in the butt stock. |
| SERIAL NUMBER | Texas Ranger Commemoratives are serial numbered from 1 on up, located on the front underside of the receiver. A total of 5,000 (including 150 special guns) were made in the New Haven plant. |

### Special Note

The 150 special-edition models have hand checkered, full fancy walnut stocks. The guns have 16-inch barrels with full buckhorn styled rear sights. Both the receiver and barrel are highly polished. The special-edition model weighs approximately 6 pounds and holds five cartridges, four in the magazine and one in the chamber.

These guns were enclosed in a special presentation case and the Texas Ranger Commemorative Star was mounted inside the presentation case instead of on the gun. The 150 special-edition Winchester Texas Ranger Commemorative Model 94 rifles were available through the Texas Ranger Association at a cost of $1,000 per firearm.

# CANADIAN WINCHESTER COMMEMORATIVE ISSUES

While the Canadian '67 Centennial Rifle and Carbine Commemorative Models were primarily designed for the United States market (see previous section on domestic commemoratives), it was obvious that there was a considerable, but at the time unestimated, potential among Canadian sportsmen and collectors. The Canadian '67 Model sold very well in Canada, as might be expected during the Dominion's 100th anniversary celebration in 1967. As a consequence, Winchester Canada Ltd., based in Cobourg, Ontario, took an increasing interest in the possibility of more limited edition commemoratives with a strictly Canadian theme. As a result, the Northwest Territories Centennial Commemorative Rifle (1970) and the Royal Canadian Mounted Police Centennial Rifle (1974) were produced. A Klondike Commemorative Carbine, commemorating the Canadian Gold Strike of 1896 and the Klondike Gold Rush of 1898, will be introduced during 1975. All of the above firearms were or will be packed in special cartons designed to promote the theme or historical event being celebrated.

# NORTHWEST TERRITORIES CENTENNIAL RIFLE

*196. NORTHWEST TERRITORIES CENTENNIAL RIFLE (1970)*

In 1870, the Canadian Arctic and Rupert's Land officially became known as the Northwest Territories. Encompassing more than a million and a quarter square miles, this vast land has remained virtually unchanged since man first set foot on it. It is as magnificent today as it was almost 5,000 years ago when the Denbigh people began settling there. The land of northern lights, caribou, polar bear, musk ox, tundra and sea ice, the Northwest Territories is the last frontier.

In tribute to this great land and its people, Winchester produced a special Northwest Territories Centennial Commemorative rifle in 1970, the year of centennial celebration.

Patterned after the early Winchester lever-action rifle which played such a key role in man's fight for survival against the harsh elements of the Northwest Territories, this special Winchester was offered in a limited edition, available only in Canada.

Winchester also provided the Northwest Territories Centennial Center with a number of special patrons' rifles to aid the natives of the Territories. These patrons' rifles helped to fund many projects aimed at supporting the cultural, educational and financial independence of the native people.

As a salute to the Northwest Territories, Winchester commissioned a painting by Toronto artist Claire Offen — uniting in one sweeping panorama a colorful story of life in the Northwest Territories. A full size reproduction of this painting appeared on the packing sleeve of the special Styrofoam box containing the N.W.T. Centennial Rifle.

## GENERAL SPECIFICATIONS OF THE NORTHWEST TERRITORIES CENTENNIAL RIFLE

| | |
|---|---|
| TYPE | Lever action, repeating, center fire Model 94. |
| STYLE | Rifle only. |
| CALIBER | 30-30 Winchester only. |
| MAGAZINE | Tubular, under barrel; capacity, 5 cartridges. Two-thirds length. Magazine plug blued. |
| BARREL | 24-inch octagonal. No barrel bands. |
| RECEIVER | Receiver, lower tang and hammer gold-plated. Lever blued. Receiver roll-engraved with border scroll and left side has engraved picture of an Arctic polar bear. |
| TRIGGER | Gold-plated. |
| MEDALLION | Gold-plated medallion, a replica of the special centennial seal of "Arctic Unity," is embedded in the stock. |
| STOCK | Satin-finished American walnut. Half-pistol grip and fluted comb. |
| SIGHTS | Bead-post front; semi-buckhorn open rear. |
| BUTT PLATE | Brass; crescent-shaped, diamond embossed. |
| FOREARM | Long carbine style; gold-plated forearm cap. |
| WEIGHT | Approximately 7¼ lbs. |
| SERIAL NUMBER | Begins with "NWT 1," located on front underside of receiver. |

### Special Note

The Northwest Territories Centennial Rifle was made in the New Haven arms plant. Approximately 3,000 were made, making this model the rarest of the special Canadian and other International commemoratives produced by Winchester since 1970. Only the domestic Wyoming, Nebraska and Alaska Models have lower production numbers.

# ROYAL CANADIAN MOUNTED POLICE CENTENNIAL CARBINE

*197. ROYAL CANADIAN MOUNTED POLICE CENTENNIAL CARBINE (1973)*

Winchester Canada Ltd. introduced a special commemorative honoring the hundredth anniversary of the Royal Canadian Mounted Police in 1973. It is interesting to quote from an advertisement of that year:

> The Force began with a call to duty: The mandate to bring law and order to Canada's turbulent "Western Empire." The year was 1873. The men . . . North West Mounted Police. Over the years, The Force has kept pace with Canada's growing needs, becoming the Royal North West Mounted Police in 1904; and since 1920 bearing the proud name: Royal Canadian Mounted Police. The R.C.M.P.
>
> From 1878 to 1914, The Force answered every call to duty with a firearm whose name became a watchword for men of courage. The name was Winchester, in use longer than any shoulder arm ever issued to The Force.
>
> To salute The Force on its hundredth birthday, Winchester proudly recalls its link with Canada's by introducing the Winchester Model 94 R.C.M.P. Commemorative Rifle, patterned after the famed MP original Winchester Model '76 . . .

## GENERAL SPECIFICATIONS OF THE R.C.M.P. CENTENNIAL RIFLE

| | |
|---|---|
| TYPE | Lever action, repeating, center fire Model 94. |
| STYLE | Rifle only. |
| CALIBER | 30-30 Winchester only. |
| MAGAZINE | Tubular, under barrel. Capacity, 6 cartridges. Full length. No magazine plug. |
| BARREL | 22-inch, round. One gold-plated barrel band. |
| RECEIVER | Receiver and lower tang gold-plated. Hammer and lever blued. Receiver roll-engraved. |
| MEDALLION | Gold-plated medallion honoring N.W.M.P., R.N.W.M.P. and R.C.M.P. embedded in stock. |
| STOCK | Satin-finished American walnut. Straight grip. All stocks had letters "MP" cut into the wood at the butt end. |

| | |
|---|---|
| SIGHTS | Blade front; musket-type rear. |
| BUTT PLATE | Gold-plated. Top wrap-around style. |
| FOREARM | Musket style; gold-plated forearm cap. |
| WEIGHT | Approximately 7 lbs. |
| SERIAL NUMBER | Begins with "RCMP 1" for general public issue; begins with "MP 1" for special issue to members of R.C.M.P. See special note below. Serial number located on front underside of receiver. |

*Special Note*

All of the R.C.M.P. Centennial Rifles were produced in the New Haven arms plant. A total of approximately 9,500 were produced for the general public with an "RCMP" prefix before the serial number. In addition, and most importantly from a collector's standpoint, an additional approximately 5,100 guns were specially produced for distribution only to members of the R.C.M.P. These special firearms had all of the features of the standard "R.C.M.P." rifles except for the serial numbers which used only the letters "MP" in the prefix. Therefore, a total of approximately 14,600 rifles were made. A special set of commemorative art reproductions illustrating historic scenes from The Force's past were also available from the Cobourg headquarters of Winchester Canada Ltd.

# KLONDIKE
# COMMEMORATIVE CARBINE

*198. KLONDIKE COMMEMORATIVE CARBINE (1975)*

Continuing their line of commemorative rifles and carbines based on strictly Canadian historical themes, Winchester Canada Ltd. plans to introduce a Klondike Commemorative Carbine honoring the Canadian Gold Strike of 1896 and the Klondike Gold Rush of 1898 during 1975.

## GENERAL SPECIFICATIONS OF THE KLONDIKE COMMEMORATIVE CARBINE

| | |
|---|---|
| TYPE | Lever action, repeating, center fire Model 94. |
| STYLE | Carbine only. |
| CALIBER | 30-30 only. |
| MAGAZINE | Tubular, below barrel; capacity, 6 cartridges. Full length. Magazine plug blued. |
| BARREL | 20-inch, round. Barrel bands gold-plated. |
| RECEIVER | Receiver and lower tang gold-plated. Hammer and lever blued. |
| MEDALLION | Gold-plated medallion commemoratng the Gold Rush and Strike embedded in stock. |
| STOCK | Satin-finished American walnut. |
| SIGHTS | Ramp and hood front; open rear. |
| BUTT PLATE | Gold-plated. Top wrap-around style. |
| WEIGHT | Approximately 6¾ lbs. |
| SERIAL NUMBER | Begins with "KGR 1," located on front underside of receiver. |

### *Special Note*

The Klondike Commemorative Carbine will be manufactured at both the New Haven and Cobourg, Ontario, arms plants. It is estimated that approximately 10,500 will be made. Specially packed 30-30 ammunition in a Klondike Gold Rush Commemorative box will be made available and can be purchased separately from retailers.

# EUROPEAN WINCHESTER COMMEMORATIVE ISSUES

As Winchester fully grasped the success of its first national commemorative models — the Centennial '66, the Canadian '67, the Buffalo Bill and others — in the last years of the 1960s, the company was concurrently investing more effort — and some of the commemorative profits — in overseas expansion. With the increased interest in overseas markets and Western Europe's sudden reawakened fascination with the American West, it was only a matter of time before the two were joined in some sort of catalyst — in this case, a special Winchester lever action rifle glorifying the "Old West." The result was the Yellow Boy Indian Carbine introduced in West European markets in 1973. The Centennial '66, marking Winchester's first 100 years from 1866 through 1966, recalled that the Indians had nicknamed the old Model 1866 "Yellow Boy" because of its brass receiver. Western Europe — mainly France and Germany — was undergoing a sort of Wild West boom. There were western dude ranches, indian and cowboy replicas, special stores catering to western-style clothing, "frontier towns" and special vacations based on an "Old West" theme. The Yellow Boy Indian Carbine, mainly based upon extra parts and variations of the Centennial '66 Model, was an instant success and rapidly sold out. It was followed by the Apache

Carbine in 1974 and the Comanche in 1975. All of the above commemorative firearms were or will be packed in special cartons designed to promote the theme or historical event being celebrated.

# YELLOW BOY INDIAN CARBINE

*199. YELLOW BOY INDIAN CARBINE (1972)*

The Yellow Boy Indian Carbine was the first commemorative Winchester conceived specifically for the West European market. Introduced in 1973, each Yellow Boy was supplied with a package of brass tacks. Customers were advised that these tacks could be placed in the butt stock or forearm by a competent gunsmith in designs similar to those decorations found on Indian-owned Winchester Repeating Rifles of the late 1800s and early 1900s.

## GENERAL SPECIFICATIONS OF THE YELLOW BOY INDIAN CARBINE

| | |
|---|---|
| TYPE | Lever action, repeating, center fire Model 94. |
| STYLE | Carbine only. |
| CALIBER | 30-30 Winchester only. |
| MAGAZINE | Tubular, under barrel; capacity, 6 cartridges. Magazine plug blued. Full length. |
| BARREL | 20-inch, round. Barrel bands gold-plated. |
| RECEIVER | Receiver, lower tang and hammer gold-plated; lever blued. Receiver roll-engraved. |
| STOCK | Walnut stock and forearm; package of decorative brass tacks supplied. |
| SIGHTS | Beaded blade front; musket-type rear. |
| BUTT PLATE | Gold-plated. Crescent shape style. |
| FOREARM | Long carbine style. No forearm cap. |
| WEIGHT | Approximately 6¾ lbs. |
| SERIAL NUMBER | Begins with "YB 1," located on front underside of receiver. |

### Special Note

The Yellow Boy Indian Carbine was manufactured in the New Haven arms plant. Approximately 5,500 were made.

# APACHE CARBINE

*200. APACHE CARBINE (1974)*

Impressed with the acceptance of the Yellow Boy Indian Carbine, Winchester International introduced its second special western-style, Indian-motif carbine — the Apache — in Western Europe in 1974. A full color Apache poster was supplied with each Apache Carbine.

## GENERAL SPECIFICATIONS FOR THE APACHE CARBINE

| | |
|---|---|
| TYPE | Lever action, repeating, center fire Model 94. |
| STYLE | Carbine only. |
| CALIBER | 30-30 Winchester only. |
| MAGAZINE | Tubular, under barrel; capacity, 6 cartridges. Magazine plug gold-plated. Full length. |
| BARREL | 20-inch, round. Barrel bands gold-plated. |
| RECEIVER | Receiver and lower tang gold-plated. Hammer and lever blued. Receiver roll-engraved. |
| MEDALLION | Gold-plated medallion commemorating the Apache Indians embedded in stock. |
| STOCK | Walnut stock and forearm. |
| SIGHTS | Ramp and hood front; open rear. |
| BUTT PLATE | Gold-plated. Top wrap-around style. |
| FOREARM | Short carbine style. No forearm cap. |
| WEIGHT | Approximately 6¾ lbs. |
| SERIAL NUMBER | Begins with "AC 1," located on front underside of receiver. |

### Special Note

The Apache Carbine was manufactured in both the New Haven arms plant in the United States and the Winchester plant in Cobourg, Ontario, Canada. Approximately 8,600 were made.

# COMANCHE CARBINE

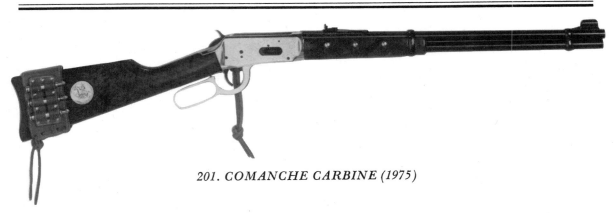

*201. COMANCHE CARBINE (1975)*

Continuing the successful marketing of limited edition Indian-theme commemoratives, Winchester International is introducing the Comanche Carbine in Western Europe in 1975. Each Comanche Carbine forearm will be embedded with three decorative brass tacks (reminiscent of the unique designs on Indian guns of the Old West) on each side. A leather, three-cartridge butt-stock bandolier (with impressed designs) plus a leather saddle-ring thong will be supplied with each firearm. Lastly, a special full-color Comanche poster will be packed with each gun. It should be noted that Winchester has varied each year's model with some sort of innovation or extra accessory — or a combination thereof.

## GENERAL SPECIFICATIONS FOR THE COMANCHE CARBINE

| | |
|---|---|
| TYPE | Lever action, repeating, center fire Model 94. |
| STYLE | Carbine only. |
| CALIBER | 30-30 only. |
| MAGAZINE | Tubular, under barrel; capacity, 6 cartridges. Magazine plug blued. Full length. |
| BARREL | 20-inch, round. Barrel bands blued. |
| RECEIVER | Receiver, lower tang and lever gold-plated. Hammer blued. Receiver roll-engraved. |
| MEDALLION | Gold-plated medallion commemorating the Comanche Indians embedded in stock. |
| STOCK | Walnut stock and forearm. |
| SIGHTS | Ramp and hood front; open rear. |
| BUTT PLATE | Blued. Top wrap-around style. |
| FOREARM | Short carbine style. No forearm cap. |
| WEIGHT | Approximately 6¾ lbs. |
| SERIAL NUMBER | Begins with "CC 1," located on front underside of receiver. |

# SPECIAL MODELS FOR FOREIGN MARKETS

## General Background

During the 1960s and the first half of the '70s, Winchester took an increasingly active role in international markets. The old Cooey Firearms Company of Cobourg, Ontario, long Canada's only domestic sporting firearms producer, was bought in 1961. A shotshell and rim fire loading facility was added in 1965 and a new arms plant completed in 1970. Winchester Canada Ltd. became an increasingly successful part of the company's worldwide operation and made significant contributions to overseas markets and to Winchester's United States operations. As pointed out earlier in this book, first the Model 370 and now the Model 37A, both single shot, single barrel shotguns, were two important Canadian-manufactured additions to the Winchester domestic line. Similarly, the last standard model introduced and covered in this book is the Canadian-designed and manufactured Model 490 Automatic (autoloading semi-automatic) repeating 22 rim fire rifle. In addition, again as mentioned earlier, Winchester Canada has taken an important role in both developing and maufacturing special commemoratives not only for its own markets but for other international areas as well.

Concurrently, Winchester took a position with a Japanese manufacturer of quality over-and-under shotguns in 1961 and Olin Kodensha Ltd. was formed. The result, of course, was the introduction of the various Model 101 shotguns, many still in the line and most recently represented by the excellent Model 101 Pigeon Grade Trap gun first listed in 1974.

In other international developments, Winchester built a shotshell plant in Italy in 1965-66 and established both shotshell and rim fire facilities in Australia in 1966, both ventures highly successful. An Australian-designed and manufactured action was incorporated in the Model 310 single shot and the Model 320 clip loading 22 rim fire rifles covered in prior chapters.

Most recently, Winchester has entered into an agreement with Laurona, a prominent Spanish manufacturer, to produce two double barrel shotguns — one side-by-side and one over-and-under — under the Winchester label for marketing in international markets, including Canada. Since it is inevitable that some of these Winchester brand foreign-made shotguns will end up in the United States — either from Canada or brought back by returning servicemen from overseas — the editors of this book felt it appropriate to include these latest models, due to be introduced some time during 1975.

# MODEL 22 DOUBLE BARREL
# SIDE-BY-SIDE SHOTGUN*

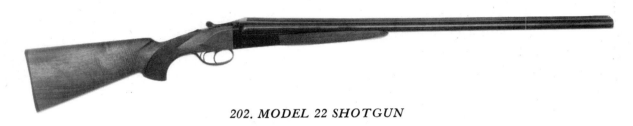

*202. MODEL 22 SHOTGUN*

The Model 22 Field Gun, a side-by-side, double barrel shotgun, is a Winchester brand name quality firearm manufactured by Laurona in Spain. Designed and manufactured to Winchester's specifications, the Model 22 was planned to provide a moderately priced, fine quality double gun for international markets. Priced within the reach of most hunters, the Model 22 contains many custom features: oil-finished hand checkered walnut stock and forearm; hand engraved receivers and trigger guards. Full pistol grip stock; semi-beavertail forearm. New black chrome finish on all metal parts. Winchester Proof Steel. The Model 22 will be available with double trigger, matted top rib and brass front bead. In 12 gauge only, the Model 22 has 28-inch (71-centimeter) barrels, choked modified and full. The gun has an overall length of 45⅜ inches (115 centimeters) and 2¾-inch (70-millimeter) chambers. The weight is 6¾ lbs. (3.1 kilograms).

# MODEL 91 DOUBLE BARREL OVER-AND-UNDER SHOTGUN*

*203. MODEL 91 SHOTGUN*

The Model 91 Field Gun, an over-and-under, double barrel shotgun is also a Winchester brand name quality firearm manufactured by Laurona in Spain. Like the Model 22 above, the new Model 91 has been designed and manufactured to Winchester's specifications in order to provide a moderately priced, finely crafted double gun for international markets. The Model 91 has many of the custom features listed for its companion side-by-side from Spain. It has a hand checkered, oil finished stock and forearm combined with hand engraved receiver and trigger guard. The guns also have a new black chrome finish on all metal parts for longer lasting protection from foul weather conditions. Winchester Proof Steel barrels. The Model 91 features a single inertia gold-plated trigger plus ventilated rib with front brass sighting bead. Chrome-plated chambers, bores and chokes eliminate rust and leading problems. In 12 gauge only, the Model 91 has 28-inch (71-centimeter) barrels, choked modified and full. The gun has an overall length of 44¼ inches (114 centimeters) and 2¾-inch (70-millimeter) chambers. The weight is 7¼ lbs. (3.3 kilograms).

*As of June 1975, the final specifications of the Model 22 and Model 91 shotguns have not been finalized in every detail. There may be some in-process changes or variations in the final production requirements for these two models. There may also be some differences in finishes for both wood and metal parts for different market areas.